Voices of a Thousand People

Voices of a Thousand People

The Makah Cultural and Research Center

Patricia Pierce Erikson,

with Helma Ward

and Kirk Wachendorf

Foreword by Janine Bowechop

University of Nebraska Press • Lincoln & London

Library of Congress Cataloging-in-Publication Data
Erikson, Patricia Pierce, 1962–
Voices of a thousand people : the Makah Cultural and
Research Center / Patricia Pierce Erikson with Helma Ward
and Kirk Wachendorf ; foreword by Janine Bowechop.
    p. cm.
Includes bibliographical references and index.
ISBN 0-8032-1824-9 (cloth : alk. paper)
1. Makah Cultural and Research Center.
2. Makah Indians—Ethnic identity.
I. Ward, Helma. II. Wachendorf, Kirk. III. Title.
E99.M19 E75 2002
305.8979—dc21
2001034760

This book is dedicated to Grace Gruger and Margaret Irving, two extraordinary women who have shared with me their passion for history

Contents

Illustrations

Foreword

As you read this book, you'll learn quite a bit about the Makah Tribe's experience and experiments with cultural anthropologists. Not all of the interaction has been bad. In fact, some research has proved very valuable, despite the bias and misconceptions you have to maneuver around to get to cultural truths. Typically, Makah experience with anthropology has been give and take—Makah people have given incredible amounts of cultural knowledge, and the anthropologists have happily taken it with them in order to earn degrees and write esoteric papers. Whether or not their studies benefited our community has not always been of concern to the researchers, except of course when we hired them to research a specific topic. Believe me, I do not come from a family of anthrophobes —my great-grandmother was a close personal friend of Dr. Erna Gunther's, my dad earned a bachelor's degree in anthropology, and I, too, studied anthropology in college. I always felt it was more meaningful to offer criticism from within than to wage a blind war from afar.

In spite of our location remote from heavily populated areas (the development of which wiped out many lives, or at least traditions, of Indian tribes) and because of our impressive history as whalers and our rich ceremonial activity, we have been very, very studied. I need not attempt to compete with some of our relations in the Southwest, but as northwesterners, we have been examined over and over again. From reading this book you will learn that Makah people are skilled negotiators and sophisticated traders. I would argue that these skills have been transmitted to the current generations expressly for the purpose of dealing with cultural anthropologists and government agencies.

Now that our tribe has the Makah Cultural and Research Center we are able to regulate research activity conducted on reservation, and even off the reservation in many cases. These days the researchers not only have to explain exactly what they are interested in but they are also required to explain their proposed methodology, their method of compensation for resource people, and the benefit of the study to the Makah Tribe. They are required to sign agreements that govern their conduct while they are on the reservation and stipulate that the MCRC have review authority prior to any publication.

Patricia Erikson was willing to comply with all these stipulations and more. She offered her skills with endowment planning and fund-raising and even went the extra mile and transcribed all her interviews before depositing them in the MCRC Archives. Sometimes she'd even make cookies for the staff, but usually they had a bit too much nutritional value. She did learn to cut fish, though, and had she stayed around a few more years she would have undoubtedly learned to cut whale.

While *Voices of a Thousand People* is important for non-Makah people to read for too many reasons to list here, I am especially pleased that Makah people, both on and off the reservation have easy access to this book. Community members can read *Voices of a Thousand People* at the MCRC research library, purchase it in our museum gift shop, or access many of the full transcripts of the interviews located in the MCRC Archives.

Voices of a Thousand People seems like a lifetime of work. In it Dr. Erikson reveals the thinking behind the creation of our treasured Makah Cultural and Research Center, the ways our governing systems have changed, the process through which we came to value both traditional and formal education, and how remarkable it is that we survived at all. Most Makah people are very proud of our rich cultural heritage and cling tenaciously to our identity as ocean-going people, but we are so busy living our lives that many of us do not have the time, energy, or training to compile the record of our history like she has. We are truly blessed by her accomplishments, and I know, too, that her life has been profoundly changed by the folks out here from whom she learned.

JANINE BOWECHOP

*Director of the Makah Cultural
and Research Center*

Acknowledgments

Without the support of many individuals and institutions, this work would not have been possible. I begin with those who are conventionally listed as last but not least. My parents deserve prominent acknowledgment, since their personal sacrifices enabled me to attend college and graduate school—a first in our family. They have always adjusted gracefully to the different directions my work has taken me; their unqualified support has been a source of inspiration. To my husband, Johan, I offer unlimited gratitude. He supported me whenever I exhausted or doubted myself and helped me to press on—even at the expense of living apart for two years. He has been an extraordinarily patient and forgiving life companion. I thank other family members, too, including my "grandmother," Grace, and my aunt and uncle who both generously opened their respective homes while I researched at the University of Washington and the Smithsonian Institution archives. Despite my all too frequent retreats to the computer, our time together gave us a cherished opportunity to grow closer.

My research depended on the support of many on the Makah Indian Reservation and at the Smithsonian Institution. I was fortunate to receive the friendship of and professional support from numerous generous members of the Makah Nation. I would like to thank the Makah Tribal Council, the Makah elders, and heads of families for extending the hospitality that enabled me to live and work in

Neah Bay for a year. I am particularly grateful to Mary Greene and to George and Ione Bowechop for arranging places where I could live. I am indebted to those members of the Makah Cultural and Research Center (MCRC) Board of Trustees who in 1995 approved my proposal to research and volunteer there: Meredith Heilman, Oliver Ward (now deceased), Hubert Markishtum, Greg Colfax, Jeanie Johnson, Gary Ray, Chad Bowechop, Dave Sones, Bobby Rose, Steve Jimmicum, and Dean Parker. Additionally, the MCRC staff offered me infinite opportunities to learn through listening, hard work, and laughter. Each worked to keep me on track but also allowed me to explore and find my own way. I hope I learned well. I would like to thank them for their support and good fellowship: Janine Ledford Bowechop (director), Joyce Morden (former director), Keely Parker, Kirk Wachendorf, Helma Ward, Maria Pascua, Cora Buttram, Yvonne Burkett, Greig Arnold, Theresa Parker, and many others who worked there on a volunteer and contract basis.

I am also indebted to the participation of elders Isabelle Ides (now deceased), Ruth Claplanhoo, Irene Ward, Margaret Irving (now deceased), Mary Greene, and Hildred Ides (now deceased). They were good and generous teachers, as well as delightful companions. The following generously shared insights, knowledge, and friendship with me during my fieldwork: Andrea Alexander, Greig Arnold, Leonard Bowechop, Ernest Cheeka, Ed and Thelma Claplanhoo, Wilbur and Muzzie Claplanhoo (both now deceased), Mary Lou Denney, Deanna Gray, Meredith Heilman, Edie Hottowe, Mary Hunter, Sadie Johnson, Shirley Ward Johnson, Batch Lachester, Joseph Lawrence, Blanchard Matte, Jo Jo McGimpsey, Ted Noel, Bobby Rose, Frank Smith, Donna Wilkie, and Lance Wilkie. A special thanks to Janine and Chad Bowechop for introducing me to Neah Bay in the first place. Several others who had strong ties to Neah Bay, but who did not live there, played important roles: Jean André, Steve Brown, Mimi Washburn Curtis, Richard Daugherty, Ruth Kirk, Jeffrey Mauger, James Nason, Sandra Johnson Osawa (Makah), George Quimby, and Gary Wessen.

This project also benefited from the support of several different departments at the Smithsonian Institution. William Merrill of the Department of Anthropology and Nancy Fuller of the Center for Museum Studies (formerly known as the Office of Museum Programs) generously hosted me and mentored my research there. They not only guided my progress but also helped me navigate through the Smithsonian. I am also indebted to Karen Cooper of the American Indian Museum Studies Program of the Center for Museum Studies for allowing me to accompany her to a training program in Cherokee, North Carolina, and for sharing a multitude of sources with me. My research relied heavily upon the expertise of archival staff, and I was fortunate to have the support of staff at the Smithsonian Institution Archives, National Anthropological Archives, and Museum Reference Center. Finally, I would like to thank Joallyn Archambault, Tamara Bray, John Ewers, William Fitzhugh, Jane Glaser, Candace Greene, Rayna Green, Rick Hill, Tom Killion, William Merrill, Paul Perrot, William Sturtevant, Herman Viola, Dave Warren, Rick West, and Patricia Zell for their contributions to this project. Each in their own way have shared memories, resources, criticisms, and insights.

Three colleagues and dear friends from the University of California–Davis have my utmost respect and appreciation: Deborah Cahalen, Norman Stolzoff, and Circe Sturm gave countless hours in reviewing earlier drafts of this manuscript. Our collaborative consumption of chocolate and other unmentionables fueled many late-night and heartfelt discussions about our work and its relation to life. My appreciation also extends to other graduate student colleagues in the anthropology department and in the Hemispheric Initiative of the Americas group, especially Sylvia Escarcega and Mimi Saunders. A number of faculty members at UC–Davis not only supported this particular project but profoundly shaped my life. They include John Beaton, who had faith in the very beginning and gave me the opportunity to join the ranks of anthropologists. Without his support, I never would have turned a critical corner in my career. Thank you also to Charlie Hale, whose integrity and devotion to social justice has been an inspiration. The energy he puts into the lives of others, including my own, truly makes a difference. I am also indebted to Carol Smith for her critical acumen, loyal support, and invaluable good advice in all matters. On innumerable occasions she charted a course for me through unfamiliar territory; she has been one of my important touchstones.

I was also privileged to work through this research in an interdisciplinary environment with faculty from other departments. Stefano Varese in Native American Studies extended my intellectual training and field research into Mexico, thus making my experience more hemispheric in scope. He is a gracious mentor and graceful activist-scholar-parent who opened many doors for me and cemented my commitment on a number of counts. Steven Crum of Native American Studies gave many hours of guidance—from teaching and the ethics of academia to the history of Native Americans. His excellence in these matters shaped my intellectual development, and he saved my sanity in the midst of chaos more times than he knows. Finally, I am indebted to John Walton in the sociology department for his unwavering support and for all the times he bothered to challenge me when he felt I needed it. His involvement always improved whatever I was doing, a privilege I hope to receive in the future.

I carried out field research while holding a National Science Foundation Dissertation Improvement Grant, a Smithsonian Institution Graduate Research Fellowship in the Department of Anthropology, a Jacobs Fund Research Grant (Whatcom Museum Society), and fellowships from the UC–Davis Department of Anthropology. Predissertation research on indigenous community museums in Oaxaca, Mexico, was funded by a master's level field research grant from the Inter-American Foundation, a UC–Mexus research grant, and a UC–Davis humanities research grant. My Mexican research experience profoundly shaped my observation that the struggle for control over representation of identity between indigenous peoples and nation-states is a hemispheric and global phenomenon.

Lastly, I acknowledge Smith College and its support of my research endeavors. Reference librarian Sika Berger and student research assistants Burke Murphy, Leana Dagan, and Kathy Wicks deserve special thanks, as they have all been essential to preparation of the final version of this manuscript.

Although all of the above participated in or supported my research, I take responsibility for all opinions presented here as well as any errors or omissions.

Voices of a Thousand People

Introduction

I was visiting with Margaret Irving at her kitchen table when she asked me to grab a letter from another part of the room. I could hardly reach it for the boxes of dried bear grass, *čibap* (pronounced "chi-bup"; also known as swamp or blade grass), and seaweed stacked on the floor. Margaret was a basketweaver, a "master basketweaver" according to the invitation from the Washington State Museum to participate in a statewide basketry exhibition and conference. Margaret had woven baskets for nearly all of her eighty years. It was her passion for weaving that strengthened her resolve to travel to this conference despite her ailing health. I didn't know it at the time, but I would become her chauffeur for the five-hour journey, her roommate for late-night conversation in the Olympia hotel, and "an East Coast lady friend" for the remaining years of her life.

On that day four years ago, Margaret asked me to sit down and record the information the museum needed. She spoke to me of how her mother, Mary Allabush, taught her and her sisters how to weave:

It seemed like I just came to myself and I was making baskets. I already knew. The funniest part is I can't remember when. I remember her showing me how to do designs. She showed me how to put the color in and let it go. We used to all get down together. She'd soak bear grass in the morning, and it would be ready by evening. Then she'd pull it through her teeth to take off the groove. There used to be bottom-making parties with all the ladies to make bottoms for this person and then for that person. But each one of us have our own feel for the thickness of the bark. I couldn't pick up someone else's basket and weave. Get-together times were a time for my mother to let us know if we did something wrong or how things were done. She used to say, "This is the way it should be done." (Irving 1995)

Margaret's gift was in making solid-woven twine baskets with designs representing whales, canoes, ducks, elks, whirlwinds, and much more. These stunning baskets (see figure 1) are twined with bear grass, čiˑbap, and seaweed — all of which I was stepping over in her home. Cattail stems are used for the basket floor, or bottom.

In her conversations with me (and with anyone else who would listen), Margaret criticized the techniques popular among contemporary weavers. She admonished that proper Makah basketry should be more than "just" the plaiting of cedar bark — a technology and art form whose antiquity was established when an archaeological excavation at the Makah village of Ozette unearthed baskets many centuries old.

Margaret focused her passion for weaving on solid-twine weaving, a style shaped and controlled by Euro-American tastes. Early in Margaret's lifetime, a local trading post known as Washburn's store used to trade solid-twine Makah baskets for groceries. Old Man Washburn, as the proprietor was known, had a part in modifying Makah basketweaving so that baskets would fare better on the market as "Indian curiosities." Margaret remembers clearly how Washburn's General Store influenced Makah weaving customs: "They [the Washburns] made us use bear grass — they didn't like čiˑbap. Twenty-five-cent baskets, fifty-cent baskets, and dollar baskets each had a size. They measured them, and they had to be exact. . . . When I had my own family, I had to keep making baskets for groceries, but I didn't have time to teach. I feel it's something we survived on way back. It should be kept alive. We still sell baskets to survive" (Irving 1995). Making solid-twine baskets was a way for the Makah people to

1. Solid-woven twine basket with whirlwind design on cover woven by Margaret Irving (Makah) and curated in the collections of the MCRC. Photo by Eric Long and Keely Parker. Courtesy of the MCRC.

adapt to a rapidly changing economy. Yet Makah women also made it their own. Margaret felt a connection between the present and the adaptations made in the past; she was anxious for this weaving style to be passed on to younger generations and for this reason taught basketweaving at the community museum called the Makah Cultural and Research Center.

Margaret's passion for solid-twine weaving demonstrates the complexity of identity. Solid-twine weaving could be considered tourist art, somehow less authentic because it was developed in the context of a cash economy. But making such a judgment would be to constrain and define "real" Makah culture, boxing it into a precontact past.[1] While women maintain such traditions as gathering and weaving by teaching these to their daughters, other traditions, such as weaving aesthetics and technologies, have been generated anew.

Selling to the curio market enabled families to put food on their tables. Because making solid-twine baskets was interwoven with the daily lives of families, it eventually became part of what "being Makah" is all about today. While solid-twine weaving may be a newer technology than that used in precontact basketry, it is a tradition representative in some way of Makah identity and is thus considered worthy of preservation. As Margaret put it: "I want to hand down what was taught to me. Basketweaving is part of our history. It's our tradition. It should be taught so you don't forget where you come from and who you belong to" (Irving 1995).

The opportunity to befriend Margaret Irving arose because I had traveled to Neah Bay, Washington, in 1995 to live on the Makah reservation for one year and conduct research at the MCRC. MCRC's collections of precontact artifacts from Ozette village and several other traditional Makah sites are internationally famous. The expressions of material culture curated by the tribal museum/cultural center extend beyond the better known Ozette artifacts. The collections include a variety of reservation-era (post-1855) Makah material culture, including the type of baskets that Margaret wove. The MCRC also curates song recordings, oral historical tapes or transcripts, and tapes and transcripts in $q^wiq^widiččaq$ (the Makah language).

In caring for these different expressions of Makah identity, the MCRC embodies the historic processes of cultural adaptation and cultural continuity that Margaret addressed in her oral history. Like the swamp grass that Margaret used to weave her baskets, Makah identity and the museum that represents it are rooted, yet they bend with the currents. By *rooted* I mean it having a continuity with the past, not static or pristine. And by *cultural continuity* I do not mean a lack of change but that contemporary lifeways and belief systems bear a relation to what we might consider the distant past. Makah people perceive a connection with the past and make that connection a reality. Recognizing cultural continuity does not preclude recognizing cultural change, however.

A people's land base and the collective memory associated with it are among the roots of culture. People around the world, in a mind-boggling range of cultural diversity, attribute special meaning to landscape. Communities in both urban and rural settings in both industrialized and underdeveloped countries designate certain places as sacred and as pilgrimage sites, monuments, parklands, or retreats. In all cases, these special places speak to people and, by evoking powerful nostalgia, connect the past to the present and future.

For the Makah people, particularly meaningful places might include former village sites, the former location of Washburn's store, and customary fishing grounds in seemingly unmarked locations many miles out to sea. This book is the story of how a community museum/cultural center entered the network of places and things that are highly symbolic and "rooting" for the Makah people. Whereas Native American peoples were once positioned by museums as objects of study, Native American peoples now position themselves as active agents, employing museums as tools, or even living forces, that counter alienating and homogenizing social forces.

Voices of a Thousand People explores aspects of human experience — sense of place, collective remembering, museum representations, politics of representation — as it documents the nature of the Makah people's cultural survival. Memory is popularly perceived as a static, passive storage space that can be full, empty, or full of holes. Kuchler and Melion (1991) refute this dominant philosophy and argue that memory is an active process. The process of transmitting memories from one person to another is itself a form of memory. In other words, the process of memory, or the mnemonic process, becomes embodied in image production and material representation — painting, carving, and dancing, for example. Memory is a daily, patterned practice involving bodily experience and usually interaction with material culture (Nora 1989; Rappaport 1988).

In order to better understand (and celebrate) the nature of cultural survival of the Makah people, we must turn to the idea that the museum is a window onto a web of sociocultural processes. How is the MCRC related to Makah sense(s) of place and collective memories? Why has a museum emerged as an appropriate means to surviving culturally? What does the appropriation of museums by Native peoples teach us about the prospects for diversity in an era of globalization? These questions are at the core of this book.

My vantage point for observing and analyzing the processes of cultural change and continuity has been from museums. This museum case study, or museum ethnography, belongs to a field of inquiry known as the anthropology of museums. In the anthropology of museums literature, the museum is considered an arena for social relationships between and among diverse peoples of often unequal social status. James Clifford has called the museum a contact zone (1997, 192). Museums—whether ethnic, mainstream, or national—are ideal places for theorizing how representation, identity formation, and power relations work. They are an ideal place for recognizing what Arjun Appadurai (1990, 4) has called "node[s] of a complex transnational construction of imaginary landscapes," where the tension between cultural homogenization and cultural heterogenization plays itself out.

The sections below introduce themes that I will discuss in greater depth in subsequent chapters: the nature of the Makah experience with American colonization and the influence of that experience on present cultural preservation initiatives (chapters 1 and 2); the importance of the Ozette excavation to the establishment of the community museum and to groundbreaking Native/non-Native working relationships (chapter 3); and, finally, the degree to which an institution with quintessential European roots can become indigenized and used to forward Native American goals of self-determination (chapters 4 and 5).

Sense of Place and Makah Colonial Experience

When William Katz edited a compilation of writings by James Gilcrest Swan (1971), he titled it *Almost out of the World*, a phrase that captured American pioneer perceptions of the remoteness of the Makah reservation on Cape Flattery. The cape is a point of land that is not only the tip of the Olympic Peninsula in Washington State but also the northwesternmost point of what we now call the lower forty-eight states. Today, members of the Makah Indian Nation who inhabit Cape Flattery still hear references to their homeland as "the end of the world." I have heard tribal members say, "No. It's the beginning of the world," thus countering popular imaginations that perceive them at the margin of maps, and even of society.

The MCRC has become an important tool for addressing this perception of Native peoples as at the periphery. This tribal museum and cultural center allows the Makah Nation to represent themselves and their way of seeing the world. Clifford has remarked that mainstream museums have historically imagined themselves as a "center" where information discovered at the "periphery" is concentrated (Clifford 1997, 193). Since 1979, when the MCRC opened, the Makah people have challenged this imaginary by founding a museum whose curatorial voices emerge from Neah Bay rather than from "centers" of the nation, such as Washington DC.

It would be an oversimplification, however, to call the MCRC an alternative and independent center of knowledge-making that counters official historical and cultural accounts. As chapters 4 and 5 demonstrate, Makah curatorial voices are not completely independent from the museum profession nor from representations circulating on the national level. Even when I was living in Neah Bay, it took some time before I could make the conceptual leap from Neah Bay as "almost out of the world" to Neah Bay as a creative and lively community engaged with the world around it, indeed, shaping the world around it. For those unaccustomed to Neah Bay, the landscape and climate can create a sense of isolation. Flanked by the Strait of Juan de Fuca on the north side and the open Pacific Ocean to the west, the rocky shores and sandy beaches of the Makah reservation are pounded by surf (figure 2). The temperate rain forest of fir, hemlock, spruce, and cedar crowds the shoreline and stretches to the western slopes of the Olympic Mountains. The rain forest is fed by rainfall amounting to as much as ten feet annually. (That's feet, not inches.) When Farmer Jones, an employee of the U.S. government, tried to clear land at Neah Bay in 1862 to make room for gardens and homes, he commented: "It was the worse piece of land to clear I ever saw. [T]he soil was good, yet [it] was covered with a very heavy thicket of brush, among which were some logs, stumps, and fallen timber

2. Map showing the location of the five traditional Makah villages. Contemporary Neah Bay is located between *di·ya·* and *bi?id?a*. Drawn after map in the introductory gallery. Printed by permission of the MCRC.

and standing trees, some of which measured ten feet through at the but" (Riley 1968, 68). One has to work much harder now to see a forest anywhere like the one that thwarted this man.

Today, driving west on highways 101 and 112, the old-growth forest is no longer visible. Clear-cuts and second- or even third-growth forests flank the roadway mile after mile. At more than one point during my fieldwork on the reservation, winter rains gauged huge chunks of land out of these denuded hillsides and dumped them onto the narrow, hairpin turns, closing the road for a day or more. These same winter storms flung about tribal fishing boats, occasionally sinking them in Neah Bay's harbor. During my residence on the reservation at least two community dinners were held to muster support for the families of fishermen who had lost the means to their livelihoods in this way.

The towering giants in the rain forest enabled Native peoples of the Northwest Coast to become widely traveled maritime peoples. Among these, the Makah people skillfully pursued fish, seal, and whale for sustenance as well as trade. Through diligence and ingenuity, people converted giant cedars into dugout canoes that could reliably carry many individuals tens of miles out to sea or that could, just as capably, ride the steep surf as they returned to shore. Smaller versions of these canoes plied the quieter waters of estuaries and freshwater rivers that drained the rain forest and provided easier access to other resources such as fur-bearing animals, berries, and plant fibers.

Given this terrain, it is perhaps not surprising that the traditional Makah name for themselves is $q^{w}idi\check{c}\check{c}a\text{?}a\cdot t\check{x}$, or People Who Live by the Rocks and Seagulls. An anglicized pronunciation of their name is roughly "kwi-deech-cha-ahtkh." The Makah people are related by language, culture, and kinship to the Native peoples on the southern side of Vancouver Island in British Columbia. Anthropologists have referred to these peoples who straddle the U.S.-Canadian border as the southernmost speakers of the Wakashan language family, or Nootkan peoples (Renker and Gunther 1990, 422).

As with colonized landscapes everywhere, names and places have a way of getting scrambled. On one of my breaks from working in the museum archives, Makah elder Helma Ward told me the story of how in the eighteenth century Capt. James Cook misnamed Northwest Coast peoples as he entered a sheltered area along what is now known as Vancouver Island. At its closest point, the shoreline of the Island (as it is referred to in Neah Bay) is no more than ten miles away from Neah Bay across the Strait of Juan de Fuca. Captain Cook encountered Native peoples when they paddled out to him in their dugout cedar canoes. Helma told me the story as it was told to her by Adam Shiwish of Vancouver Island:

The people were all gathered together at Friendly Cove. While they were there it was foggy. After a while, they heard "ding-ding." They'd never heard a bell before. They didn't know what it was. "Ding-ding." They said, "let's get in our boats and see what that is." They started out to look at what it is. "Maybe it's an animal. Maybe we'll be killed!" What they saw was a man looking through a window. "Ding-ding." They got scared. He had hair all over his face. They had never seen a boat before. They were keeping their distance. Men came out on the decks and were talking. They didn't know what they were saying. Then the men motioned for them to come. A couple went onto the boat. They came back with eyes big. "They got everything there — something to see through" [a window]. They were asked, "What is your people's name?" They responded, "nootka." They thought the men wanted to get out of where they were. So they were saying "nootka," telling them to go out around the island. But the men decided to stay. So they stayed and were fed. The next day they were told again how to leave — "nootka" — go out around the island. So they've been called Nootka people ever since. (H. Ward 1995)

Cook, and explorers who followed him, not only charted the territory and collected samples from nature but also mapped the Native peoples of the Northwest Coast, inscribing names for them onto maps and collecting items of their material culture. Some of these misnomers, like *Nootka* and *Wakashan* took hold. It wasn't until 1980 that the Vancouver Island relatives of the Makah Tribe changed their collective name from Nootka to Nuuchahnulth (Arima 1983).

Colonial inscriptions and the misunderstandings that accompany them can be hard to counteract. The name *Makah* is as much a colonial product as the name *Nootka*. The term *Makah* happens to be one applied to the people who called themselves qʷidiččaʔatx̌ by the Clallam, a tribe further east along the Strait of Juan de Fuca (Renker and Gunther 1990, 429). Yet because the Makah people are related to the Nuuchahnulth peoples, much Makah basketry and carving located in museum collections nationwide are categorized as Nootkan.

3. After three decades of collecting from tribal communities in the Northwest Coast, James Gilcrest Swan's office was brimming with "Indian curiosities," Port Townsend, 1891. Courtesy of the Medford Historical Society.

The explorers, sea merchants, and early ethnologists who followed compiled these ethnographic collections (Gunther 1972). The Northwest Coast is only one of many regions to be charted, ordered, and symbolically controlled through collecting (Arnoldi 1992; Bieder 1986; Boone 1993; Defert 1982; Hinsley 1992, 1993; Stewart 1984; and Thomas 1989). Some of these earliest ethnologists — people like James Gilcrest Swan — researched Native American cultures on the side while carrying out jobs as teachers, missionaries, merchants, or Indian agents (figure 3). While juggling his responsibilities to the U.S. Office of Indian Affairs in the latter half of the nineteenth century, Swan collected Makah material culture and documented customs for the Smithsonian Institution. His work culminated in the publication of a monograph, *The Indians of Cape Flattery* (1870), the first monograph written about a single Northwest Coast Native people.

When James Swan arrived on the Makah reservation in the late 1850s he was the personal embodiment of a large-scale project to map and control Washington Territory. The Makah people were, not surprisingly, uneasy with some of Swan's actions. Swan wrote the following about his effort to make a census of the five Makah villages:

Here [at Wa'atch] I found the first evidence of a determination on their part not to give me their names. They said if they did, that the Bostons [Euro-Americans] would come and bring with them great herds of cattle, which would eat up all their grass and berries. . . . [They] finally declared that I should not take their names, for if I did, they would all grow sick and die. . . . [And at Ozette] the old chief then said the Indians were afraid if I took their names that they would have the smallpox. They thought all I had to do, was to blow in my book on their names, and I could bring any sickness on them I desired. (Swan 1971, 111–13)

Clearly, charting, naming, and mapping were perceived by the Makah people as associated with malevolent forces. However, as he did on many occasions, James Swan used his personal charm, patronage, and titular status to persuade the Makah people to consent to his requests.

Researchers such as James Swan represent an untrained or amateur stage of anthropology. Later ethnologists would be considered professional scholars and founders of American anthropology. Franz Boas was one of the most prominent. By the late nineteenth century, Northwest Coast scholars, such as Franz Boas, were devoting themselves fully to researching and documenting Native peoples and to designing museum exhibits to represent them (Hinsley and Holm 1976; Jacknis 1985). Whether we refer to Swan or Boas, the context for early material culture collecting and early anthropology was colonial (Cole 1982, 1985).

An example from Makah history illustrates why many tribes associate museums with the history of their colonization by Euro-Americans (Clifford 1997; Cole 1982). In 1875 Indian Agent C. A. Huntington of the Neah Bay Agency traveled for three weeks with a group of Makah children from the Ba'adah boarding school. First they traveled by canoe to Victoria, on Vancouver Island, to visit various missionary projects. Then they continued to Olympia, Washington, by steamer. Along the way, Huntington took the children on tours through industrial shops they had never seen before. They visited a sawmill in Port Ludlow. In Olympia they visited printing offices, shoe shops, a flour mill, and other businesses. In part, this tour appears intent on revealing non-Indian lifeways to these children. Yet the tour also provided an opportunity to display the children as exemplary products of a civilizing project. While in Olympia, Huntington was invited to bring the children to a public meeting that was assembled especially to see the children from Neah Bay. There, the children entertained the audience for two hours by singing and rehearsing scripture lessons. One Olympia Sunday school superintendent commented to Huntington that he thought the Makah children did better than their white counterparts would have.[2]

These performances, which were intended to show the progress made by Indian children at boarding schools, were a direct outcome of American political and economic control over Indian territories across the country. These types of performances — displays of Western visions of progress and civilization — were by no means restricted to Washington Territory. Throughout the United States, museums and world's fairs were important means for representing Native American peoples in late-nineteenth- and early-twentieth-century popular culture. Between 1876 and 1915, more than one hundred million people in the United States attended world's fairs which usually featured Native American and other peoples of non-European descent (Howard and Pardue 1996, 70).

The same year C. A. Huntington was touring Makah children through the Northwest Coast region, collections of Native American artifacts were being amassed for the Centennial Exposition in Fairmont Park, Philadelphia. This exposition would open in May 1876 to commemorate the centennial of the American nation's independence. Congressional funding to support a U.S government exhibition enabled Spencer Baird at the Smithsonian Institution to purchase artifacts directly for the exhibition. Since the Indian Bureau of the Department of the Interior was planning an exhibition of Indian cultures, Baird argued that the bureau should collaborate with the Smithsonian and combine efforts to effect a more exhaustive display.[3] Through this collaboration, Baird secured sufficient funds to commission James Swan, who by now lived in Port Townsend, Washington. Swan would become the first salaried and commissioned collector on the Northwest Coast secured by the U.S. government specifically for ethnological collecting (Cole 1985, 19–22; Trennert 1974, 120; Zegas 1976, 163). Swan eventually amassed about five hundred objects for the exposition; his was considered the most extensive and valuable collection from the Northwest Coast at that time (Cole 1985, 27–28).

Makah material culture items and Makah persons were on Swan's collecting checklist. That year, and subsequent years, when James Swan was collecting vast quantities of material for expositions, the Indian agent in Neah Bay commented that Makah women were selling sea grass table mats and baskets and that there was a ready market for what was then called "Indian curiosities." Swan also commissioned the production of items such as fully equipped, model-size whaling canoes.[4] Thus Makah whaling, fishing, woodworking, and dance materials were among the tons of Northwest Coast items shipped to Philadelphia for display. When the exposition was over, those materials on display were added to the Smithsonian's collections.

Swan envisioned more than just displays of artifacts at the Centennial Exposition, however. He envisioned at least three sets of Native Americans paddling their canoes on the Schuykill River that bordered the exposition park. Makah whalers in a Makah whaling canoe were among those Swan felt would make fine living examples of Native civilization; however, Swan did not succeed in presenting the whalers (Cole 1985, 26). Although by the standards of their day the ethnologists who created the displays were empathetic to Native American peoples, they were operating from a perspective now considered not only limited but dangerous to human rights. Baird wrote in 1876: "So far as the ethnological display is concerned, it is quite reasonable to infer that, by the expiration of a second hundred-year period of the life of the American Republic, the Indian will have entirely ceased to present any distinctive characters, and will be merged into the general population" (Trennert 1974, 127). This worldview assumed that Native American peoples would inevitably progress toward Euro-American civilization.

By the World's Columbian Exposition in 1893, living Native American peoples were arranged for display. Several Indian boarding schools from around the country provided children for some of these living exhibitions — performances of progress that resembled those orchestrated by Reverend Huntington of Makah children. Boarding school children sang, recited, played music, and displayed their written exercises at the world's fair. Proficiency in farming and various trades, such as wagonmaking, blacksmithing, and broommaking were demonstrated in the hopes of disrupting the public's stereotypes of Indian people and of convincing them that Indian children could be educated (Lomawaima 1994).[5] These Indian school exhibits were well patronized, with as many as sixteen to twenty-three thousand visitors passing through exhibits daily. As many scholars have written, world's fairs cast Native Americans in few roles, roles that revealed Euro-American sensibilities about savagery, civilization, and progress (Benedict 1983; Ewers 1958; Hinsley 1981 [1994]; Lester 1972; Trennert 1974; Yengoyan 1994; Zegas 1976).

The long history of efforts to redefine Native American civilization and replace indigenous ways of knowing with Euro-American ones led to contemporary Native American critiques of museum representations and their correlation with colonialism. Like countless others, the Makah Tribe's material culture was subjugated to intense ethnological interest. Ethnologists preserved Makah material in the face of anticipated cultural extinction, while missionaries and employees of the U.S. government hastened the assimilation process. Through these interwoven efforts, Makah ways of knowing became what Foucault has called *subjugated knowledge* — a set of knowledge that has been disqualified (1974, 203), one shown to be mere superstition or primitive thinking, for example.

Given these associations between past museum practices and colonial history, why would the Makah people turn to the museum format to express their own visions of Makah history and identity? To understand this we need to return to the generations of women who modified their basketweaving to accommodate the market of Indian curiosities, a market they tapped primarily through Washburn's store. The solid-twine weaving Margaret so passionately cared about embodied the adaptation of values and skills to a changing Euro-American-dominated economy and political environment. Nonetheless, the new weaving tradition still made sense to Makah women, who perceived its continuity with past lifeways. Like the baskets, the Makah community museum/cultural center represents the adaptation of traditional values and skills to a changing economy and political environment. In each case, something at once new and traditional is created: both the baskets and the museum are products of a dialogue with non-Native, or Western, ways of thinking.

Native American community museums such as the MCRC operate in a larger social context dominated by what Clifford has called a *Western temporality* (1988, 232). Western temporality is a Western sense of time and civilization that expects progress and modernization to move human civilization "forward," leaving indigenous lifeways "behind," stuck perpetually in a timeless past. This linear framework has largely shaped the representations of Native peoples, including the Makah people. The tradition of ethnographic representations of indigenous peoples produced by anthropologists has trapped in an "ethnographic present, this timeless, distant, and exotic Other" (Fabian 1983).

Throughout the nineteenth and early twentieth centuries, Native American culture was earnestly collected; the assumption was that Native American culture — like a finite supply of sand in an hourglass — needed to be preserved before it ran out. Despite dramatic improvements in museology and anthropology, representations of indigenous peoples in a timeless past, or as curiosities, still exist. Coco Fusco and Guillermo Gómez-Peña discovered, for example, that their performance art installation — designed to satirize the colonial history of representing indigenous peoples — was repeatedly experienced by viewers as a genuine museum display of savages in a cage (Fusco and Heredia 1993). Such visitor expectations should force us to question whether or not museums are *post*colonial yet. Although anthropologists and museologists are quick to highlight the improvements in our profession (and there are many), counteracting a colonial legacy that has permeated not only museums but also popular culture is not a simple matter, as some curators have painfully discovered (Cannizzo 1989).

In spite of the problematic history of Native American representations in museums, more than one hundred Native communities in the United States have chosen to establish their own museums; approximately fifty have done the same in Canada.[6] Additionally, I have estimated there are nearly fifty indigenous community museums in Mexico (Erikson 1996a). If Native American communities consider museums, a Western institution, to contain problematic representations and practices, why do they use them? Consider that these communities have been subjected to sometimes extreme external control. From this history has come a heightened awareness of the dangers inherent in being defined by others.

Communities might also expect economic benefits from these institutions. In Neah Bay, for example, the museum provides professional jobs for a number of Makah people whose other employment choices include commercial fishing, commercial logging (and the salvaging of stumps for "shake bolts"), artistry, tourism-related retail businesses, tribal government, the Indian Health Service, the Neah Bay public school system, or the Clallam County Correctional Facility (as well as other major off-reservation employers). Despite these seasonal and year-round opportunities, the unemployment rate is approximately 51 percent, with 49 percent of reservation households below the poverty level (Renker 1994, 327). Although tribal museums offer job opportunities and stimulate a tourist economy, they are very expensive for tribal governments and operate at a high financial risk.

Tribal museums/cultural centers offer hope for far more than economic benefit. They offer an opportunity to represent one's own identity through a media that is globally respected as a knowledge-making institution. In a nation-state arena, museums help empower national identities by offering individuals a perception of shared culture (Anderson 1991). They seek to counteract cultural and political invisibility and bolster self-esteem. By appropriating the museum format, Native American communities can represent themselves to external others and to themselves within the Makah community (both on and off the reservation).

How does the MCRC translate Makah identity to external others and yet still speak to its host community? Two material culture elements in Makah historical and contemporary experience are useful for answering this question: canoe and *longhouse*, both of which are used metaphorically by the MCRC.

Welcome to This House: The Makah Cultural and Research Center

Welcome to this house, all of you who have traveled near and far.
Welcome to our beach; we tie up your canoe.

With these words of welcome the MCRC—also known as the museum—connects itself to two important elements of Makah identity: it offers hospitality to visitors who have traveled to this small, coastal village and likens itself to the longhouse. The MCRC is a place for representing and performing Makah identity, for strengthening existing social ties, and for creating new ones. In this sense the museum and cultural center presents itself as and functions like a modern version of a traditional longhouse.[7]

In addition to welcoming visitors, this museum/cultural center develops and hosts various cultural programs in the Makah community and provides Makah artisans with an outlet for selling their work, which includes baskets, carvings, screenprints, and beaded items. The museum's remarkable collection of precontact artifacts from Ozette, a now uninhabited Makah village site, is one of the primary attractions on the reservation. The MCRC bolsters the cultural tourism sector of the reservation economy by drawing fifteen thousand to twenty-two thousand visitors each year (Dean Runyan and Associates 1995; MCRC n.d.).

In the twelve months that I lived on the reservation and researched at the museum, I observed that tourists quieted as they passed through the museum entrance, darkened to enhance preservation of the rare Northwest Coast artifacts on display. While their eyes adjusted, tourists often stood rooted at the entrance, where remarkable totem poles and a house post spire upward toward the dim ceiling, the carved faces turned toward the guests in a well-practiced stance of greeting.

These dramatic carvings were created by a Makah man named Young Doctor, c̓uyʔiˑ, born in 1851. Young Doctor is said to have carved with the guidance of spirit helpers who came to him in his dreams (Densmore 1939; McCurdy 1981). Nearly a century ago, these cedar sentinels greeted visitors to Young Doctor's longhouse, or pot-latch house, located on the street facing Neah Bay harbor. Another of the many functions of Young Doctor's longhouse was to display artworks in a museum, like fashion for tourists and collectors.[8]

Today, Young Doctor's carvings are located in an institution that projects itself as a modern version of a Northwest Coast long-house. The architectural features of the MCRC's two main buildings (galleries/administrative offices and storage facility) evoke the cedar plank siding of longhouses indigenous to the Northwest Coast cul-ture area (figure 4). The MCRC grounds host a smaller third building on the front lawn — a reconstruction of a postcontact longhouse. The MCRC makes this facility available to the community as an al-ternative gathering place to the community hall at the other end of town.

The expression of the museum as a longhouse extends far beyond the architectural level. The MCRC projects its sense of self as a cul-tural center, a gathering place for fostering a *living* culture. As Wayne Suttles describes it, the Northwest Coast longhouse "was not merely a dwelling: it was a food-processing and storage plant, and it was a workshop, recreation center, temple, theater, and fortress" (1991, 214). Based on my experience, MCRC hosts nearly all of the ac-tivities typically associated with a longhouse. Because I researched at the MCRC, I was pressed into service on the museum's grounds cut-ting fish, cooking potatoes, and serving ceremonial dinners. Partici-pant observation at the MCRC was a challenge in keeping up with all that went on; it meant attending language classes, helping move ceremonial gear stored there, and enjoying the many expressions of Makah identity, such as formal speeches, dances of blessing, and prayer offerings. Yet for all of this activity, the longhouse meta-

4. View of the MCRC, Makah reservation, Neah Bay, Washington. Photo by Patricia Pierce Erikson.

phor refers to more than its architectural style and social role in the community.

Narratives of the MCRC history usually begin with the contents of ancestral longhouses being washed into the sea. In 1970 winter storm waves slammed a coastal area of Makah territory known as u·se·ʔiłt, or Ozette (see figure 2). Ozette had been one of the tribe's five main villages. However, by early in the twentieth century Ozette's permanent residents had abandoned it and moved to another of the five villages: Neah Bay. The mandatory schooling of children in Neah Bay, and the centralization of commerce there propelled consolidation of the five villages. Since then, Ozette has been used for seasonal residence and subsistence use. Makah people still live at two other village sites: waʔač̓ and c'u·yas.

Leaving Ozette has become an important part of remembering Ozette. Given that Ozette land passed out of Makah control and had to be regained further complicated Ozette's association with the history of territorial rights. While living in Neah Bay my sense was that Ozette had become a highly charged site of memory, one associated with the history of colonization. The Makah museum, whose exhibits focus primarily on Ozette has by association also become a crucial place for remembering. Indeed, a desire to remember was a fundamental motivation for establishing the museum.

In 1970, when winter storm waves exposed the remains of a longhouse in the village embankment and hikers from nearby Olympic National Park began walking away with artifacts, the Makah Tribe decided to excavate and preserve the Ozette village site (Claplanhoo 1994; Daugherty 1995). What followed was one of the most important excavations ever done in the Northwest Coast, one conducted jointly by Washington State University and the Makah Tribe (Cutler 1994; Daugherty 1995). Archaeologist Richard Daugherty and journalist Ruth Kirk persuasively communicated the extraordinary nature of this site to the public and to Congress (Kirk 1975). Their efforts were matched by the strong leadership and moving oratory of several Makah Tribal Council members and elders. Collectively, their efforts significantly raised public awareness of the Makah people.

After ten years, the excavation had uncovered more than 55,000 artifacts from several longhouses. The mudslide that had entombed Ozette village longhouses five hundred years earlier created what archaeologists call a "wet site" situation that preserves organic materials to an extraordinary degree (Mauger 1991, 32). Preservation enabled archaeologists to uncover not only house structures and material possessions but fine details characterizing the daily environment: beetles, green leaves, and, at a carver's work site, cedar shavings (Mauger 1994). While the excavated materials can be called artifacts, they can also be called family possessions. The excavated longhouses were the homes of a Makah community caught in the wake of the landslide. In this sense, the museum has become the new home for these possessions.

The effects of the excavation were many. By 1979 the tribe established a museum — governed by an all-Makah board of trustees — to care for these artifacts. In addition to establishing a museum, new working relationships with archaeologists were formed that continue to provide a model for other projects around the country. The newly established tribal museum played a significant role in making the Makah people more visible and placing them on the cultural tourism map. In an interview with me, archaeologist Richard Daugherty described the importance of the Ozette archaeological excavation to establishing a presence in the literature and in the public mind:

> In the Northwest Coast, you know if you look around and watch how anthropology and archaeology develop . . . the groups that you learn about are those that have been studied. You know, the Nootka became very well known because Drucker did a great study. Boas's thing [ethnographies] and so forth, the Tlingit, the Haida, . . . they had all this kind of material. Well now we find out that it's just as good down here [in Makah culture]. It's just as elaborate. You only know about these people or they only get into the textbooks if something has happened or someone has done something or there's something spectacular about them. (Daugherty 1995)

The renown of the excavation (in addition to the reservation's remote location) made the MCRC a desirable tourist destination.

Among the exhibits planned for the galleries of the new museum was a reproduction of one of the fifteenth-century Ozette longhouses — the building and its contents. I interpret this indoor longhouse exhibit as another expression of the museum's concept of itself as a longhouse. When the longhouse exhibit was first constructed, it was assembled and weathered outside the museum. Before it was moved indoors, a potlatch-style party inaugurated it after the fashion of longhouse dedications (cf. Cranmer Webster 1991). Even after officially becoming an exhibit, the building functioned like a Makah longhouse by hosting events that marked turning points in tribal members' lives, such as high school graduations and weddings. In essence, the longhouse exhibit added another ceremonial space to the options available in the village (see right side of figure 5). The Makah community diverged from conventional museum representations of Native American peoples, instead produc-

5. View of the "Chief's Corner" *(left)* and Ozette longhouse *(right)* in the permanent exhibitions of the MCRC 1998. Photo by Eric Long and Keely Parker. Courtesy of the MCRC.

ing an exhibit that not only represented a longhouse but was a longhouse used by a living community.

It was in this longhouse exhibit, while tagging along with a tour group, that I realized how important the museum is as a place for remembering, for retelling oral histories, and for teaching anew those who are unfamiliar with Makah history and culture. Leading this tour was a member of MCRC's board of trustees. She was recounting a few moments of the Makah encounter with colonialism for the two families of tourists who stood quietly in the darkened interior of the longhouse. Fragrant, dried salmon hung in strips from the rafters over their heads. Reproductions of Ozette cedar bark mats and kerfed cedar storage boxes rested on the sleeping bench beside them and awaited their touch. The tour guide explained how the qʷidičča?a·tx̌ people did not know what to make of the European trading ships at first. She said they thought they looked like houses floating on the water. So they called the people who came from the ships *babałids*, which means, literally, "house-floating-on-the-water-people." She pointed behind her, up the hill beyond the museum, and told how one of the five traditional villages, known as biʔidʔa, used to stand there. That was until a box of blankets came ashore, blankets contaminated with smallpox. The disease ended up wiping out biʔidʔa.[9] Overall, she said, more than 60 percent of the population was lost.

The tour guide recounted further that "the Spanish were among the first to land here. They built a fort, but our men ran them off." On August 1, 1790, Spanish naval officer Alferez del Navio Quimper named the village of Neah Bay, Bahia de Nuñez Gaona (Gunther 1972, 65). The fort referred to by the museum guide was built by Salvador Fidalgo, who arrived on May 29, 1792, on the *Princesa Real*. The Spanish hoped Bahia de Nuñez Gaona would provide a badly needed defensive site. Upon settling they planted a cross, built a bakery, set up a blacksmith's shop, mounted guns, and cultivated a plot of land only to abandon it in September because of difficulties with its location and uncooperative residents (Hayes 1999, 70; Gunther 1972, 67–72; Riley 1968, 61).

I was reminded of the tour guide's narrative of colonial encounters later that year when I was researching Makah artifact collections at the Smithsonian Institution. It was while photographing each artifact for the MCRC that I came across a brick. This brick had been collected by James Swan over a century earlier. The brick was labeled as having come from the former Spanish fort site in Makah territory. Elsewhere, Swan documented the brick as follows: "Colchote then spoke of the ancient Spanish settlement at Neah Bay, which has long since gone to ruins. He said the house was a brick one, with a board or shingle roof, and after the Spaniards left it was burned down by the Indians. He pointed out to me the site, and one of his slaves, after digging a couple of feet in the soft soil, found one of the old Spanish bricks, which he gave me; it is thin like a tile, slightly burned on the outside, but the centre is dark and looks like the adobe clay of California" (Swan 1971, 84). This brick, curated carefully in a padded metal drawer at the Smithsonian Institution, represents several moments: a moment of failure in the Spaniards' colonizing efforts on the Northwest Coast, and, conversely, a moment of success in the American colonization of the region. It also embodies a moment when the Makah people represented themselves and their history to James Swan. After reading Swan's diary of his time in Neah Bay, it seemed to me that the Makah people did this often when the opportunity arose.

Whereas Colchote recounted episodes of Makah history for Swan on the beach, contemporary Makah people often share Makah oral history in the context of the MCRC. Sometimes they do this formally as a Makah tour guide and sometimes, especially those who are not on the museum staff, by escorting family members, visiting friends, or dignitaries through the museum galleries. They give their account of Makah history, usually drawing from the oral history of their own family.

Based on the diverse Makah narratives shared in the museum galleries, ties to specific places on the Makah landscape or to specific objects are a common denominator in the Makah memories of colonial encounters. As Julie Cruikshank has argued, oral history is not an object to be collected and stored for later, synchronic analysis. Both material culture objects and stories have dynamic, continuing lives, "not so much the 'same stories' as ongoing ideas, continually reinvested with new meaning" (Cruikshank 1992, 7).

In representing Ozette and caring for the contents of several village longhouses, the museum has become a dynamic link to these memories and to the landscape. A Makah father mentioned to me that he brought his daughter to one of the remarkable beach dioramas in the museum and that together they had placed a stone with the others in the beach diorama. He said that stone was there so she could remember their time together. That started me thinking about how the MCRC had become an altogether new place on the landscape for being Makah and for remembering that experience.

Museum Subjectivity

The anthropology of museums — a highly interdisciplinary concentration in cultural anthropology — distinguishes itself from its older relative: museology. It acknowledges that museums have been valuable sites for practicing science, in general, and anthropology, in particular. Historically, museology conducted an archaeology of objects — the discovery and recovery of the "original" meaning of an object, or the reconstruction of ancient cultures using material remains. From this perspective, material culture seemed to offer a transparent representation of the cultures collected.

The anthropology of museums, emerging most dramatically in the last twenty years, has reframed the concept of a museum. The museum is now a place for attempting to understand how identity is formed and represented, how social inequalities are established, reproduced, and disrupted. One effect of this reframing has been a theoretical interest in the "biography of things," or the history of an object's social life (Kopytoff 1986). The anthropology of museums has analyzed how objects are repeatedly recontextualized throughout the stages of creation, collection, exhibition, and viewing. Michael Ames has suggested that objects in museum collections can be seen as palimpsests, literally, writing tablets used repeatedly after earlier writing has been erased. (A modern example of this would be a chalkboard.) Objects or works of art are like palimpsests: layers of meaning are superimposed upon objects, each layer failing to completely obliterate the previous one. Similarly, layers of meaning are laid down upon the museum itself.[10] Despite this layering process, some meanings, or interpretations, are given greater credence than others.

In the large body of literature concerning itself with how some ideas become dominant ways of seeing the world, museums are identified as one of the types of institutions through which standards of truth, beauty, and history are established. Throughout their history, museums have primarily represented elite tastes and ideologies. Yet the public can be socialized to dominant ideas through the museum such that these ideas or sentiments become "natural," unquestioned, or hegemonic elements of collective consciousness or memory.

Collective memory refers to a set of memories held in common by a group of people, a set of memories that serve as a basis for group identity. Holidays, hardships, and heroes are all examples of the many possible events, conditions, or icons that constitute collectively held memory. Collective memory is often located spatially, connected to certain landmarks, monuments, homes, and so forth. Anthropologists have paid special attention to how dominant elites use museums to foster perceptions of shared kinship in the nation-state (Anderson 1991; Duncan 1991; Dominguez 1990; Handler 1985; Haraway 1989; Hinsley 1992, 1993; Hooper-Greenhill 1991, 1992; Karp and Levine 1992; Lomnitz-Adler 1992; Norkunas 1993; Sacco 1996; Yengoyan 1994).

Native American identity, material culture, and bodies are among the things that have been appropriated for nation-building. This is not the whole story, however. Native American peoples have also tried to survive culturally, economically, and politically through their interactions with museums. Today, Native peoples enjoy some control in their own museums — tribal museums, community centers, urban cultural centers — where they can represent themselves and use these self-representations to disrupt stereotypes. Given the authority of museums in Western societies to establish truth, beauty, and history, museums are ideal places for these disruptions to take place and for critical consciousness to emerge.

It is no longer enough to say that museums are agencies of social control that have served dominant interests. In the introductory chapter to *Theorizing Museums* Sharon Macdonald argues that recent social changes call for more nuanced analyses of museums. She highlights changes such as the dramatic proliferation and relative democratization of museums globally. While the association between museums and dominant social sectors is still strong, theorizing museums must also account for the many cultural logics that have appropriated the museum model (Macdonald and Fyfe 1998). The anthropology of museums has developed a number of analytical tools for understanding that museums can be both powerful authors and a space or terrain where social relations and contestations are played out (Jones 1993; Kaplan 1996).

Voices of a Thousand People uses an ethnography of the MCRC to argue that Native American museums/cultural centers are hybrid embodiments of Native and non-Native perspectives. As a synthesis of cultural forms, they reveal a process of collaboration between diverse peoples amid conditions of unequal empowerment. Native American museums/cultural centers are both translators and translations, agents of social change and products of accommodation.

Key contributors to my analysis (and to the anthropology of museums literature in general) are Mary Louise Pratt and James Clifford. In 1992 Mary Pratt published *Imperial Eyes: Travel Writing and Transculturation*, and through Clifford, who translated Pratt's theory to museum analysis, Pratt's writing has enriched the theorizing of museums. Drawing upon sociologist Fernando Ortiz, Pratt offered a theory of contact zones,[11] describing them as a space of colonial encounter involving "conditions of coercion, radical inequality, and intractable conflict" (Pratt 1992, 7). She modeled a contact zone as:

> an attempt to invoke the spatial and temporal *copresence* of subjects previously separated by geographic and historical disjunctures, and whose trajectories now intersect. By using the term *contact* I aim to foreground the *interactive*, improvisational dimensions of colonial encounters so easily ignored or suppressed by diffusionist accounts of conquest and domination. A contact perspective emphasizes how subjects are constituted in and by their relations to each other. . . . [It stresses] *copresence, interaction, interlocking understandings and practices, often within radically asymmetrical relations of power.* (Pratt 1992, 6–7; emphasis added)

Pratt's model of contact zones preserves the experience of inequality, yet allows that those who are colonized need not remain passive. Instead, they may select and create from elements of the dominant culture, using them as a way to engage with the dominant culture. She calls this self-made cultural portrait *autoethnography* (Pratt 1992, 7).

Following Pratt's model, Clifford argued that museums are more than tools for inevitable colonization, globalization, or homogenization of particular ways of knowing and representing the human past (1997, 216). Museums may also be considered autoethnographic — a means to negotiate and counteract dominant trends in a society. By calling museums contact zones, Clifford highlights the museum as a place where different systems of meaning encounter one another and where its collections and exhibitions are the product of their negotiation with one another: "When museums are seen as contact zones their organizing structure as a *collection* becomes an ongoing historic, political, moral *relationship*—a power-charged set of exchanges, of push and pull. The organizing structure of the museum-as-collection functions like [Mary Louise] Pratt's frontier. A center and a periphery are assumed. The center a point of gathering, the periphery an area of discovery" (Clifford 1997, 192–93). Historically, national or mainstream museums have been the center, the terrain where *non*-Native paradigms have been institutionalized and legitimated, leaving Native American cultures as the periphery or zone of discovery (Jonaitis 1991; Cranmer Webster 1991).

Clifford illustrates museums-as-contact zones with a 1989 encounter between curators of the Portland Museum of Art in Oregon and several Tlingit elders serving as consultants to the museum. Clifford (also in the role of consultant) and the curators expected the elders to comment directly on the objects in the Rasmussen Collection. Instead, elders used the objects as mnemonic devices, or what Clifford calls *aides-mémoires*. In a somewhat spontaneous ceremonial event, members of different Tlingit clans performed songs and stories demonstrating their respective rights and privileges related to the ceremonial objects.

It became obvious to Clifford and the museum staff that the objects in the Rasmussen Collection were far more than aesthetically pleasing objects with cultural meaning. The Tlingit referred to them as "'records,' 'history,' and 'law,' inseparable from myths and stories expressing ongoing moral lessons with current political force" (Clifford 1997, 191). Suddenly the categories of *artifact* and *art* seemed inadequate. Indeed, looking at tribal museums and cultural centers allows us to recognize them as the product of ongoing contact between divergent ways of seeing the world. They are points of articulation between local and global forces and identities (Erikson 1996c). *Voices of a Thousand People* draws upon concepts such as contact zone and autoethnography to theorize the dialogic processes that create museums. As concrete institutional embodiments of dynamic and diverse social processes, museums have complex identities I term *museum subjectivity.*

Understanding museums requires understanding who they are and how as an institution they perceive and construct their own identity. In offering the term *museum subjectivity* I am drawing from feminist theories on the complexity of human identity. Just as with human subjectivity, museum subjectivity is neither innate nor independent of its contexts. It is relational. Linda Alcoff describes human identity as "relative to a constantly shifting context, to a situation that includes a network of elements involving others, the objective economic conditions, cultural and political institutions and ideologies, and so on" (1997, 349).

In parallel fashion, museum subjectivity is the product of interactions between the institution, individuals, and organizations and of broad, social processes. The concept of museum subjectivity, then, refers to the institution's sense of self as related to and shaped by the world around it. As Hooper-Greenhill has said (1992, 191): "There is no essential museum. The museum is not a pre-constituted entity that is produced in the same way at all times. . . . Identities, targets, functions, and subject positions are variable and discontinuous. Not only is there no essential identity for museums . . . [but such identities] are subject to constant change as the play of dominations shifts and new relations of advantage and disadvantage emerge." In 1979 when Edward P. Alexander (1979, 14) called attention to a Metropolitan Museum curator's ideas on the hybrid nature of museum personalities, he, too, seems to have been contemplating the parallel complexities of identity between individuals and museums.

Theorizing museum subjectivity is a necessary part of understanding how museums contribute to processes such as knowledge-making, remembering, and reinforcing or dismantling social inequalities. Pertinent to my interest in tribal museums has been Foucault's definition of subjugated knowledge, which I earlier described as a set of knowledge disqualified as inadequately or insufficiently elaborated, naive, or beneath the level required of science (Foucault 1972, 203). The historic position of Native American ways of knowing relative to official forms of knowledge, such as science, is an excellent example of subjugated knowledge. Foucault's project was to make visible the struggles that silenced some ways of knowing and established others as true knowledge and scientific discourse (Dreyfus and Rabinow 1982, 107–10). The writings of Eilean Hooper-Greenhill (1989, 1992) have translated Foucault's analysis of knowledge and power to museum settings.

In the history of the United States, and of many European societies, the museum has been one of the places where particular versions of knowledge have been legitimated and others have been categorized as primitive folklore or myth. For those of us whose childhood experience includes visiting museums, it is likely that museum exhibits have played a significant role in shaping our concept of Native American peoples. In the wake of post-1960s awareness about Native American issues, docents have noted that children are often confused by ethnographic exhibits and come away with notions that the people are stuffed or dead (Doxtator 1985). While museum exhibits have drastically changed to include representations of contemporary, living Native Americans, many institutions, including the Smithsonian Institution, have aged exhibits that they cannot afford to replace. These exhibits, although themselves artifacts of a former era, continue to communicate messages considered problematic today.

One could say that the Native American movement has been attempting to participate more fully in the social processes which make knowledge about them to make their own knowledge more valid to both an external and internal audience. Establishing their ways of knowing as valid has for Native peoples become an important part of an emancipatory or self-determining process.

Transnational Currents

Although this book focuses on a small community museum/cultural center on a Native American reservation, it notes how this tribal institution is part of a broader social movement and how it participates in cultural and political processes that extend beyond national boundaries. Indigenous intellectual traffic throughout the

Western Hemisphere is not new, of course. We know that, at least since the 1960s, Native intellectuals have encountered and been inspired by self-determination strategies across national boundaries and have returned home with an enlarged repertoire of ideas (Warren 1995; Fuller 1992, 340).

In the latter half of the twentieth century, Native American cultural preservation and self-determination movements emanating from the local level have intersected at national and international levels at an increasingly rapid pace. Increasing access to technologies such as telephone, television, radio, air travel, video, and the internet partly explains the hemispheric and global networking between members of self-determination movements. Participation in professional organizations — whether anthropological or museological — also provides an effective means for indigenous people to link together across national boundaries. Museums/cultural centers are one of the important places where this intersection is taking place. In addition to forwarding self-determination through museum settings, Native American peoples are transforming these institutions.

In Canada, Mexico, and the United States, indigenous peoples have been challenging the precepts of the museum profession as they pertain to indigenous cultural resources. Ownership of material culture, for example, has increasingly become a point of contention between museum professionals and indigenous peoples throughout the Western Hemisphere. Dominant notions about national heritage and national property have been destabilized, notions that have long awarded indigenous antiquities the symbolic equivalency of Old World ancient civilizations (Hinsley 1993, 133). Some indigenous peoples throughout the Western Hemisphere envision the museum as a potential means for self-determination. For example, Canadian indigenous peoples — who refer to themselves as First Nations — have pressured for repatriation of land as well as human remains and cultural materials in museums. Two groups pressured museums for the repatriation of potlatch materials that were seized in 1922 due to Canadian federal law prohibiting potlatches. In 1979 and 1980 the Kwakiutl Museum at Cape Mudge and the

U'Mista Cultural Centre in Alert Bay were opened to receive the repatriated materials (Cranmer Webster 1988).

Some First Nations, such as the Lubicon Lake band of Cree of northern Alberta, have successfully called for international boycotts against exhibitions in order to draw worldwide attention to corporations and governments who simultaneously exploit indigenous natural resources and sponsor celebratory cultural exhibitions (Ames 1988; Assembly of First Nations 1992; Cooper 1996; Harrison 1988). In the United States, tribal councils, religious leaders, elders, and activists from rural and urban Native communities have been mobilizing in great numbers to establish their own community museums/cultural centers. This North American mobilization — what I have called a Native American museum movement (Erikson 1996a) — has had a phenomenal impact on museology in the United States and Canada.

The strategies used by the Native American museum movement include

protesting museum exhibition of and storage/curation/ research of Native American bodies (commonly called *human remains*);

protesting exclusionary exhibit production processes;

pressuring for the repatriation of excavated grave material so that it can be reburied;

pressuring for the repatriation of other materials (forms of knowledge such as songs, oral history, ceremonial descriptions), now known as *cultural patrimony*, that were inappropriately alienated from the community. These developments can now be enforced through the legislation known as NAGPRA — the Native American Graves and Repatriation Act;

entering into the museum profession in order to reform it from the inside;

establishing rural and urban community museums/cultural centers;

raising public consciousness about the history of museums and indigenous peoples (e.g., Farmer 1994, and "Museum Cases" by the a cappella women's trio Ulai).

A variation of these movements also exists in Mexico — a *movimiento museo comunitario*. Pueblo cultural institutions have been bolstering indigenous claims for cultural, economic, and political self-determination. In some states, such as Oaxaca, the establishment of *museos comunitarios* represents widespread appropriation of and conversion of the Western museum model. A dozen of these Oaxacan *museos comunitarios* are networking with each other and linking with grassroots projects from other Mexican states, as well as other nations (Erikson 1996a, 1996b; Morales Lersch et al. 1987; Morales Lersch and Camarena Ocampo 1991, 1993). In the summer of 1998, for example, the small Zapotec pueblo of Santa Ana del Valle hosted a delegation of Mayans from Guatemala who wished to add a community museum to their strategies for cultural and political survival (Erikson 1998). To a lesser extent, then, a *movimiento museo comunitario* is also occurring in Guatemala, Brazil, and other nation-states despite ongoing and often brutal repression of indigenous peoples (Richardson 1996).

Aside from the hemispheric geographic distribution of indigenous community museums, there is a hemisphere-wide trend of transforming relations between indigenous peoples and museums that is based on both transnational and international forces.[12] I discuss two transnational components of the movements here. The first transnational component — that concerning repatriation of cultural materials and human remains — stems from the fact that cultural relations straddle national borders. The bounding of nations has generated transnational affiliations by either dissecting traditional indigenous territories or by dislocating portions of populations from their traditional territory, thus separating them from relations left behind. Although the policy of repatriating cultural material is a U.S. policy, transnational cultural affiliations are extending the policy beyond national borders. Since repatriation was mandated at the Smithsonian Institution in 1989 (and throughout the United States in 1991), negotiations have begun, and in some cases completed, for transnational repatriations.[13] This is a trend that is likely to increase. A hemispheric perspective contributes to understanding alternative cultural centers for two reasons. First, many Native American populations straddle international boundaries. By virtue of their inclusion in the cultural category Nootka, the Makah people are an example of those tribes involved in border-straddling relations.

Secondly, the transnationalization of indigenous family networks and economic exchanges — particularly between Latin America and the United States — is influencing forms taken by autoethnographic expression. As indigenous community life stretches across national boundaries as a strategy for economic and political survival, museum exhibitions follow. In 1994 the Union de Museos Comunitarios de Oaxaca sent an exhibit to the Plaza de la Raza in East Los Angeles. This exhibition represented each of the dozen Oaxacan pueblos that are developing or have developed their own *museos comunitarios*. Members of the indigenous pueblos traveled with the exhibition so they could explain the history and traditions represented in the exhibit, particularly to those children born "on the other side" who they did not want to forget their ancestry (Erikson 1995).

The hemispheric nature of this indigenous museum phenomenon is supported by international factors as well. Given the hemispheric extent of museum collecting practices over the past century, contemporary collaboration between museums and indigenous communities are necessarily occurring across national boundaries. For example, Jonaitis and Inglis (1992) describe how the American Museum of Natural History in New York has been collaborating with the Mowachaht band on Vancouver Island in British Columbia. The National Museum of the American Indian (NMAI) at the Smithsonian Institution is also contributing to the international character of this collaboration. NMAI is carrying its community-collaboration philosophy across national boundaries by establishing constituents throughout the Western Hemisphere. The extent of this collaboration mirrors the hemispheric scope of their collections. Since 1991, nine representatives from indigenous communities in Latin America have worked to design, interpret, and install NMAI's initial exhibits; in 1995, twenty-six representatives convened at the Smithsonian and in Santa Fe, New Mexico, with North American Native peoples to discuss new avenues of communication and collaboration (NMAI Report 1996).

Through such means, indigenous peoples of Latin America are experiencing qualitatively different working relationships with foreign national museums, such as the Smithsonian Institution. They are concurrently establishing, with northern indigenous peoples, common interests and strategies regarding self-representation through museum formats. The director of the MCRC, for example, traveled to Bolivia to meet with indigenous intellectuals and assisted in hosting a Quechua delegation's visit to the Makah reservation. Given these developments, it is likely that national museums in Latin America will experience increasing pressure in the future from indigenous peoples, as has occurred in Canada and the United States.

Incorporation into systems that span the globe is not a new phenomenon for Native American peoples, although the pace and degree of that incorporation is, without question, currently more rapid. Native American peoples, like Third World populations, have long been incorporated into global-scale processes (Wallerstein 1974; Wolf 1982). The economic and religious interests of colonial powers have moved people, plants, animals, goods, and ideas across great distances for many centuries. In the 1790s, for instance, Alferez del navio Quimper mentioned that five foreign vessels had come to Neah Bay over a one-year period to trade large sheets of copper for sea-otter skins (Taylor 1969, 17), and in 1861 James Swan recorded that he spent an evening at Ozette village with a Makah man named Jackson. He reported that Jackson had sailed as a crew member on ships to the Columbia River, San Francisco, and the Sandwich Islands (Swan 1971, 111). For more than half a century before ceding land to the Americans and coming under their political control, Makah people — as individuals and as a group — were participants in economic trade that connected far reaches of the globe.

Theories of globalization — the interlinking of cultural, political, and economic systems across the globe — call attention to the homogenizing pressures on local cultures. This homogenization is encouraged since much cultural contact and adaptation has occurred under neither democratic nor egalitarian circumstances. *McDonaldization, Disneyfication, Americanization,* and *Westernization* are some of the terms that point to the infiltration of Western-manufactured goods and consumer desires throughout the world. However, a number of authors have asserted that neither colonization nor globalization should be equated with simple homogenization of cultures. For example, Appadurai offers the term *indigenization* in his discussion of globalization: "at least as rapidly as [homogenizing] forces from various metropolises are brought into new societies they tend to become indigenized in one or another way" (Appadurai 1990, 5).[14] In other words, while some cultural forms (such as the system of capitalism or museum representations) are adopted, they can become localized and given new meanings and functions.

Recall my earlier discussion of Makah solid-twine basketry, the type woven by Margaret Irving and others. While one could say that the creation of Makah trade baskets indicates the assimilation of the Makah people and their greater incorporation into the cash economy, it would be more accurate to note the baskets as creations of a *compromise culture* (Small 1997, 36–37). A compromise culture occurs where both Makah culture becomes more Western and Western cultural elements become indigenized (see Pratt's discussion of transculturation, 1992, 6). Baskets become modified to meet Western tastes, and cash begins to circulate through a logic that supports "being Makah" in a meaningful and appropriate way. Margaret's solid-twine baskets, her "bread money," became a means for both cultural adaptation and cultural continuity. So, too, has the MCRC become a means for engaging with the dominant sectors of society, for adapting and persisting.

I mentioned earlier that the history of the MCRC is often narrated as beginning in 1970 when a storm exposed part of the Ozette village site. This storm spawned the archaeological excavation that catapulted Makah cultural history into the national and international media. This book, however, begins the story much earlier — in the 1850s. This museum ethnography portrays a community museum/cultural center as embodying the ever-changing identity of a group of Native American people and the tension between their self-image and the identity assigned to them by others. In this case, it is a window onto a history of cultural survival.

Part 1

1 Anthropologists in Neah Bay

Past and Present

Colonialism and the Collecting of Makah Culture

It was January 1863, the rainy season, and James Gilcrest Swan was preparing dried sponges, evergreen boughs, and whale skin barnacles to ship to the Smithsonian Institution in Washington DC. Swan was a teacher for the Office of Indian Affairs Agricultural and Industrial School in Neah Bay, Washington. For more than a year he had been collecting natural history specimens, with assistance from some Makah individuals, and he intended the items for the national museum's natural history collections.

Several other government agents, travelers, and residents across the western territories had, like Swan, been solicited by the Smithsonian to gather collections from the field (Cole 1985, 12). Before 1863, Swan had focused on collecting what we would readily recognize today as natural history specimens: rocks, plants, fish, sand, and other aspects of the natural environment. Although Swan had not yet focused his collecting on expressions of Makah culture, in January 1863 he slipped into the shipping crate a cedar bark mat, baskets, and a description of how black alder bark was chewed to make a dye.[1] This was Swan's first foray into collecting Makah culture — both material culture and traditional knowledge. Soon, however, the focus and fervor of his collecting would center on Native American cultures on the Northwest Coast.

Not long after packing this crate in January 1863, Swan received a circular from the Smithsonian Institution titled *Instructions for Re-*

search Relative to the Ethnology and Philology of America. The circular informed Swan, and the others who received it, of a search for the origin of America's indigenous peoples that would "trace the migrations and conquests of the various nations that composed it from one part of the continent to another, to disclose their superstitions, their manners and customs, their knowledge of the arts of war and peace — in short, to place before us a moving panorama of America in the olden time — such is the purpose which the scientific ethnologist has in view, and to accomplish which he neglects no source of information that promises to cast even a single ray of light into the obscurity with which the subject is surrounded" (Gibbs 1863, 7). This circular would significantly change the direction of Swan's collecting.[2] It was a call to assist the Smithsonian in "extending and completing its collection of facts and material relative to the Ethnology, Archaeology, and Philology of the races of mankind inhabiting, either now or at any previous period, the continent of America" (Joseph Henry in Gibbs 1863, 1).

The circular bolstered Swan's eagerness to collect what were then called "Indian curiosities." In response to it, Swan wrote to Spencer Baird, assistant secretary at the Smithsonian:

> I noticed in Mr. Gibbs paper in the report of the Smithsonian Institution relative to the collection of Indian curiosities the fact that all such collections will be of interest. There are few Indians that have come under my observation who have more of such articles than the Makah people. Everything pertaining to their fisheries both of whale and smaller fish, their canoes, spears, harpoons, ropes and lines, fish hooks, knives, mats, baskets, dog hair blankets, bark blankets, wooden ware, tools, etc. all are objects of interest, and a collection of these with description of their manufacture and uses could not fail of being attractive objects in your collection.[3]

This letter became just one of many Swan wrote to express his personal interest in Northwest Coast cultures and his eagerness to serve as an ethnologist who would collect from and document these cultures.

Swan's correspondence with Baird and others reveals his perception that the Smithsonian Institution embodied a heroic scientific project, one he was both enamored with and humbled by. Self-conscious about his perceived lack of appropriate training for his task, Swan referred to his collections and ethnological contributions as "trash." In a letter to Baird he confessed that his "desire to be of some service, however humble to the scientific world, is great and you may rest assured that while I remain here I will endeavor to fulfill your expectations."[4]

Beginning with the first recorded contact between Northwest Coast Native peoples and Europeans late in the eighteenth century, collecting Indian curiosities was one of the duties of government-backed expeditions — such as those of Alejandro Malaspina for Spain and George Vancouver for England. Since the sixteenth century, the main motivations for colonial expeditions in or near the Pacific Northwest had been exploring and claiming territory, finding more efficient navigation routes, and identifying new trade goods and markets (Hayes 1999). In the late eighteenth and early nineteenth centuries sea otter furs became one of these highly sought after trade goods. On these expeditions, explorers traded for items that were integral to Native daily and ceremonial life (Gunther 1972). Explorers and merchants also commissioned the creation of objects especially for collections, and they took items from grave sites (Cole 1985, 1–8).

The collecting associated with colonial expeditions constitutes a significant stage in the history of museums and their relationship with Native American peoples. A large portion of these expeditions predate the profession of anthropology, but they are linked nonetheless. Nation-building projects and scientific collecting have shared a symbiotic relationship in many locations around the world (Anderson 1991; Cole 1982, 1985; Handler 1988; Pratt 1992; Trennert 1974). Projects to map and claim territory, such as the Wilkes Expedition in 1838 and the Cascade Mountains Route Survey, provided incentive and support for blossoming scientific professions (Richards 1990; Viola 1985, 23). In turn, science has offered to expeditions various methodologies to further national interests. The cultures of Native American peoples were valued by a young American nation hungry for a ready-made human history of some antiquity. Hinsley has argued that monumentalizing Native American cultures created "symbolic capital for the legitimation of a grounded national culture" (1993, 112).

In this sense, Swan's natural history collecting was an extension of the efforts being made to colonize Washington Territory and incorporate its indigenous populations. The material culture and knowledge of Makah and other peoples were considered part of this natural history. Developing a taxonomy of Native peoples was another aspect of charting colonized terrain. In his correspondence with the Smithsonian Institution, Swan describes the ties between himself, Washington Territory governor Isaac Stevens, the Indian Bureau, and the Smithsonian. Swan was relying on the same politico-economic systems related to treaty-making and territorial settlement would support the collecting of Makah culture in the five villages of the tribe (see McDonald 1972 and Cole 1985, 9–47).

When Congress established the Smithsonian Institution, it charged it with receiving all specimens belonging to or thereafter belonging to the United States (Rhees 1901, 433). Hence, Smithsonian secretary Joseph Henry asserted in an 1870 letter to the secretary of the Board of Indian Commission: "the duty of this country [is] to collect and preserve all the relics possible of the races-of-men who have inhabited the American Continent. . . . [The tribes] are rapidly disappearing and their original modes of life continually undergoing changes" (in Cole 1985, 13). In order to preserve the essence of this early American history, any and all objects that might help to discover and monumentalize the indigenous inhabitants were collected. There was an urgency to this collecting of Indian knowledge and material culture that stemmed from the Vanishing American paradigm: the belief that Native Americans were a vanishing race due either to physical or cultural extinction.

The popular concept that Native tribes were passing away was supported by several factors, only two of which I'll mention here. First, tribal populations across the country were being decimated by diseases of European origin from which they had no immunity. Baird asserted that, in essence, collecting was salvaging the remains of these dying Indian cultures (Lohse and Sundt 1990, 89). The

Makah people were not exempt from extreme population losses. Records from earliest contact suggest the Makah population may have numbered in the thousands. George Gibbs reported that a Makah named Flattery Jack, or Yallakub, spoke of times prior to smallpox when the Makah people had five hundred *fighting men*. Flattery Jack contrasted that with their total population in 1853 of five hundred individuals (Taylor 1969, 20).

A second factor encouraging the Vanishing American paradigm was that Native Americans were adopting and adapting objects of non-Indian manufacture and substituting them for traditional items. The Smithsonian circular conveyed this urgency to Swan: "the tribes themselves are passing away or exchanging their own manufactures for those of the white race. It is hardly necessary to specify any of particular interest, as almost every thing has its value in giving completeness to a collection" (Gibbs 1863, 4). These patterns of consuming European goods began as early as the eighteenth century (Gunther 1972). Swan reports that early in the Makah reservation's history, in the 1860s, Makah people were using Euro-American items as luxurious courtship gifts and as specialty foods at feasts.[5]

A portion of the nineteenth-century urgency for collecting was directed at human skeletal material. The first item listed on the Smithsonian circular that Swan read was *human crania*. The argument went that massive quantities of skeletal, or human osteological, data were needed in order to chart out what were called the different "stocks" of the "American race." Thus, the Smithsonian Institution asserted that the discovery and mapping of this racial history would require accumulating "as many [cranial] specimens as possible of each tribe" (Gibbs 1863, 3). The circular forewarned Swan that "The jealousy with which they [Native peoples] guard the remains of their friends renders such a collection in most cases a difficult task" (Gibbs 1863, 2). Despite the warning that Native Americans would resist grave robbing, the Smithsonian encouraged collectors to proceed "without offense to the living." This included collecting from graves of extinct tribes, relocated tribes, victims of war, and slaves. Based on Swan's correspondence with the Smithsonian, and on the Smithsonian's collection records, we know that Swan followed the directive to collect Makah human remains. Like other collectors, he collected from graves. Swan recorded that he gathered what he "believed to be heads of chiefs or prominent men, as no slaves are ever buried in that place [where he gathered them]."[6] This material, discussed in Bray et al. (1994) has been subsequently repatriated to the MCRC and reburied.

In addition to human skulls, the Smithsonian sought Native weapons, implements, utensils, clothing, and other manufactured goods. Over a twenty-year period, Swan complied with these instructions by sending a plethora of Makah materials to the Smithsonian: cradles, headdresses, mats, baskets, model canoes and gear, dog hair blankets, bark capes, and much more.

Makah people were not passive victims of Euro-American policies and practices, however. Certainly, Makah sealers, fishermen, students, and artists interacted extensively with Euro-American agents, businessmen, teachers, and missionaries beginning with early contact in the 1700s and intensifying in the 1850s in the treaty and reservation period. The traces of their conversations with each other in diaries, reports, and oral history show a considerable amount of resistance and accommodation among all parties involved. Makah people resisted, adapted, and survived in a variety of ways, sometimes at the cost of creating new intratribal divisions. At other times, accommodation created new forms of cohesiveness. Not all Euro-Americans regarded Makah people in the same light.

Swan had heard that the Makah people had previously assisted British collecting expeditions off the west coast of Vancouver Island. Perhaps in response, he solicited their aid in his natural history collecting.[7] Swan's overwhelming duties as a teacher, census taker, and sometimes physician led to his nearly total reliance on Makah individuals for collecting natural history specimens. Nonetheless, Swan complained bitterly about his Makah assistants: "I have been trying to get the Indians to collect bird skins for me. I have several, but they are hardly fit to send, as I cannot as yet make the savages understand the proper method of skinning them."[8]

Since he was a teacher, Swan was most effective persuading the children to help him. Swan felt that by encouraging the children to collect natural history specimens he was teaching them a valuable lesson about the productivity of their labors and was making them "useful."[9] He hoped that while assisting in the collection and preparation of natural history specimens, Makah children would reevaluate things in nature for their potential value as commodities. He also hoped to train them in "the scientific enterprise."[10]

While some Makah people participated in natural history collecting, others apparently resisted it. While Swan encouraged the Makah people to collect shells and bird skins, eggs and nests, the elders disapproved of his using children to collect for him. In his diary Swan attributed this to what he called superstitions and the "sturdy though peaceful opposition of the old men."

To counteract Makah resistance, Swan offered what he called "considerable" sums of money to the children. Initially the children avoided Swan's requests to collect birds nests. They said they feared that taking the eggs would incite all birds to attack them and pluck out their eyes before they reached home.[11] Eventually, with ever greater financial encouragement, the children brought baskets of sand to Swan, and he picked out the shells, or sent them along to Baird — baskets, sand, shells, and all — just as the children brought them. The children seem to have found a way to negotiate between opposing points of view.

Swan's diary does not enable us to fully understand why Makah people resisted shell collecting. We can, however, get a glimpse of the distinctly different worldview that shaped Swan's view of collecting practices. In 1862 a wounded bear attacked a Makah man named Karoquot and bit him in the thigh and in the hand, severing part of his hand.[12] Swan recorded that the Makah people killed the bear and brought the skull to him after they completed a spiritual use for it. He recorded: "I wanted it for a specimen but it was not perfect as the larger teeth had been knocked out by the Indians to make medicine of to be used to cure the wounds of Karoquot."[13] Swan was concerned with the structural perfection of the bear skull as specimen. The Makah people involved appear concerned about balancing the healing powers of the bear with receiving potential rewards from Swan for providing him with a specimen.

An occasion in 1863 shows Swan's disregard for Makah religious beliefs. Swan mentions that Makah people confided to him their belief that Indians who die by drowning become owls. As proof, they cited their observation that five owls had been seen with shell and ring decorations in their bills or ears immediately after the loss of five Indians off of Ozette.[14] Despite knowing that Makah beliefs correlated owls with victims of drowning, Swan was determined that an owl would become part of his scientific investigations. A year later he wrote in his diary: "Last evening I shot a horned owl of the mottle gray species. It had lit on a pole over Old Flattery Jack's grave and I went out and shot it. This forenoon I skinned it and prepared it for the Smithsonian Institution. The Indians think owls are dead Indians and I had quite a talk with some children, who assured me that the owl was not a bird but an Indian. Dr. Davis dissected the carcass of the owl and found in its stomach two mice just eaten, probably at the time I shot it."[15] Further, in 1866, Swan eagerly investigated what he called the "whale medicine" of a Makah man named Captain John. Captain John shared with Swan the privilege of seeing the whale medicine only after ascending the schoolhouse tower with Swan and locking the door behind them. Captain John opened a box that had evidently been buried in the ground for some time. After describing the box's contents in his diary, Swan concluded: "John very grandly assured me that it was taken from a dead whale and was a great medicine and he had procured it from a Nittinat . . . so I was convinced of the correctness of my opinion that the *Hah hah to ak* is a myth."[16] Swan invalidates the Makah peoples' spiritual interpretation of their natural environment as superstition that, at times, obstructs his collecting.

From these accounts we may infer that, despite Makah participation in some collecting, there existed a significant gulf between Makah and Euro-American perceptions of the birds and animals Swan sought to collect. From what is understood about Makah cosmology, it is fair to say that Makah culture did not imagine the relationship between nature and culture in the same way as Swan did. Land and sea mammals and birds all played important roles in the origin of their people and in ongoing relationships with the supernatural world (Densmore 1939; Drucker 1951; Waterman 1920; Swan 1870). However, the scientific — rather than Makah — way of knowing was the basis for gathering and ordering specimens for scientific study in museums.

Soon after Swan received notice of the Smithsonian's interest in Indian curiosities, he bought two headdresses used in a medicine dance called Tsiack, or c'a·yiq, a healing ceremony (Swan 1870; Densmore 1939).[17] Presumably, Swan was forced to buy what he obtained, for only months earlier he complained: "These Indians will not do the slightest thing or give the most trifling article without pay of some sort, and it is only by offering them a fair price for all their articles that will enable me to make a collection of the best of each . . . [for] they are great traders."[18] Yet Swan also noted that the Makah people were not always willing to sell their gear. Objects, such as whaling gear, for example, became highly prized after successful use and so Swan was often forced to commission the creation of new whaling, fishing, and hunting gear for the Smithsonian (Cole 1985, 46).

We know that Swan stubbornly obtained human skulls, owls, shells, and other items despite objections. We also know that in later travels through Haida villages in the 1880s, Swan encountered significant resistance to the idea of selling ceremonially active regalia. Nevertheless, Swan prevailed in his collecting, largely due to differences of opinion within families (Cole 1985, 44). It is difficult to say whether Swan was able to obtain ceremonially active items from the Makah people, but the research required to decide this is currently under way at the MCRC. Swan records that family items were sold to obtain critical supplies when hardship and harsh weather conditions coincided throughout the five Makah villages.[19] The correlation between economic need and selling family possessions to collectors has been recorded elsewhere on the Northwest Coast (Cole 1985). In the low points of some family's experiences with political and economic restructuring of their societies, ceremonial items they were unable to hold onto were recontextualized as *curiosities* or *scientific specimens*.

Even though Swan circumvented Makah resistance to collecting, he sometimes launched his own critiques of the scientific process. From Neah Bay, Swan, too, critically eyed the anthropological profession. At times, Swan doubted the research questions he was directed to pursue with tribal community members. The study of genealogy or of kinship systems, for example, seemed particularly pointless to him. He wrote to Baird in 1864: "I must confess that I cannot see what possible benefit to science it will be to know what the Indians call their grandmother or great aunts. I am inclined to think that a great deal that passes under the name of scientific discovery is of no more practical use in science than the discoveries of Mr. Pickwick respecting the Tittlebats." [20] He also disdainfully distinguished between himself and "closet students" — also known as "armchair anthropologists" — or those who studied and wrote about the culture of others without ever having seen them or having had prolonged contact with them. Swan cited, again in a letter to Baird, the frequent errors in translations of indigenous vocabularies to English: "closet students are apt to be misled by the careless observations of worthy people, who, without ever having given any attention to the real manners and customs of a tribe while they were with them, are likely to conform their recollections when they return home, and attribute to one tribe, customs that strictly belong to others." [21] In this case, Swan criticized linguistic research on the Northwest Coast based on data gathered by explorers in fleeting exchanges, rather than long-term community exposure. Swan observed that such fleeting exchanges led to misunderstandings that could end up in print.

Even when ethnologists lived with Native American peoples for long periods of time, as Swan did, they still experienced some resistance to research or collecting. From Swan's diary we learn that Makah language consultants deliberately offered him incorrect information when he was conducting research. In 1863 he wrote: "It is characteristic of an Indian when he finds an interpretation given which appears ludicrous to him, to keep up the delusion for the sake of a joke, rather than make an explanation and when we recollect how difficult it must have been for the early explorers, and the Indians, to have understood each other, it is easy to account for the mistake." [22] The ludicrous interpretations Swan refers to apparently are the efforts of settlers, missionaries, and ethnologists to understand Makah language and culture. Reading Swan's writings, I am inclined to think that these jokes, or he he names, reflect not only Makah humor but the nature of passive resistance to anthropological research in the nineteenth century.

How easy it is in the twenty-first century to criticize early ethnologists, to point out the folly of classifying human culture as part of natural history or of persuading or tricking people to go against their traditions and beliefs for the sake of forwarding research. Yet contemporary anthropology is not free from ongoing ethical concerns in its ethnography of Native American and other peoples. Nor is contemporary anthropology free from the local memories of past actions taken by anthropologists.

In the Footsteps of My Anthropological Ancestors

While researching Makah cultural history in Neah Bay, I was continually running into anthropologists of prior generations — both in person and in spirit. The actions of prior anthropologists — allegedly unethical or idiotic actions — were frequently mentioned to me. The retelling of stories about my anthropological ancestors seemed to serve as warnings that I should not repeat their actions. By virtue of my title as anthropologist, I had to fight my way out of a stereotype. These encounters with my anthropological ancestors forced me to consider to what degree I was, or was not, following in their footsteps.

One spring morning in 1995, I had an appointment to record oral history with Makah elder Helma Ward at the MCRC. Since I was living in the center of the small village of Neah Bay, I could walk to the museum at the eastern edge of town by following Front Street, which bordered the curved harbor beaches. I walked past a variety of homes and businesses: clapboard homes that had been in the same family for generations; mobile homes — both new and spacious and small and worn; and brand new homes with commanding views across Neah Bay harbor looking toward the snowy peaks of Vancouver Island, British Columbia. The sportfishing resorts and cappuccino bar were still slumbering in off-season, but the Makah Maiden Café and Washburn's General Store bustled with morning diners and shoppers. After passing these, I came to the three-building cluster that makes up the MCRC.

Taking a shortcut, the first building I passed was a newly con-structed reproduction of a longhouse. Its cedar plank walls and dirt floor embrace various gatherings—both ceremonial and educa-tional. I headed for the museum building that housed the galleries, gift shop, and administrative offices. The architecture of that build-ing and the collections storage building facing it was reminiscent of cedar plank longhouses. Entering the front door, I stepped under the vaulted ceiling of the museum. I greeted interpretive specialist Kirk Wachendorf, who sat on the left orienting visitors and administrat-ing the gift shop burgeoning with carved masks, baskets, beaded olivella shell necklaces, and screenprint clothing. Bypassing the en-trance to the permanent galleries, I walked to my right toward the temporary exhibit gallery and turned into the museum's classroom.

There, in the classroom beneath a Makah (qʷiqʷidiččaq) syl-labary, I met with Helma Ward. Helma is in her eighties and works part time as a cultural specialist and language mentor at MCRC. She is one of the few elders left who is fluent in qʷiqʷidiččaq. Because of my frequent encounters with stories of past generations of anthro-pologists, I asked her if she could tell me what she had heard about anthropologists who had worked previously in Neah Bay. Her answer led me full circle back to one of Swan's letters to Baird:

[Elizabeth] Colson was known for always asking questions, and people used to say that she was a spy. [Erna] Gunther worked on genealogy, but she worked using only a couple of people. There were lots of sources, like county records, that she didn't use. That created lots of errors — like so-and-so didn't get married or have children and that was just plain wrong. . . . They [anthro-pologists] always write wrong things about us. All the time. But they never come back and change it. Photos get the wrong names on them and then families want to believe it's true. . . . We had to go through and fix Swan's vocabulary. It was full of bum words. Swearwords. People were giving him the wrong in-formation just to be mean to him. (H. Ward 1995)

As we have learned, Swan knew that the Makah people would per-petuate inaccuracies created by Euro-Americans for the sake of a joke. Despite his awareness of this passive resistance to his research, Swan's list of Makah vocabulary words (included in his Makah ethnography and published by the Smithsonian in 1870) apparently includes several of what Helma identifies as swearwords. The theme in Helma Ward's story was repeated by many others whom I inter-viewed in the community.

On another morning, I interviewed Ted Noel in his home. He had agreed to think through some of my research questions over a cup of coffee together. I asked him about the various roles of the mu-seum and how it affected the public perception of the Makah people and about the tribe's prior history with anthropologists who con-ducted research in the community. It was cold and rainy outside, and I was grateful for the hot cup of coffee he offered me as he started remembering some stories: "There was an anthropologist here who my grandmother thought was really irritating. Everything she did, this woman asked her about it. She would say, 'Why are you doing that? Why do you put it [her coffee mug] there?' So my grand-mother would make up answers. Some of those were cited and made my grandmother laugh" (Noel 1995). It occurred to me that here I was, sitting with this man in the same kitchen where his grandmother had once conversed decades ago with another anthro-pologist. What had and hadn't changed since then? Certainly the tension over gathering information about the community had not gone away.

At her office in the tribal council headquarters, Donna Wilkie shared additional memories of an anthropologist:

[She] used to hang out on the steps of Washburn's [General Store] and she'd overhear conversations between the old men and she'd ask them what they were talking about. Then they'd feed her a tall tale and she'd write it down. My great-grandma was a medicine woman and she'd make the rounds through the village and sometimes I'd go with her. She would hear about what was going on in the village. . . . People gave anthro-

pologists untruths deliberately when they were asked questions that they didn't want to answer. Some of those untruths
have gotten into print and people have laughed over it. I think
they held the information back for two reasons. One, if the anthropologist found out the traditions, then they would destroy
it by knowing it. It would take that power away. Secondly, to
document that those traditions were alive would reveal that
the people were not conforming. I think they were afraid that
then more discipline and more civilization would come.
(Wilkie 1995)

Such stories made me wonder in what ways might I be following in
the footsteps of my anthropological ancestors?

Frequently acknowledged is the love-hate relationship between
anthropologists and Native Americans. On one hand, anthropologists have supported the goals of numerous Native American communities by conducting archival research, linguistic research, and
archaeological excavations and by offering expert testimony in
courts of law. On the other hand, anthropologists are the butt of
countless jokes and complaints in Native communities. The jokes
highlight the genuinely humorous faux pas we make in trying to
navigate another culture, but complaints center on breaches of trust
by anthropologists whose business it is to gather information and
generate knowledge about cultures.

A frequent complaint is that anthropologists often fall short in
understanding what constitutes knowledge in the host community
or in understanding how to care for that knowledge. Consequently,
we have a legion of university-credentialed scholars considered experts in the anthropology of Native Americans and numerous Native
American communities who disagree with the scholarly interpretations and are left feeling disempowered by the work of these scholars and sometimes even vulnerable to its consequences. When I
worked in Neah Bay, my Makah colleagues both criticized and lav-
ished praise on the anthropologists who preceded me. Like most Native communities, the oral history of their past experiences with anthropologists was abundant. Amid their stories, they cautioned me
that the anthropology discipline would propel me toward becoming

an "Indian expert" — that is, one who speaks authoritatively about and for them. In raising these issues, many Makah people demonstrated their ability to recognize how everyday practices could perpetuate tenacious relations of domination. They pinpointed the process of earning university credentials, gaining tenure, and publishing books or articles as the motors that drive scholars to reproduce colonial-era relationships rather than create more ethical working relations. These conversations were very important to my work since my project centered on the evolving relationship between Native Americans and museums. Conversations with Makah tribal members reminded me that through my association with universities and museums I was at risk of reproducing the historical relations that were the subject of my study.

Largely due to the critiques of indigenous and Third World peoples, anthropologists are increasingly recognizing the importance of writing about how professional academic systems and institutions affect the creation of knowledge considered "official" or "true." If official knowledge is as much a product of power relationships as accumulating and testing information, then anthropologists and museum professionals should concern themselves not only with creating knowledge about others but also with critiquing their knowledge-making processes (Dixon 1992b; Weil 1990). This angst over how anthropologists represent cultures is certainly not new.

For some time, critics have pointed out that colonial or colonially derived power relations have shaped how anthropologists represent "the other" (Asad 1973, 1986; Hymes 1969; Said 1978a). This critique led to the observation that anthropology imbues ethnographies with an authoritative aura of official knowledge. This authoritative aura obscures how ethnographies are the result of a process whereby cultures are analytically taken apart and then reconstructed into a coherent text that some have called "fiction" (Bruner 1986; Clifford 1988; Fabian 1983; Geertz 1973b; Marcus 1986; Marcus and Cushman 1982; Marcus and Fischer 1986). Feminist writers furthered these critiques, calling for finer-grained attention to how the gender or position of ethnographers in First World/Third World and Western/non-Western contexts introduced subjective perspectives into an avowedly objective science (Abu-Lughod 1993; Mohanty 1984; Ong 1988; Spivak 1987). These writings have argued that the nature of all knowledge is situated and that scientific claims to a transcendent and objectively created knowledge deserve extensive critique (Haraway 1991).

From these critiques has emerged the observation that anthropology is Eurocentric in its tendency to make monuments of "the other." Imperialist nostalgia for what one is destroying is said to drive the need for preserving those cultures which are rapidly disappearing (Rosaldo 1989). This nostalgic aspect of Eurocentrism has led anthropologists (who, until recently, were predominantly of European descent) to depict subaltern, Third World, or indigenous peoples in a time and space distant from their own (Appadurai 1988; Fabian 1983; Wolf 1982).

Any decolonization of representations — whether in museum exhibits or ethnographic monographs — is inadequate if it leaves institutionalized power structures unperturbed. In Neah Bay, I was not alone in realizing the tension between practicing anthropology and breaking out of relations of domination. Not surprisingly, I found myself entangled in a role that I was trying not to play. The Makah people thoroughly critiqued how anthropologists make knowledge about them, offering constructive challenges as they did so. Several individuals expressed critical perspectives, and their thoughts title the following subsections. Structuring this chapter according to the concerns of Makah critics is part of my effort to share their critique of the history of collecting Makah culture. It will be self-evident from these anecdotes that stepping *out* of the footsteps of my anthropological ancestors would prove more difficult than I thought.

Anthropologists don't get that it's the ones among us who say they do
know that know the least. But anthropologists don't care. They write what
they write and then it's history and we have to live with it.

As part of initiating informal interviews or formal and taped oral history sessions with Makah community members, I would explain where I was from (my homeland, university, and departmental affiliations), what my project was about, and what I hoped to achieve. To my surprise, my statement often elicited quite lengthy and unbroken narratives about the interviewee's own genealogies, specific events in family history, and the impact of these events on their personal lives, particularly in the context of rapid social change and community political life. These narratives often made me uncomfortable, as their content was intensely personal, entailing information that I considered private and often felt I should not know.

For a while, this pattern upset me because often it was visibly painful for the person to remember these family histories and to relate them to me. I wondered at this since I had not asked any questions eliciting this personal information. Because my presence was initiating these narratives, I was concerned that people felt, in some way, that I was cornering them for this information. From my uninformed perspective, there was no link between the narrations of family history and the implicit assertions of authority and so I remained confused. Thankfully, one day a Makah friend bluntly explained: "My family history is how I tell you that I know what I'm saying and that what I tell you is true."

Eventually, I realized these narratives were partly analogous to those given publicly at potlatches or at other community gatherings — they were oral forms of expressing family and tribal identity ("who I belong to") and authority ("why I have the right to speak and why I should be heard"). Following a Makah aesthetic, they were narratives meant to move the listener toward recognizing the speaker's authority and toward new or renewed understanding of what was being narrated.[23] The narratives shared with me privately were more personal in nature, however, than those I saw delivered publicly.

I eventually realized that Makah perceptions of my role as an anthropologist were triggering the personal testimonies. The assumption was that as an anthropologist I had earned an authority (or that I presumed an authority) that enabled me to author an "official history" about the Makah people based on my research there. On the one hand, their narratives were educating me on their standing in differential authority structures within the community — that is, asserting their authority to speak to me. On the other hand, they were holding up a mirror and reflecting back to me an image of my presumed role as a self-proclaimed author of their official history—an official knowledge-maker about them. I had encountered a legacy of my profession and a new challenge to overcome.

In trying to understand the series of events that led to the founding of the community museum/cultural center and the contemporary meanings the community ascribed to it, I encountered Makah etiquette for the transfer of knowledge. In the Neah Bay community, with respect to a number of subject matters, there is not a free market of knowledge transfers; rather, one's status based on lineage, class, gender, rites of initiation, and ethnic background legitimates the knowledge transfers. Like many Native American communities in the United States, one important, traditional means for transferring knowledge within the community has been by oral tradition and physical instruction, superseded only perhaps by knowledge acquired by direct observation or through sacred interventions. The reception that this knowledge receives when revealed to the community is often affected by *who* the person is.

I came to understand that the Makah sense of ownership of knowledge and of etiquette for knowledge transfer is very elaborate. Although their knowledge system would be a point of interest for many anthropologists, my intent was not to write a classic ethnography of the Makah people, one that would have included Makah knowledge systems. My intent was to focus on a more particular phenomenon, namely, how did Makah notions of knowledge, respect, and humanity shape their own community museum/cultural center? How was the nature of their community museum/cultural center the same or different compared to mainstream museums?

Makah families or individuals can *own* oral history, stories, songs, dances, and artistic designs. Ideally the ownership is transferred within Makah society under strict protocols. What are the implications then for an ethnographic discipline that seeks to textually and visually represent cultural expressions as a means to describe, understand, and explain cultural difference? Based on their historical experience, numerous Makah people expressed to me in frustration that "anthropologists don't get" how the anthropological drive to gather information and write about it to a non-Makah audience often violates a community ethic. They lamented that anthropologists will always find someone who will talk to them, whether or not the informant has the authority to speak for the tribe. They admonished that the methodology for arriving at a truth varies cross-culturally and that one cannot legitimately claim scientific accuracy within the community unless internal authority structures are honored.

Of course, respect for internal authority structures was already a concern when I approached the project. For that reason, I approached MCRC before submitting funding proposals and asked for direction on how to request permission to work in the community. Given MCRC's status as the prominent cultural institution of the tribe, the Makah Tribal Council had invested the MCRC board of trustees with the authority to review and oversee prospective research projects. Consequently, my research request was submitted to the MCRC board for its vote. Since MCRC's authority as a gatekeeper of research projects on the reservation was chartered by the Makah Tribal Council, I was instructed to file a final copy of my project with the Makah Tribal Council, as well as with MCRC. Despite these and other protocols, most Makah tribal members expressed to me that the tribe could, only with some difficulty, shape projects about them, but that ultimately they had few resources to protect themselves from whatever researchers (including myself) might write. This propelled some Makah people toward the principle that researchers were to be avoided; thankfully for me it propelled others to find subtle and overt ways to raise my consciousness about what their concerns were regarding "outsiders coming in and researching us."

Why should I tell you anything?

This was perhaps the best-framed question, and Makah community members delivered it to me repeatedly in a number of ways. At least a handful of community members chose not to wait for my answer, deciding instead not to speak with me at all. As one woman put it, "I've decided not to speak with you because I simply don't agree with outsiders coming in here and studying us. It's that simple. I'm sorry." Her repulsion of the process of being studied made clear to me that, despite my efforts to forge collaborative field-work methodologies, the whole anthropological production process was fully ensconced in a dominating relationship that had been established long before I asked for permission to research there. Others who did choose to speak with me, albeit after thoroughly challenging me, still shared her concern.

The point is that anthropologists usually arrive with a research agenda that was not constructed on the tribe's terms (Deloria 1969). Although anthropologists have ethical guidelines, various factors work against them—the publish-or-perish syndrome and notions about academic freedom, to name just two. As another Makah person said, in challenge: "No matter what your intentions, or how good they are, that doesn't make what you do right. That doesn't prevent what you write from hurting us in the long-run." Such encounters provoked some serious reflection on my part about the anthropological enterprise.

The problems of objectification, of whether or not people want to be written about, of whether anthropologists have a right to make those decisions are, of course, not new ones. For Native communities, there are a number of justifiable reasons for concern about the loss of control over information and representation as it enters the public realm. Ethnographic studies can directly influence policy planning, public opinion, and can violate, whether intentionally or not, certain ethics of community privacy. Obviously, many Native American communities are in a double-bind of needing the American public to understand them enough so individuals will vote responsibly on heated political, economic, and cultural issues. This is especially true for issues that affect their survival in local or state political arenas. Communities are negotiating between the need for Native/non-Native cross-cultural communication and excessive objectification of Native peoples that leaves little room for private domains or self-determining representations.

Mary Lou Denney (Makah), MCRC board member and former teacher, explained to me that when MCRC drew the line between public education and private cultural practice, the reception was often not favorable. I quote her explanation of this at length:

Indian ways and things that are protected with the community and with the people, I think it's different because of what happened in the past. If they weren't protected then they were commercialized. So that it *wouldn't* be commercialized, so that it *wouldn't* be taken away from the people, we had to come up with a language [a policy] so that it would be protected. A lot of times, people on the outside really did not like it. If they came in and was going to do something and then we asked them to see it first before they published it or showed it or whatever, they would really get irate about a lot of stuff. They would say "when I went to such and such a museum, I didn't have to do this." Well, they weren't at that museum anymore. They were at our museum. And because there were a lot of things that were protected, sometimes it didn't go over very well. . . . [In the past, especially before the MCRC existed] there was a lot of things that were violated — a lot of the songs, a lot of the dances, a lot of the basketry, a lot of even some of the legends that were being told. People would come in and indicate that this is what they wanted. They weren't there for themselves, they were there to let people know and be aware of what the Makah people were like. But it didn't turn out that way. When they would rewrite their stuff, some of their stuff was nothing like the first things that they wrote. We've become very apprehensive about people coming in and doing stuff. A lot of them used to just come in and they would ask for certain things [to borrow objects/information] and sometimes we wouldn't get a lot of these things returned. So we've become very leery of people wanting to do this and do that. (Denney 1995)

The "Why should I tell you anything?" response to my presence surfaced as a concern with the draining away of information from the community and with the loss of control over information. This concern was first presented to me as I sat in a Neah Bay living room looking out over the harbor. After a considerable amount of preliminary conversation about my research project, MCRC, and other topics, another former MCRC board member asked me: "Do you know what the 'helicopter effect' is?" "No," I responded. So he told me: "You, and the information you gather, get into the helicopter and fly away. That's it."

Almost every community member I spoke with was armed with anecdotes about lawyers, politicians, anthropologists, and others who, in the name of supporting the Makah Tribe, managed to leave the reservation with historical documentation such as maps and archival documents, as well as newly generated materials, such as photos, oral histories, field notes, song recordings, film, and much more. The long tradition of anthropologists taking their research materials with them has given the MCRC Archives years and years of work in tracking these materials from university archives and museums to private homes. I am describing a perception among many Native Americans that historical evidence can be drained from the reservation (both Makah and others) and centered in places — such as museums and universities — for the purpose of making official knowledge.

To counteract this perception, which holds the Makah community as periphery, I left in the MCRC Archives the tapes and transcripts of oral history interviews, field notes from formal interviews, photographs, and duplicate copies of primary archival materials and secondary publications about the Makah people that I had located as part of my research at the Smithsonian Institution and at the University of Washington library. These materials have been accessioned formally into the MCRC Archives. In addition to following the protocol of returning final reports to the tribe, this is another means to address this issue of the helicopter effect.

Another related version of the "Why should I tell you anything?" challenge identifies the ethnographic process as plagiarism. The first time ethnography was presented to me as plagiarism was when I was visiting the late Makah elder Hildred Ides in her living room one morning. I went to her to discuss how Makah elders started teaching traditional forms of knowledge to the children of the tribe in public school classrooms of the 1960s. But our conversation soon strayed from that topic, as she had very serious concerns about the ethnographic process that would record and narrate just such a history.

Following an etiquette that was widespread in the village, she did not directly address her concerns to me, but rather told me a story about an anthropologist she had worked with some years before. She left me to discover any potential parallels between my work and that of the previous anthropologists. Hildred spoke of how she had worked with this anthropologist on family genealogies, mapping out the different generations of a family or families, since it was relevant in some way to the research methodology that the anthropologist had chosen. She recounted how some time later, another tribal member had brought to her a published ethnography or article that summarized the anthropologist's results. Hildred complained to me that the anthropologist's work was presented as her own. As Hildred explained, the anthropologist didn't *know* that information; it wasn't just her own work. It was Hildred's knowledge that was recorded, but it was presented as the anthropologist's own work. Hildred named that plagiarism.

I felt that her anecdote was not only a commentary on a previous bad experience but also a commentary on how she felt about the prospect of working further with me. At that time, I did not know how I could fulfill the expectations of a dissertation committee while working with the elders in a fundamentally new way, so I didn't make her any promises. Our interactions afterward were purely social.

Hildred Ides's point is valuable to this discussion because it highlights the way ethnographies tend to downplay the knowledge and insights provided by those traditionally called *informants*. Although not worded as such, Hildred's point was that anthropologists make their careers on the people they study without sufficiently acknowledging the degree to which they intellectually take from them. Ironically, her point was the opposite of some presented in the literature on critiques of anthropology. As Clifford has argued (1986), classical ethnography is a scholarly construction wherein anthropologists' assertions are cloaked as the Native point of view. In other words, writing ethnography is an assertion of power that produces the appearance of reporting ethnographic truths. The critique of this Makah elder and other Makah community members was that anthropologists present ethnographic truths as their own discovery of knowledge, rather than attributing it to its rightful sources in the community.

I responded to Hilda's critique by incorporating oral history methodology as much as possible. Oral history allows people who are both products of and makers of their cultural systems (Mintz 1996, 302) to verbalize their memories and perceptions, revealing cultural patterns in the process. The recollections of these cultural patterns are elicited through a dialogue between the anthropologist and, in this case, Makah consultants. It takes practice to establish a common vocabulary and communication etiquette so that the anthropologist can hear the appropriate meanings in the narrative (Friedlander 1996).

Oral history was once considered little more than a methodology for mining a storehouse of facts in someone's memory. It was largely discredited as an unreliable tool for reconstructing the past of groups of people without their own written history. Today, however, oral history is considered an invaluable way to include a history of classes and ethnicities of people that would otherwise be excluded. Furthermore, oral history today is valued for the way it reveals the dynamic structure of memory and perception (Cruikshank 1992; Friedlander 1996, 155).

A second response of mine to critiques of anthropological plagiarism was to acknowledge Kirk Wachendorf and Helma Ward as co-authors on two chapters. This acknowledges their central contributions of historical information, analysis, and analytical structure. Mary Lou Denney would have been designated as co-author on a third chapter, but a sudden and serious illness prevented her from collaborating beyond the stage of oral history recording.

I am well aware, however, that acknowledging these co-authors is a textual gesture. It is only a first step, one that does not, in and of itself, disassemble the unequal power relationships at the heart of the plagiarism critique.

Who are anthropologists writing for?

This next Makah-postulated question brings me to the issues of formulating research questions and imagining audience. With this question, several Makah individuals encouraged me to revisit critically the realities of the power relations in which I was embedded as a then graduate student in anthropology. That meant examining the process of the production of anthropology in which I was caught at that time as a participant striving for, but not yet having achieved, a doctoral-level credential. Members of the Makah community argued that the discipline ensures reproduction of itself, leaving little room for radical reform of the power relationships that leave the studied out of the process of formulating the research agendas, questions, methodologies, and texts.

Perhaps another way of putting this is that it is time to visit the issue of whether writing *for* the ethnographic subjects and *with them* would be of more scientific and social value than writing *about them* to an outside audience. I borrow here Watanabe's term (1995, 41) *reimagining of colleagues* to describe a process in which power relationships may be radically reimagined as a basis for reworking them in reality. Watanabe describes this process of reimagining colleagues as anthropology "address[ing] its others directly and to admit their replies" (41). In other words, "the others" need to be imagined as part of the audience of the ethnography and, presumably, as part of the collaborative writing process.

I have attempted reimagining colleagues in this book as part of the writing process. For that reason, I wrote a significant portion of the first version of this book while still in the field, distributing chapters to approximately twenty Makah individuals before returning to the university. This enabled me to include their concerns, responses, and advice. But this is not enough and, therefore, in no way can I hold up the resultant product as the ideal. The ideal would entail change in the greater disciplinary processes and structures in which I am embedded. I am suggesting that we go beyond textual solutions to this dilemma and address the institutional contexts in which anthropology is produced and reproduced. Reimagining our colleagues means more than representing our dialogues with the studied in the text; it means more than using their metaphors to structure our text; it is more than including the studied in the writing process.

The reimagining of colleagues has occurred as indigenous peoples have entered museums and universities in increasing numbers and, through becoming colleagues, disrupted traditional paradigms and representational strategies in anthropology and museology. The following quote by Michael Ames (1994, 15) reveals the degree to which some museum professionals are responding cooperatively to Native American calls for significant reform:

> If the purpose of allowing many voices to be represented in an exhibition is to move towards a greater degree of equality between an institution and the peoples it represents, then more drastic measures are required than simply balancing non-Native curators with Native consultants, like counterpoising so many cowboys and Indians. . . . Equal collaboration more likely will require the restructuring of the entire enterprise and its value system. . . . This will not be an easy move to make, for it will involve, as Loretta Todd warns, a decentering of those in control (ourselves) and of their (our) institutions, and therefore, in a real sense, a certain loss of power and privilege.

By decentering our knowledge-making institutions we are reimagining the sites where anthropological knowledge is produced, seeing Native American communities not as a frontier of discovery or somewhere "almost out of this world" but as new zones of contact in which Native American peoples choose to initiate or participate in dialogues that create knowledge about them. Over the past three decades, Native Americans have increasingly exercised their right to proclaim their own humanity, identity, and history in public forums. They are creating autoethnographies (Pratt 1992, 7), representations of themselves that engage with dominant cultural systems yet still have a degree of local control. Tribal museums are one of the many strategies that Native communities are using to rework what constitutes "official knowledge" about them.

My argument is that tribal museums, which have emerged mainly since the 1960s, are rooted in processes of resistance and accommodation that stem from the colonial era. In reaction to a long, colonial history of disrupting traditional knowledge systems, Native American communities are adopting and reforming the museum media to create cultural centers they hope will assist them in reaffirming and representing Makah identity. In order to fully understand how the MCRC grows out of colonial-era struggles over ways of knowing, the next chapter will explore the Makah experience with American colonization.

2 Redefining Civilization

Struggles over Ways of Knowing on the Makah Reservation

with Helma Ward

Nearly a century after the display of living Native peoples at the World's Columbian Exposition, Native American performing artist James Luna (a Luiseño/Diegueño tribal member from the La Jolla Indian reservation in California) heightened public awareness of the colonial legacy embedded in mainstream representations of Native Americans. Luna's performance art created alternative museum exhibits that challenged the public's perception of Native peoples. In his San Diego exhibit *The Artifact Piece* (1987–90) he made himself into an exhibit. Clothing himself in only a breechcloth and standing in an exhibit gallery of the Museum of Man in Balboa Park, which otherwise frames Native Americans in what Luna called "typical, anthropological fashion," Luna played with public expectations of American Indian representation. A couple of years afterward he reminisced:

> I was actually exhibited in a natural history museum in San Diego and was actually on display outside the California room, which I guess is a kind of coup. The exhibit was not announced which was good because of the element of surprise. . . . Then these people [who] came, just "Joe Family" on a Saturday to the museum, were, like, totally blown away. That told me something about the power of the piece, and also about what people

come to museums for. They don't come to see living things, they come to see dead things. I've been requested to do it numerous times and I've refused because it's a really emotional piece for me. (Farmer 1994, 20)

Like Luna, the Makah people counteract the colonial legacy in mainstream representations by *representing themselves* in their own museum/cultural center. In the process, they appropriate museology while disrupting some conventional tenets. In the previous chapters I mentioned some examples of Native American peoples' attempts to disrupt popular expectations about Indianness, especially those historically conveyed by museums. One of the distinctive features of the contemporary Native American museum movement is its commitment to serving and representing living cultures and promoting cultural survival.

This chapter highlights a portion of the historic struggle over who would determine the future of what being Makah looks and feels like. This struggle continues today and manifests itself in debates over treaty rights, intellectual property rights, and ownership of Native American material culture. The Makah people did not passively experience having their culture targeted for collecting and "refinement." As with other tribal groups, the Makah people actively negotiated these pressures, and today their memories of resistance and accommodation to colonialism (including the practice of ethnology) are an important aspect of their identity.

The following sections describe some American colonial strategies meant to disrupt traditional Makah ways of knowing and restructure Makah sensibilities. MCRC cultural specialist and Makah elder Helma Ward assisted me in structuring this chapter; her thorough understanding of Makah experience with Euro-American perspectives and practices made clear to me the frequent tensions between nontribal and tribal management of Makah material and intellectual resources. My conversations with other Makah elders and tribal members were also invaluable for connecting historical experience with recent, proactive efforts by the tribe to control its own heritage.

Daily I moved back and forth between conducting interviews and reading Office of Indian Affairs documents, Indian agent diaries, and other archival materials. Historical documents that seemed remote to me were grounded in the deeply personal memories and experiences of Makah oral histories. In my work with elders and other tribal members, I have tried to honor their decision to share their personal experiences with me. This has meant carefully illustrating a history of Makah relations with non-Natives who challenged, transformed, collected, and managed Makah culture. In this sense, non-Natives, or what the Makah people call *babałids*, are as much — if not more — the subject of study here.

Education and Techniques of Isolation

In October 1862, the same year the Neah Bay Indian Agency was formally established, James Swan and two other employees of Indian Affairs began supervising the construction of a day school. According to Swan, the old men of the traditional village of *di·ya·* (now known as Neah Bay) were opposed to the construction of the school building behind their longhouses. Swan recounted in his extensive journals:

Today Mr. Brooks, William Ingraham and myself finished setting the posts for the main building of the school house and when we had all ready, which was at noon, I told Capt. John to call the Indians. Some 25 or 30 came out . . . the sticks were lifted into their places and the whole of the sills for the main building fastened together in about an hour. I told John that when the buildings were done Mr. Webster would give them a treat to pay for the good feelings evinced on this occasion. They have been opposed to having the building erected back of their lodges and I have had a deal of explanation to make to do away with the superstitious prejudices of the old men. But by the exercise of a great deal of patience I have succeeded in inspiring them with a confidence in me, which makes them believe not only what I tell them is true, but what we are doing is for their good.[1]

The founding of this school launched more than fifty years of educational programs directed by the Office of Indian Affairs and various religious sects.

The Makah Treaty of 1855 ensured that the federal government would educate Makah children in exchange for Makah land. The history of transformation in Makah traditional lifeways is scarred, as it is for other tribes, by boarding schools and day schools. However, the proximity of day schools and sometimes of boarding schools, enabled some tribes, including the Makah Tribe, to maintain a significant sense of community identity in spite of the schools' missions (McBeth 1983). When Helma Ward and I were discussing the history of schooling in Neah Bay, she found many parallels between her personal experiences and those of previous generations. I showed her a statement written in 1893 by Indian Agent John P. McGlinn that began: "I am more than ever convinced that the great civilizing element, coupled with moral and religious training, are the schools." Helma Ward reflected upon how she had to move back and forth between Makah teachings and the mandatory education she received in day schools and boarding schools. "There were two different worlds," she said. "We still live in two worlds. It's hard, but that's how it is" (H. Ward 1995).

Swan was the first teacher at the Neah Bay Agency; missionaries followed when his day school was assigned to the Christian Church in 1871. Three years later, the day school was abandoned and a boarding school was constructed. By 1885 the government had founded numerous off-reservation boarding schools, such as Chilocco in Oklahoma, Haskell in Kansas, Genoa in Nebraska, and Chemawa School in Oregon (which many Makahs attended) (Lomawaima 1994). By 1896 federal aid to mission schools was on the decline, and the Ba'adah boarding school for Makah children was closed. The day school model returned once again to the Makah community and stayed until 1931 when Makah students were incorporated into a public school system.

To encourage allegiance to the expanding nation, the nationwide education of Native American children sought to silence local history and customs. This was as true for immigrants to the United States as it was for Native Americans. Throughout the late nineteenth and early twentieth century, the boarding and day school attempted to increase the cultural distance between Makah parents and their children, as physical distance was considered one way to culturally isolate the children.

Government schooling did more than force cultural assimilation, however; it also stimulated Makah discontent and resistance. In the day school's first year, 1863, attendance was poor, and Swan sent for a Makah man named Youaitl (Old Doctor) and explained the purpose of the school to him. Swan recorded his presentation to Old Doctor as follows:

> I told him that the Government at Washington had been at great expense to have the school house built and now I wanted the children to come and be taught and wanted him to let his second son Kachim come and board with me . . . that his board and schooling should cost nothing, that I proposed to teach Jimmy's class by themselves and then teach the smaller children who could come as day scholars. . . . I also told him that the old men were dying off and these boys would shortly take their places and if they would come and learn now they could be useful when they grew up and could better adapt themselves to the white man's customs than the old men.[2]

Swan's diary reveals his perception that some Makah parents responded positively to his arguments: "Old Kachook came into school today and expressed himself as very much gratified that his boy was learning. Chealu said he is a great chief. He is a chief among the Makah people and also among the Cowitchans. The old fellow grunted and clucked awhile to express his pleasure and after having made a short speech to the boys, the purport of which was to have them behave well and learn fast."[3] Yet, according to Swan, other parents did not readily accept the purpose of the day school. Some parents felt that what was really needed to survive were the skills to kill whales and catch halibut. They also harbored much greater fears:

Andy's father, Kloopoose came up with the boys and told me that the Indians had talked over the subject of sending their boys to school but some of them had an idea that I wanted to get the boys and send them off to California or somewhere else and they were afraid to let them come and told him he was a fool to let Andy come. I think this impression has arisen partly from what they were formerly told by agents, that their children were to be sent to school at Tulalip reservation and partly from enquiries that have been frequently made by masters of vessels and others for boys to be taken to California as servants.[4]

When U.S. Indian Agent E. M. Gibson arrived in Neah Bay in 1871 he practiced a much less tolerant policy than Swan did. With the backing of the Christian Church, Gibson began to separate children from their parents so that Euro-American lifeways could more easily influence their morality. Gibson complained that the proximity of the longhouses to the school permitted the "old Indians," who did not agree with the benefits of the school, to hold the children back.[5] This motivated Gibson to open a boarding school in 1875 at biʔidʔa (also known as Ba'adah or Bahada; figure 6), one of the five traditional villages (see figure 2). Ba'adah was abandoned in the early 1850s due to a smallpox epidemic and subsequently occupied by H. A. Webster's former trading post. The agent at Ba'adah hoped for more successful immersion of children in Euro-American culture. As Indian Agent Willoughby put it three years after the boarding school was constructed: "to educate the children of these Indians is the best and surest way to civilization; and in order to do this, none other than a boarding school (such as at present exists) will answer. The children must be kept entirely from the homes of their savage parents."[6] The boarding school teachers attempted to replace the home life and education provided by Makah parents with a new set of Euro-American habits and sensibilities. C. A. Huntington moved his own family to

6. "Indian School, Neah Bay" shows the boarding school at Ba'adah Point that opened in 1875 and closed by 1896. Photo possibly by Jesse Thomas. Courtesy of the Washburn family collection.

Ba'adah Point and took Makah children into their home, teaching them to live in the way of his own family.

Although Indian agents stationed at Neah Bay sought to block the transmission of Makah language, customs, dances, and personal habits from one generation to the next, their efforts apparently did not meet their goals. In 1965 Makah elder Alexander Greene recounted that during his attendance at the Neah Bay boarding school between 1885 and 1892, his training in tribal customs was not ceased. His father was still able to teach him dances and songs at home (McDonald 1965, 7). Parents would increase contact with their children by visiting them at Ba'adah. When Isabelle Ides and I discussed her family's experience with boarding schools, she described the following: "My father had gone to the boarding school at Ba'adah, but it was gone in my times. Only the dormitory building was left where they used to hold dances. He used to say that the food was so poor there. Just rice and lima beans. Those kids were eating so poor that they were malnourished. They were dying. Just rice and beans, that's what he said. My Dad thought that those lima beans had maggots so he never ate them. Parents knew how poor it was up there so they packed food up in their baskets and carried it up the hill to their kids at that school" (1995). Agents complained that general classroom absenteeism intensified in spring and summer, when families left, taking their children with them, for their seasonal camps for fishing, curing, hunting, and gathering. Toward the turn of the century, absenteeism was also high in the fall due to family participation in distant migrant labor.

After the Ba'adah boarding school had been open more than ten years, Agent W. L. Powell became frustrated that the youths educated there for five to ten years were ridiculed for their "civilized habits" once they reentered Makah social life. Thus he pondered even more extreme measures of cultural isolation: "it would advance these people many years toward civilization could a reservation be set apart for all old Indians, say all that are over fifty-five years of age. Let them live and die together, having no intercourse with the younger ones except at long and rare intervals. By the time the old ones die off, my belief is that the other would be living in as civilized a manner as the same class of white people. . . . It certainly would, I think, be an economical solution of the Indian question."[7] Although this plan was never implemented, the agency did resort to other extreme measures.

Eventually, the Neah Bay Agency used force to counteract the stubborn resistance of Makah parents and children. In 1872 Agent Gibson reported that parents were strenuously opposing school since it made the children unfit for the "hardy pursuits" of Makah life.[8] In 1877 Agent Huntington imprisoned a parent for two nights and one day in order to coerce the surrender of a child to the school. He reports that after he imprisoned the parent, others "exhaust[ed] every device imaginable to induce me to yield to their wishes."[9] In 1888 agents reported that police — sometimes Makah police — were used to bring children to the boarding school at Ba'adah Point.[10]

The agency day and boarding schools did threaten some Makah values and lifeways, but they ensured others and generated new ones. One example is the transformation of the five-village structure of their tribe. The determination of Makah parents to avoid parent-child separations contributed to consolidation of five traditional villages into one at *diʸya*, near the Indian Agency. Helma Ward explained to me the important link between staying together as a family and the traditional way of educating their children: "We didn't have books. We learned by being told over and over. We were told at home, not in public. That was *huhuʔaq'it*, [which means] an old saying and teaching from way back" (1995). This desire to stay with their children and continue the old sayings from way back led families to relocate.

By 1917 all families with children who still lived at Ozette, the most southerly of the five villages, had relocated to Neah Bay. Before she passed away, Meredeth Parker (Makah) shared her family's experience with how mandatory schooling hastened the abandonment of the Ozette village and even *waʔač̓* (also known as Wa'atch or Wyatch) (Marr 1987, 48). Although families without children stayed longer at Ozette, a new tribal tradition emerged: occupying Ozette seasonally, in May and June, to smoke fish, salt fish, and gather clams (Marr 1987, 48). One enduring effect of the agency school system, then, was to associate Ozette with memories of mandatory schooling and relocation. These memories would pique the Makah Tribe's emotional response to the need for protecting artifacts washing out of the Ozette site.

Indian agents, other agency employees, and missionaries implemented a variety of strategies to redefine Makah civilization. Silencing qʷiꞏqʷiꞏdič̓č̓aq was another means to break the transmission of traditional knowledge.

Silencing the Language

During one of our oral history sessions at MCRC, Helma Ward concentrated her account of American colonialism on language. I showed her a statement by Huntington made in 1874 that read: "The Indian tongue must be put to silence, and nothing but the English allowed in all social intercourse." Helma virtually snorted a reply: "If they did that to us [English-only policy], did they do it to themselves? Did they tell themselves that they should *never* learn and speak any foreign language? That the English would *always* speak *only*

English? No!" (1995). Historical documents and oral history record that Neah Bay Indian Agency teachers discouraged Makah children from speaking qʷiqʷidiččaq in school by belittling and physically punishing them. Huntington clearly articulated his belief that the English language was not simply a subject matter to be mastered but a means to reconstruct the minds of the children. He felt that in order for the children to understand proper social and religious life, philosophy, and morality they must be taught in English.[11]

Makah oral history is layered with multigenerational memories of prohibitions against qʷiqʷidiččaq extending from the nineteenth into the twentieth century. Elder Ruth Claplanhoo remembers that an older companion, Nora Barker, had her mouth washed out with brown soap in the Neah Bay day school early in the 1900s as punishment for speaking qʷiqʷidiččaq (1995). Other elders, such as Irene Ward, experienced the soap punishment firsthand (I. Ward 1995). Helma Ward still winces when she remembers how she and her classmates experienced yet other forms of punishment: "When I was in first, second, and third grade, our teacher told us not to speak Makah in class. My teacher's husband (who taught the older grades) would hit our hands with rulers if we still spoke it. That's when I decided to go away to boarding school [in Tulalip] for a few years. I couldn't stand him" (1995). At least by 1894, Neah Bay School superintendent John Youngblood began requesting transfers of five Makah boys and seven girls to boarding schools, such as Chemawa and Carlisle.[12] Boarding schools accelerated language loss actively (through policies prohibiting Native speech) and passively (through separations of children from their families).

Children's experience at boarding schools off the reservation varied, depending on the government contract school. Isabelle Ides's oral history recounted a more lenient atmosphere at Cushman School in Tacoma:

In 1912 I went to government boarding school in Tacoma. I was there for almost three years. . . . There were Indians there from *all* over at that school — Montana, Alaska. And there were thirteen girls there from Neah Bay. Those Indians from Montana would be together as a group talking in Indian. And we'd be together as a group talking. They let us talk in Indian. Not like the agency in Neah Bay that didn't. We didn't come home for Christmas or for other holidays. We were too poor to come home. Only when school got out did we come home. But then I got sick, real sick. I came back to Neah Bay then.

Makah students at other boarding schools, however, were severely punished, and these hardships drastically affected the transmission of language from one generation to the next.

In her oral history, Mary Lou Denney recalled how her father's experience affected her:

I never learned Makah, so English was the only thing I knew. The other thing is that we used to ask our parents, how come we never got to learn Makah? Their reply was that when they were growing up, they were not allowed to speak their own language. They were punished very severely if they were caught speaking it. I think I'll always remember when my father had indicated that . . . he was speaking Makah to another one of the boys that were in the same barracks, because they were sent away to school, and when he was caught, they took him outside and it was raining. The weather was very bad and they put him to a harness and they had to walk around just like animals when they were, I don't know what they would do, but anyway they just kind of walked in a circle and they were chained. . . . They didn't have a coat on, just their clothes that they wore to class. He said he'll never forget that because there were some pretty sick kids that were having to do the same thing. So him and my mom decided that they wouldn't allow us to go through that kind of treatment and that we would learn the English. (1995)

Concern about punishments and public shaming encouraged many Makah families to support their children's acquisition of English. Some stopped speaking Makah in their children's presence (Greene 1995, Sadie Johnson 1995). This dramatically interrupted the rate of fluent acquisition of qʷiqʷidiččaq. Still, some people who were children in the early 1900s were raised by grandparents who knew little English. These individuals became the few fluent speakers of qʷiqʷidiččaq and have carried it into the next generation. These speakers — some of whom have lived a century — have been critical to the language preservation and survival programs of the MCRC over the past twenty years.

In 1931 the Neah Bay community considered granting land to the public school district in order to end the educational segregation of their children from the white children who lived on the Coast Guard base. Parents wanted their children to receive a less vocational education. However, Makah concerns about handing land over to county and state jurisdiction and the resistance of Coast Guard parents to desegregation were among factors that led to a lack of Makah consensus on land donation.[13] Then, a Makah named Luke Markishtum stepped forward and deeded a piece of his land in the village of Neah Bay to the public school district.

Early-twentieth-century Indian education policy still centered on assimilation, but the strategy had shifted from special Indian schools to desegregated public schools. Superintendent Raymond Bitney felt that since agriculture had never been and was still not promising in Neah Bay, and since fishing "[would] not last forever . . . the problem is one of education and assimilation — we must prepare the Indian to leave the Reservation and earn his living on the outside in competition with the White man. With this in mind we have completed the present project — the Neah Bay public school."[14]

In contrast, Makah tribal members, such as Luke Markishtum, saw the public school as a way to educate the next generation without removing them from their families and culture. If anything, public school was considered by at least some Makah people as an alternative to assimilation (E. Markishtum Hottowe 1995). Both contemporary oral history and historical documentation suggest that when Makah people participated in government or public schooling, they saw it as a way to add to the children's educational experience, a way to enhance their adaptability and survival. In contrast, Euro-American observers seem to have anticipated that education would divorce the children from "Indianness."

In addition to targeting traditional education and language, nineteenth- and twentieth-century Indian Affairs policies also sought to incorporate Makah people into regional and national economies, transforming mentalities and lifeways in the process. Like strategies of the government, commercial market forces also encouraged Native American peoples to incorporate themselves as individual entrepreneurs and rub against strong, kinship-based economic and social structures.

Economy and Governance

When the whites came here to civilize us, to teach us how to farm, they gave us pitchforks. The weather here is not good for farming. Too much rain. Our men decided to take the tines of the pitchforks and bend them into fishhooks.

HILDRED IDES

From the Office of Indian Affairs perspective, the mid-nineteenth-century Makah economy — characterized by fishing, sealing, and whaling for subsistence, trade, or cash — was considered neither industrious nor civilized. Economic forces and Indian policy must have seemed schizophrenic to the Makah people. On the one hand, national Indian policy demanded agricultural development on the reservation; while on the other hand, numerous incentives encouraged adaptation of their traditional whale, seal, and fish economies to the cash market.

Some of the more astute agents lobbied Indian Affairs to consider the particular situation of the Makah community. As early as 1865, Henry Webster noted the disparity between Indian Affairs policy and local economic reality: "one of the most practical and practicable methods of directly benefiting these Indians is by aiding them in their fisheries; they are an anomaly in the Indian service. . . . The waters of the Pacific and Straits of Fuca teem with life . . . and forms the principal food of the natives. What the buffalo is to the Indians on the plains, the whale is to the Makah."[15] Just two years later, Webster requested fifty-ton to seventy-five-ton fishing vessels for the

Makah people. He felt that the act of providing the vessels would show the moral superiority and civilized nature of the government.

By 1869 non-Indians had hired Makah sealers to accompany them on sealing expeditions. At this point, the Makah people were not well equipped to enter the commercial market independently. Throughout the 1860s and 1870s, agents inconsistently recommended that the government support the commercialization of Makah subsistence activities, such as sealing, whaling, and fishing.[16] In 1873, at the urging of the Makah people who were expecting treaty-provided fisheries assistance, another agent requested a schooner of at least fifty tons. Such a schooner would carry Makah canoes further out to sea for whaling and sealing, thus enabling the modification of traditional methods and more successful marketing of the seal products.[17] The government was never forthcoming with aid for schooners, a point keenly remembered in Neah Bay today.

In 1879 Agent Willoughby notes that Makah disinterest in agriculture was not due to their indolence but to their ability to calculate higher returns and lower risk from their marine economy. Willoughby confessed that he was willing to carry out his orders to shift their attention to agriculture but that their fisheries industry would be more favorable for them.[18] Ironically, incorporating the Makah people into the American economy began by dismantling a rapidly adapting and lucrative indigenous economy. In 1877 Agent Huntington indicated that the "country is impatiently waiting for the promised harvest of social reform, of moral regeneration, and of material prosperity among these burdensome people."[19] We might thus suppose that Makah material prosperity was equated with incorporation into a commercial industry and wage economy.

The schooners that took the Makah sealers away from agency surveillance could carry anywhere from eight to fourteen canoes apiece, with each canoe manned by two Native sealers. These schooners cruised from two to eight days, returning to harbor only in bad weather. In the late 1880s they were gone longer hunting in the extreme north. In 1882 it was reported that these sealers could earn the extraordinary sum of forty dollars per day sealing commercially.

Surprisingly, some agents saw commerce as a corrupting factor in the Makah civilization process. Agents complained that commercial demand for fish oil and sealskins and demand for wage labor in canneries and fish-packing companies provided immediate gains and deterred Makah agriculture.[20] During the 1870s and 1880s they also complained that white-owned sealing schooners were "anxious to secure a complement of these Indians, and the demand is generally greater than the supply. Consequently, every conceivable move is resorted to induce them to take to their canoes and join the fleet. . . . Flushed with their success, and the money they have earned, they look coldly upon work harder and less remunerative, and the proceeds of which must be waited for, and uncertain."[21] In pushing to make the Makah people into farmers, the agency simultaneously discouraged them from their fisheries for the sake of their "civilization" and encouraged them to commercialize their fisheries so that they would become more industrious and economizing, also for the sake of their civilization.

Incorporation into the regional, market economy did not necessarily discourage the practice of traditions as agents had hoped. Makah people could reinvest profits in such a way as to reinforce social ties and maintain social ranking as was traditionally done through potlatching. As Makah elder Helen Peterson has remembered: "Long ago you had to keep up your name, you know. When they came back from sealing, they gave lots of parties, they gave away calico and other things" (Marr 1987, 25).

In 1885, with an accumulation of savings from commercial sealing and other wage labor, Makah sealers began to invest their earnings, purchasing their own schooners so that they could better compete with non-Indian sealers.[22] In 1887 it was reported that a Makah-owned schooner was sealing in the extreme north with an entirely Indian crew.[23] Just as the Makah people began to gain this ground, non-Indian hunting methods shifted from spearing to shooting. Agent Powell reported that 1888 was a sparse season, attributable to, according to the Makahs, the schooners from San Francisco and Victoria that had introduced shooting and scared away the seals.[24] By 1893 the Makahs owned seven schooners, including those used for fishing.[25] These Makah schooners generally carried all-Indian crews, with the exception of white navigators, and sailed as far as the Bering Sea.[26] Some invested their earnings into stores, hotels, or trading posts. In 1892 three reservation businesses were Makah-owned — one hotel and two stores (one was obtained by buying out the white trader's stock with three thousand dollars cash).[27]

In 1897 a treaty between the United States and Great Britain banned fur seal hunting, except from canoe (Marr 1987, 25). Within a few years, several Makah schooners were seized for purported violation of the treaty. Due to confusion about the dates for open season, two Makah schooners were seized and impounded until the customs fines were collected. The record is unclear, but others may have been seized and sold.[28] This sealing restriction, combined with a collapse in the whale oil market and the halibut industry, initiated a period of prolonged economic hardship of a kind the Makah community had not previously known.[29] The transition from subsistence and trade economy to a regional market economy led to participation in the rapid extraction and depletion of natural resources. (Nineteenth-century capitalism had few, if any, safeguards for resource sustainability.)

The strains on natural resource industries encouraged Makah participation in various wage labors, such as picking in the hop fields of Puget Sound and laboring in logging camps, lumber mills, and barge canneries.[30] During the hop-picking season, individuals or entire families left Neah Bay for weeks at a time. In 1884, after the hop-picking season was finished, families continued through the fall harvesting other crops. They "return[ed] home with their canoes laden with flour, sugar, potatoes, and other vegetables."[31]

As with sealing, manufactured goods purchased from hop-picking wages were incorporated into traditional Makah exchanges. As Meredeth Parker (Makah) remembered, "They used to go to town during berry-picking season clear up to hop-picking season. Before they came home, they'd buy things for the winter. They bought some of their clothing, and they also bought calico to sew with. And in their parties they used to give away a lot of calico. We have a song that says as long as that song lasts they pulled out their calico, another bolt of it and another bolt of it, until that song was done with" (qtd. in Marr 1987, 19).

The hop-picking tradition continued into the twentieth century. In one of our interviews, Isabelle Ides remembered her family's participation in this seasonal labor early in the century:

It was hard to get money here. Money was real hard to come by then. I went hop-picking twice. Once when I was really little and once after I was married and had my first baby. Dick Williams [Makah] got a lot of people from here to go hop-picking. It was at Auburn and Orton. The first time we took a gas boat to Port Angeles and then to Seattle. The second time we caught a steamer that came here once a week and it took us to Tacoma. They took all the hop-pickers on a train from Tacoma out near the farm. We walked the rest of the way and they had all our stuff hauled out to where we went. That first time my grandma didn't make the train and she got left behind. Oh, I cried! She came the next day, but I never knew how she lived or where she slept that night. My mom said that before we were born, when they would travel to the fields, they would stop in Port Angeles. They didn't have a tent in those days, so they used cattail mats for a tent. She told us those mats kept the water off real good. But we didn't use those. The people at the fields gave us houses to live in. Lots of families lived together in one house with partitions between. There was a table and a stove. . . . My mom picked and me and all my sisters. We'd get one dollar per box. It was a *great* big box. We had to pick fast in order to fill it. I think we picked two boxes per day. We'd first put the hops in our spruce roots baskets and then use those to carry it over and fill that big box. My mom used to work at the cannery. She saved the collars from the fish and salted them. She took that along and we ate that. Lots of people wished for them and she gave some to them. But that's what we ate. Other people who come from where there are lots of clams, they dried those and ate them. There used to be a fish truck that would come by. One time the man was selling silver salmon and my dad said "that's not silver salmon, that's dog salmon." That man said "shhh, here take this" and he wrapped up that dog salmon in paper and gave it to my dad so that he would keep quiet and not tell that it was dog salmon. There was a store there and we would go and buy some of the things. It was fun living there. People were there from *all* over. . . . It was late summer [when we went to the fields]. We'd be finishing right when the Puyallup Fair started. We were too poor to go the fair, but I remember people talking about it. So I guess we would be there picking a couple weeks — until the hops ran out. Then we'd come home. (1995)

Hop-picking was only one of several migrant labor opportunities. In 1894 Makah-owned schooners took many people from the Makah reservation to Westminster, British Colombia, to catch salmon for the canneries. Reportedly, the reservation was left with only children, women, and elders, who caught large quantities of halibut.[32]

Many more opportunities were open to women and young girls at the turn of the century than for women of earlier generations who primarily wove baskets, dried fish, or landed lumber and other supplies from steamers in the harbor using dugout canoes (R. Claplanhoo 1995).[33] Ruth Claplanhoo, who was born just after 1900, remembers that when she was young girls and women could do piecework, such as packing fish into cans or running canning machinery. The Makah commute to the barge cannery out in the harbor emptied the village of a significant part of its population during those days (R. Claplanhoo 1995). Women also traveled with other family members, following the barges to other processing sites such as Irondale and Astoria (R. Claplanhoo 1995). Their work was largely organized by Puget Sound businessmen and sometimes Chinese foremen (R. Claplanhoo 1995).

Unable to control Makah labor, the agency attempted to control economic decision-making by systematically restructuring traditional forms of Makah family, village, and tribal governance. It was thought that dismantling qʷidičča?atx̌ power structures would prevent the Makah people from aligning with others, such as the British or their Nootkan (now known as Nuuchahnulth) relatives on the northern side of the Strait of Juan de Fuca. Americans also feared alliances with other tribes in Washington Territory or Oregon.[34] During the negotiations for the treaty with the Makahs, 1855, Governor

Stevens selected one of the village chiefs to be a head chief; concentrating authority in fewer hands in tribal societies had proven beneficial to the Hudson Bay Company, and the Americans sought to duplicate this (Gibbs 1855, 424). By 1878 the agency challenged the hereditary chief system by instituting elections, the idea being to encourage representative government and elect headmen analogous to town selectmen.[35]

Despite these controls, the Makah people, individually and collectively, *did* make economic decisions. The point here is to recognize that they were forced to make these decisions within the extremely confined parameters allowed them and with the information made available to them by the Indian Affairs bureaucracy. The rapid changes in the Makah economic system, along with the prohibitions of cultural expressions, would redefine greatly the value and destiny of various Makah material culture items.

Cultural Expressions and Citizenship

For more than a century, Euro-Americans have tried to transform Makah society by suppressing Native language, controlling children's education, and modifying Makah economy. The spiritual foundations of Makah society were also targeted, and because spirituality was intertwined with daily life, Euro-Americans criticized traditional medicine practices, midwifery, bone gaming, Makah singing and dancing, and potlatching, activities not only spiritual but also social and economic. Non-Natives living on the reservation labeled Makah beliefs "superstitious" and their activities "uncivilized," "savage," and "heathenistic." As late as 1931, a U.S. Indian agent commented that the potlatch was the "curse of the Coast Indians."[36]

The Neah Bay Agency records reveal how Euro-Americans imagined the civilizing process as disrupting Makah traditional social systems and severing their social ties with the past. The integrity of the Makah belief system was not acknowledged; it represented little more than a threat to Euro-American authority or an unacceptable eruption of uncivilized behavior. For example, the Makah people considered physical and spiritual health to be intimately related;

thus healing was not a secular process. Although healers had considerable respect in the villages, from the Euro-American perspective they were the antithesis of civilization. In the minds of observers, the curing itself functioned as a kind of social disease (Bracken 1997, 71). Agent Willoughby revealed his contempt for medicine men in his 1882 report to Indian Affairs; "To destroy their belief in medicine men, who are ever the enemy of whites, inasmuch as the presence of the latter is a signal for their overthrow, is to make a huge stride toward civilizing the Indians."[37] With these attitudes before them, the agency ridiculed and punished Makah healers for their practices in the name of Makah social evolution.[38]

Hostility toward traditional medicine continued into the twentieth century. As late as 1931 the agency reported that field nurses were needed in order to discourage pregnant women from going to the "filthy, brutal, ignorant mid-wives."[39] In contemplating the history of this repression, Helma Ward noted the irony: "They weren't filthy or ignorant. They were very concerned with hygiene and sterilizing themselves and towels and sheets before the birth. They knew how to turn breaches. Now the [white] doctors are returning to midwifing and returning to the use of herbs that they outlawed years before. What can I say?" (1995).

Indian songs, dances, and potlatching were strictly forbidden beginning mainly in the 1880s. James Swan attended many winter ceremonies and was admittedly fascinated by them. These were referred to as *tomanawas* (also *tamanos*, *tamanowes*, and other variations). The word, derived from a Chinook term for beings endowed with supernatural power, was used by whites to refer to spiritual ceremonies or shamanistic acts, which included some dancing. The term was also used to refer to the guardian spirits themselves (Bracken 1997, 11). As an ethnologist, Swan collected many of the ceremonial items made for these dances. To a certain extent, he made himself a part of these gatherings, even attempting mask painting. At one potlatch he publicly presented a shawl and rattle to declare himself godfather to the children of a former student.[40]

Swan's fascination with Makah culture was not widely shared by other agents, however. Swan notes in his diary that in 1878 the "physical mutilation practices" of ƛuˑkʷaˑliˑ dances (also historically referred to in anglicized terms as Dukwalli, Koquallies, Cloqually, or Kloquallys) disgusted the white women present and made them faint.[41] The X̌uk̓ʷaliˑ dance was a wolf ritual ceremony whose practice was shared with the Makah people's relatives on Vancouver Island (Ernst 1952; Drucker 1951). Willoughby boasted that the Kloquallys are carried on with "perfect decency in respect to the wishes of the agent." He reports taking a "determined stand" against the cutting, lacerating, and skewering of skin.[42] Willoughby's perceptions parallel those of officials in British Columbia who abhorred the allegedly cannibalistic tendencies of the feasts (Bracken 1997, 73).

By the 1880s various ceremonies were not only discouraged but had become the "target of a whole apparatus of outright coercion" (Bracken 1997, 69). During the 1880s and 1890s, the agency established an Indian police force and used it to leverage the community's compliance with Indian Affairs.[43] In 1890 it included one lieutenant and seven privates. Agent McGlinn used this police force to stop the immoral influence that Cloqually dances and potlatches supposedly had on the schoolchildren. Although he admitted that potlatching had stopped on the reservation, he did note that the Makah people still went out to Tatoosh Island — a pattern of resistance that would continue well into the twentieth century (figure 7).[44]

The Makah people did not live through these prohibitions passively. In 1881 Agent Willoughby exclaimed that each "still clings to the ways of his ancestors with a tenacity only terminated with death."[45] Although medicine men were forbidden, their services were still quietly sought or the white man's medicine refused.[46] Bone games and potlatches were moved off the reservation, where the agent had no jurisdiction, or were held in places inaccessible to the agent, such as Tatoosh Island (see figure 7). Makah elder Isabelle Ides remembers one of these occasions in the early 1900s when the agency restrictions were evaded: "[The agent] didn't allow Indian dancing. No Indian dancing, no Indian singing, no Indian parties. He didn't say why. The agency was still strict back then. Even after about 1918 when I was married. I remember these people wanted to have a party but couldn't. They decided to have it out on Tatoosh Island. I was there. There was a salmon bake and dancing. But then the beach got real rough and we had to leave. We would have been stuck

7. In the late nineteenth and early twentieth centuries, the Makah people evaded
prohibitions on their cultural expressions by holding potlatches and other ceremonies on Tatoosh Island. This photo, ca. 1899–1905, was taken by Jesse Thomas,
who worked as one of the lighthouse keepers on Tatoosh Island. Courtesy of the
Clallam County Historical Society.

there if we didn't leave. The waves were pounding on the beach"
(1995). Ruth Claplanhoo's memories of the resistance to agency restrictions on these gatherings are also vivid: "We couldn't have Indian dancing. No parties. Except at night or something. I remember
when Dodge was agent, it came Makah Days and he wouldn't let
us do anything. Most of us were working for a floating cannery out
here in those days. That floating cannery gave us a whole bunch of
salmon. We took it out to Tatoosh. We baked those salmon and some
potatoes. Just then a torrent came up. We had to leave. We didn't get
to eat all that salmon. They say the tide came up and those potatoes
were floating out there" (1995).

The Makah families continued with their cultural practices as
best as they were able under the restrictions. The preservation of privacy in domestic spaces was one of the means to continue. Isabelle
Ides remembers one home that regularly served as a space for singing and, therefore, as a sheltered space for keeping songs alive:
"When Dodge left, that's when the songs came back. Before then,

there weren't any parties. There was singing at home, though. Lizzie [Claplanhoo], Wilbur's mom, she was laid in bed with arthritis for eighteen years. I remember that they used to sing to her *every* night. They would sing to her in bed. That was Helma's mom and dad, Nora Barker, maybe Alec Greene, and Randolph Parker. They would sing all kinds of family songs. That's why Nora knew all those songs later. She heard them there and had them all in her head" (1995).[47] Traveling off the reservation in order to participate in wage labor — such as hop-picking — also provided the opportunity to create a space sheltered from the agency restrictions. Isabelle Ides remembers the bone gaming at the hop fields near Auburn, Washington, where she picked with her family early in the century: "People were there [at the hop fields] from *all* over. I remember one night, when I was there the second time, I heard bone gaming. My husband said 'let's go see the bone game' and so my mom took care of my baby so I could look. But she woke up and I had to come back. . . . When the men were being festive, they would decorate their hats with hop leaves. Just to be decorative" (1995). The annual cycles of migrant agricultural labor, then, provided another intertribal social space for continuing cultural expressions (see Tollefson 1994).

In the period immediately surrounding the American Indian Citizenship Act in 1924, hope for cultural freedoms was high in Neah Bay. In 1924 an agency employee noted that "Once a year the older Indians give a celebration on what they call Makah Day. This is the day set aside by the Rodman Wanamaker Expedition some years ago."[48] The Rodman Wanamaker Expedition traveled to a number of Indian reservations in the summer of 1913 to present tribes with an American flag as "a prophecy"—"let us hope of their coming citizenship and uttermost blending with the civilization that crowns the age" (Wanamaker 1913, 4). Makah Days is an annual celebration that continues today (figure 8). Some agency employees interpreted the Makah Day dances "by the old folks" to be distinctly less threatening than the dances of previous decades: "Makah Day is celebrated along patriotic lines [and] some years the Indians hold a pageant of the past which is very colorful and harmless."[49]

The public display of Makah culture had apparently increased between 1924 and 1930, at which point Superintendent Raymond H.

8. Makah girl in dance regalia at Makah Days, 1995. Photo by Patricia Pierce Erikson.

Bitney began "closing down on them more and more." He was more inclined to see Makah Days as a continuation of past values rather than a so-called harmless pageant. His reasoning is nearly identical to his nineteenth-century counterparts: "There is no doubt as to the harm of these Indian parties where they give away money, clothes, etc. . . . The potlatch, which is masked as a birthday party, christening party or wedding party is going to be very difficult to stop at once. . . . The Indian Police were instructed to arrest anyone giving away money at a party or playing the bone game for money."[50] It is clear that Bitney did not feel Makah Days was merely a monument or pageant of the past. He saw it as a continuation of tradition, one white supporters external to the agency had enabled them to continue: "The Indians have enlisted the aid of Indian sentimentalists, politicians, and cheap grafters to be 'allowed to carry on their innocent pastimes and exhibit their culture.'"[51] Despite his efforts, Bitney, like his predecessor Dodge, was not successful in stopping such gatherings since the Makahs would just move off-reservation or to Vancouver Island.[52]

Makah elders remember at least two of the occasions when agency restrictions were avoided. Ruth Claplanhoo remembers one incident under Superintendent Dodge:

My husband's oldest brother lived out at c'uˑyas raising cattle. This was early in the twenties. He invited some older people over. He killed a beef. We were bone gaming, just for fun. Not for money. Some could bet seafood or berries. Around nine or ten at night, there came a knock at the door. It was a warning that Agent Dodge was upset. No one had showed up at the show hall [movies]. We got scared. I don't know why. It was just older folk. But we did. We all scattered. Some went to Anderson Point. Viola's grandfather was an old man then. He had to go up river in his canoe. He got his kerchief caught on a bush trying to get away. We found it there the next day. The [agency] police did show up and they had guns. (1995)

Ruth's sister, Isabelle Ides, also shared her firsthand account of avoiding bone gaming restrictions that continued under Superintendent Bitney: "Another time, I went to a bone game at Bowman Beach. The road was open by then [at least 1931]. We were playing the La Push [people]. We could go to Bowman because it was off-reservation. The agent couldn't say anything there" (1995). Finally, when Indian Commissioner John Collier passed the Indian Reorganization Act in 1934, BIA policy ceased direct interference with religious practices, at least in theory. In the meantime, although political and economic change had an impact on nearly all realms of Makah life — especially whaling, sealing, and fishing — the cultural and spiritual significance of these practices remained encoded in songs, dances, communal sharing of food, and other social protocols. These memories of prohibitions, accommodations, and resistances formed a bedrock on which the meanings of the contemporary MCRC would later rest.

In this chapter I attempted to show how local colonial histories affect contemporary Native American concerns about identity and ways of knowing. Some of the Euro-American perspectives described above that propelled the "civilization of the American Indian" project also supported the scientific investigation of and collection of Makah culture. Within eight years of the Treaty of Neah Bay, an Indian Affairs employee named James Swan began collecting a diverse array of Makah curiosities and shipping them to the Smithsonian Institution. He did so in order to record and preserve what a fledgling anthropological science considered to be a passing way of life. Two projects — *preservation* of Native American culture and *elimination* of Native American culture — seem contrary; yet the Makah people experienced them simultaneously. Their experience with this contradiction informs contemporary political debates over the degree to which Native peoples are allowed to care for and represent their heritage.

Once treaties established reservation boundaries, outlined Indian rights to be protected, and promised various compensating services, the U.S. government, particularly the Office of Indian Affairs asserted itself as the guardian of the future of American Indian communities. Although the qʷidičča?a·tx̌ signed a treaty which they felt protected their sovereignty and way of life, American politicians, businessmen, U.S. Indian agents, and missionaries began to implement policies and practices that were based on their own ideologies.

What followed was a project that sought to transform Makah morality and industry in order to move them out of what Americans perceived to be a state of savagery. This entailed not only dramatic changes in the volume of trade, the identity of trading partners, and the methods of procuring resources but also in the balance of how much material goods were accumulated and how much were given away in potlatching. The intent in discouraging the so-called curse of the potlatch was not only to encourage individual financial saving and reinvestment but also to break tribal and intertribal economies and social ties that were a stubborn basis for resisting change.

To encourage what was considered a more civilized morality, Americans proceeded to transform Makah social and personal space in order to holistically transform the "Indian mind." The intent in reshaping Makah personal habits was to ready the spirit and identity to follow. The most personal details of bodily cleanliness were closely scrutinized and criticized. The American vision of the transformation of the Makah people is perhaps best illustrated by the following 1881 Neah Bay Agency Report, wherein Agent Willoughby applauded some changes he was witnessing:

To prove that their advancement, which at first was slow, has been not only gradual but permanent, one has but to visit, first, the lodge of an old fossil of the tribe, of which there are but few remaining, who still clings to the ways of his ancestors with a tenancy only terminated with death, and for one moment take in the utter disregard of comfort or convenience, to say nothing of the demands of common decency, and then pass on to a large though rudely constructed cabin of split boards, roomy, well ventilated, and arranged with some degree of taste, certainly of convenience. And now to the last and latest — the neat, painted cottage. Within we do not look for mahogany and Eastlake, but we do find comfortable furniture, neat and clean blankets, and the luxury of a cook stove with its steaming pots and kettles. Father, mother, and children are well clothed, and all apparently anxious to show visitors that they know how to enjoy the comforts of civilization-a contrast so great as to seem hardly credible.[53]

This tour of domestic spaces that represent evolutionary stages — from lodge or longhouse to split-board cabin to neatly painted cottage — reveals the American vision of a linear social evolution, a very specific vision of progress that places the contemporary American society at the apex. Any survival of precontact Makah culture was considered a fading anachronism. Yet surviving anachronisms linked Makah material culture to the symbolic capital of national identity: antiquities.

Although Makah historical experience and ways of knowing were perforated by Euro-American schooling, language, and so on, the disruptions often called *language loss* and *cultural loss* do not represent complete breaks or discontinuities. Because the Makah historical experience with American colonization was embedded in ongoing Makah social relations, those moments of puncture were also moments when Makah ways of knowing could be creatively rewoven or repaired, enabling ongoing coherence, adaptation, and survival in a new politico-economic environment.[54] Of course, it is not surprising that there have been dramatic differences between Makah and Euro-American perceptions of Makah identity in the past and present. The focus here is how these perceptions were transformed by power relations and institutional environments. This struggle is part of the social fabric that informs twentieth century politics of material culture.

This chapter has briefly characterized some of the contact zones created by American colonization on the Makah reservation. Throughout the history of contact with Euro-American peoples, Makah people have forwarded self-representations in a variety of ways. Reflection on this contact and dialogue provides a critical background for my subsequent discussion of the subjectivity of the MCRC. We turn now, then, to the famous archaeological excavation of the Makah village of Ozette and the founding of the MCRC. This excavation and cultural center are contact zones that are relatively

new in comparison to those of the late nineteenth and early twentieth century that I have discussed here. The excavation and mu-
seum/cultural center became collaborative projects — new contact
zones that emerged in an era when power relations between Native
American peoples and conventional centers of knowledge-making
were shifting.

Part 2

3 Many Gifts from the Past
Elders, Memories, and Ozette Village

I no longer remember who first told me there was a little museum in the Neah Bay high school. I do remember that many tribal members advised me to go look at it when I was trying to learn the history of the MCRC. With the help of Mary Hunter, a Makah teacher, I found myself standing in the cafeteria, also known as a multipurpose complex, looking at wooden and glass exhibit cases that lined one wall. My visit to the display cases in the school cafeteria was an important part of realizing that the Ozette excavation was only one stitch in a whole fabric of cultural preservation efforts that were responsible for the founding of the MCRC. This chapter considers some of the lesser known yet remarkable moments in twentieth-century Makah history and some of the people, places, and desires that made them.

Without question, the Ozette excavation energized the community and created unprecedented opportunities for validating oral history and expressing Makah identity to the public. But this moment in Makah history rested on a firm foundation: a series of other remarkable historic moments in a long history of cultural survival. Since the time of colonial contact, the qʷidiččaʔaˑtx̌ have struggled for economic and political survival, with each family choosing a different way to adapt. Some passed down the language; others did not. Some chose to convert to Christianity; others did not. Some invested in reforming public education to make it culturally appropriate; others watched skeptically.

When I first saw the exhibit cases in the cafeteria they had been displaying family heirlooms for almost thirty years. They were built in the 1969–70 school year with funds from the Johnson-O'Malley (JOM) planning grant ten years before the opening of the MCRC. On display were items such as halibut hooks, whaling gear (harpoon and line), cedar bark baskets, and cedar mats. The label on a sealskin float indicated that the float had been collected around 1910 and acquired by the Makah Tribal Council in 1973. The council then loaned it to the exhibit. Another label told the story of a blanket received by Nora Barker's father as a potlatch gift on Vancouver Island. Another told the story of some watertight baskets made about 1910 by Ruth Claplanhoo's mother, Mary Allabush, and then donated to the exhibit by Ruth and her husband, Art.

In addition to artifacts, the cases displayed many photographs. Some were mounted on posterboard, and others were matted and hung in wooden frames. Among these is one of the most famous historic photographs of the Makah people, attributed to Asahel Curtis. It depicts a Makah whaler harpooning a whale from a cedar, dugout whaling canoe (see figure 9). More recent photos, taken by Washington State's Office of Public Instruction, documented high school students practicing dances in their old gym in the 1960s. Others showed Frank Smith teaching wood carving classes at the school in the 1970s. Still others recorded elders Nora Barker and Helen Peterson teaching the paddle dance to kindergarteners; elders Isabelle Ides, Alice Arnold, and Alberta Thompson were also photographed teaching children. Many of these elders are shown in olivella shell regalia singing and drumming for the youths before them.

Earlier I posed the question, why would the museum format be an appropriate way for a Native American community to forward cultural survival, especially since museums have been a part of the colonial experience? We have considered how collecting practices associated with museums have been zones of contact between the Makah and Euro-American peoples during the nineteenth century. Strictly speaking, the Makah people have not adopted this colonial-derived museum format wholesale. The MCRC can be considered an autoethnography — a self-portrait of the Makah people. The Makah community has selected elements of the dominant culture — prac-

9. "Neah Bay whaler fighting the whale first day." Makah whaling canoe being towed by whale. Note the sealskin float attached to the harpoon and raised over the whaler's head. Photo by Asahel Curtis. Courtesy of the Washington State Historical Society, negative no. 56519.

tices such as archaeology, museology, and linguistics — to use creatively in modified form as a way to express and continue Makah identity.

The MCRC is more than simply an outgrowth of post-1960s Native American activism and liberal federal funding. These political and economic factors are undeniably important, but their importance can be overstated. The portrayal of the MCRC in this book explores another factor — how the subjectivity or identity of this tribal museum/cultural center has been greatly shaped by a long history of autoethnography in Neah Bay. For this project, studying the MCRC has not been an end in and of itself. It has been a window onto the history of cultural survival and the experiences that give the museum meaning for the community today. To appreciate how the Makah history of autoethnography has shaped the subjectivity of the museum, we need to consider how many grandparents, parents, and teachers struggled to preserve and validate Makah traditions while accommodating rapid social change throughout the twentieth century.

The history of other Makah social spaces — such as community halls, homes, and schools — has also shaped the subjectivity of the MCRC.

Keeping the People Together

The songs and dances weren't "brought back." They never left.
MARGARET IRVING, Neah Bay, 1995

Each family had its own way of keeping tradition.
BATCH LACHESTER, Neah Bay, 1995

Around 1928 a Makah man named James Hunter built a community hall next to his house. Over the following twenty years it became known as Hunter's Hall, a community center and hub of social life in Neah Bay. Hunter invited people to the hall to practice singing and drumming their family songs or to have Thanksgiving dinners. He did this because "he just wanted to keep the people together" (I. Ward 1995). Singers and drummers, such as Sebastian LaChester, Ralph LaChester, Dewey McGee, and Alexander Greene, would come to the hall to practice (I. Ward 1995). By 1944 Randolph Parker, another of these regular drummers, decided to pass some of his family songs onto the next generation. He selected a thirteen-year-old boy named Batch LaChester and began training him. He decided to use Hunter's Hall to teach him how to dance. I caught up with Batch LaChester and we sat down at his kitchen table to reminisce about Hunter's Hall. He described his experience as follows:

> When I was thirteen, Randolph picked me to learn his dances. He used to make me run out to First Bridge and back. He taught me Ozette songs and dances. He wanted to preserve those things. He taught me the song before I even danced. "Learn the song, learn the beat, condition yourself, and then dance." He taught me the Wand Dance and the Elk Dance. He'd teach me at Hunter's Hall. For the Elk Dance I wore a leather piece around my waist with thongs that hung down. Each one had a deer hoof at the end so it clicked-clicked with each jump,

with each step. That was a solitary dance. I danced alone under a spotlight. No one there knew who I was until I hugged my grandma after the dance. (LaChester 1995)

The restrictions on Native American ceremonial and spiritual life, which ridiculed and forced underground many traditional lifeways, had begun to weaken by the 1930s. Being allowed to dance again inspired the Makah community to build an additional hall, Star Hall. Dances that were solitary, like the one described above, used to be danced at Makah Days on a platform in front of Star Hall (I. Ward 1995).

An arts and crafts store and a federal building also became important gathering places, albeit on a smaller scale. In 1952 the Makah Arts and Crafts Club was founded to pass on Makah artistry to the younger generation. The club's purpose was to teach basketry and shell artwork and provide a venue for selling these items to tourists. By 1956 the arts and crafts building was being remodeled; by 1962 the Arts and Crafts Club had opened a shop on the waterfront (see figure 10).[1] Women took turns keeping the store open. The store provided a place for women of different generations to gather, weave, and socialize (Irving 1995; I. Ward 1995). The Arts and Crafts Club was also interested in sustaining Makah language, although it did not pursue this through formal classroom instruction (Miller 1952, 270).[2] Another women's group, a Presbyterian sewing group, met in the sewing room of a federal building. Women gathered there to sew, knit, weave, or work on other projects. Young girls who went along with their mothers were exposed to the skills and oral histories shared there (Irving 1995; Shirley Johnson 1995; I. Ward 1995).

In order to remain strong, families had to adapt to new gathering spaces. Many elders early in the twentieth century understood the nature of the rapid change people were experiencing in Neah Bay. These elders encouraged gatherings in whatever ways they could. Batch LaChester identified Dick Williams as one of the many who encouraged their families to stay together despite all the changes: "My great-granduncle, Dick Williams, used to say that we lost our identity when we moved from those big longhouses — where people were

10. Ada Markishtum and Matilda McCarthy enter the Makah Arts and Crafts Store, which stood along the Neah Bay harbor beach on the west end of town, 1964. Photo by Ruth Kirk. Courtesy of the photographer.

always gathering for meals — to wooden houses. So he had a favorite saying, 'You come eat my house.' He wanted to keep the gathering going. Leaving the longhouses separated our ties, but that's what brought about the need for all the gatherings in the community" (1995). They gathered in cedar plank longhouses measuring as much as sixty feet long, thirty feet wide, and fifteen feet high. The roof was flat and constructed of planks, and the walls were planks suspended horizontally, tied between pairs of poles. Partitions normally installed for privacy could be removed for ceremonial occasions (Renker and Gunther 1990, 426; Mauger 1978).

During the transition to Euro-American-style homes, living rooms provided relatively safe havens for community members to gather to honor, pray, celebrate, or mourn in the ways of the qʷidiččaʔatx̌.

Elders today remember that in the 1930s parties were often held in the homes of families who had large living rooms. Cedar mats were placed on the floor to accommodate the bone gaming, singing, or drumming. These parties celebrated weddings and births or memorialized losses. Some of these gatherings were c'ayiq, a healing ceremony using a ceremonial rattle song (Irving 1995).

These gathering spaces, and the memories formed within them, provided a strong foundation for the traditions alive today in Neah Bay. Community halls and living rooms are just some of the active gathering spaces in the first half of the twentieth century where Makah people attempted to sustain community interaction and social ties. Important about them, of course, is what happened in these spaces — the coming together and the sharing of food, oral history, and performative traditions.

In these new gathering spaces the community experienced two new forms of social gatherings: club meetings and furlough parties. In the 1940s, 1950s, and 1960s several clubs were formed that specifically focused on preserving Makah traditions. These included the Makah Club, the Makah Arts and Crafts Club, the Slahal Club, the Hamatsa Club, the 13–30 Club, and the Warriors Club. Activities of the Makah Club are preserved in the memories of elders and in various archival records.

The Makah Club wanted to keep the culture alive; one way they did this was holding group dinners. Because they did not have tables they simply put boards on the floor (I. Ward 1995). In 1951, Makah Club members Norman Greene, Mrs. Greene, and Mr. and Mrs. Dewey McGee sought Makah Tribal Council donations to fund the Fourth of July celebration, and by 1960 the Makah Club was one of the organizations sponsoring the Makah Days celebration.[3] As Batch LaChester told me: "As I remember, the sense of that club was that the BIA [Bureau of Indian Affairs] has nothing to do with us. This is our club. They would sponsor Makah Days, Fourth of July, and other get-togethers. Their devotion was to stay together. It was to stand against the BIA. But it was also entertainment. They used to hold contests at Hunter's Hall. People loved that because there was nothing to do in the evening. So we gathered" (1995).[4]

Dancers who were active in the 1940s remember dancing almost every weekend. If it wasn't a wedding, name-giving party, or other celebration, it was a furlough party. In Neah Bay, more than fifty men participated in World War II. Their families wanted to honor them when they returned on furloughs or from duty. This community desire to honor servicemen encouraged and strengthened the public expression of traditional songs and dances. Batch LaChester remembered: "The furlough parties were pretty regular because there were so many of our boys in the service. The war years were lean for some families. So the Makah Club used to take on some of the responsibilities for hosting these furlough parties" (1995). The Slahal Club also sponsored homecoming parties for veterans. The way these Makah clubs honored veterans in Neah Bay mirrored a widespread pattern in Native American communities. Nationwide, warrior societies and ceremonies related to veterans were revitalized in association with World War I and World War II (Miller in Davis 1994, 156).

The revitalization of ceremonies for veterans — ceremonies with spiritual dimensions — touched upon some significant historical divisions in the Makah community. During the twentieth century, the Makah people maintained diverse points of view on the fundamentals of traditional Makah spiritual practices, prayer, and cosmology. Some of the Christian churches in Neah Bay encouraged their congregation to refrain from, and to disdain, non-Christian practices. Ministers preached that Makah traditions such as bone gaming and potlatches were "worldly pleasures" and "of the devil" (Ides 1995). Many Makah families chose to adopt this Christian morality. Other Christian churches at times had ministers who did not discourage Makah cultural practices. Consequently, a significant segment of the Neah Bay community continued with qʷidičča?a·tx̌ traditions; they were able to balance Makah traditions with Christianity by joining a more tolerant church or by withdrawing from active membership in a nontolerant church (Colson 1953, 240–41). Elder Mary Greene remembers the continuation of songs, despite admonitions against them:

Singing songs is something that follows you all through your lifetime. The elders would gather nightly and sing all evening and never sing the same song twice. Each family has its own set of songs. Family songs are your identity. You're only going to sing your own songs. They're too valuable to lose. . . . We'd have special occasions, like birthdays, and we'd get happy and start singing. That would happen at home, even when by yourself. You don't just sing Indian songs at a party. I see no way the songs could get lost. I can't see no way to forget them. They're too big. There are all kinds of songs: potlatch songs, guessing game songs, lullabies, prayers. . . . During the 1960s, our minister told us that we shouldn't sing or go to parties. But later, after he got to know us, he agreed that as long as the culture doesn't come first, as long as God comes first, then it's alright. He decided singing songs and going to parties was OK. He realized that himself. That's who we were anyway. He couldn't stop it. He was my uncle and he was Indian. (1995)

Some members of the community resolved these tensions with Christianity by simply remaining non-Christian and staying away from the churches.

I learned from the late Minerva "Muzzie" Claplanhoo how the World War II furlough parties related to the preservation of songs in an increasingly Christian community:

My family is one of the ones who turned away from their Indian ways. My grandparents were [Indian] Shakers. Those were the days when Shakers didn't take to the Indian culture. They put away their songs. But then when the war came (WWII) and the men came home on furlough before going overseas, then families wanted to honor them. Those who hadn't sung their songs in a long time wanted to honor those young men with a party — a welcome-home party. I had two brothers who came home like that. . . . The Slahal Club gave the party for my brothers. . . . So some families would go to Wilbur's [Claplanhoo] mom, Lizzie, and ask her family to sing their family songs for them. After that, many families kept it up and brought back their family songs. World War II got a lot of it going again. (1995)

Neah Bay had much cause for celebration after World War II and through the Korean and Vietnam Wars. Not a single Makah man was lost in active duty. The impulse to gather and celebrate, or sanctify, the launching or welcoming home of whalers, sealers, and fishermen from their expeditions at sea were continued through the new tradition of furlough parties.

Attention to Makah participation in World Wars I and II certainly reveals how the Makah community was not isolated (see Colson 1953, 148). Not only did Makah individuals leave the reservation to serve the military, but World War II in particular militarized the reservation. Bunkers, observation stations, and an Air Force base were built on the reservation, and a large number of non-Makah personnel became long-term residents, resulting in significant changes in community social life. One of the most notable was the increased rate of intermarriage of non-Native men and Makah women. Because of its location, the military considered Neah Bay strategic with respect to any potential Japanese invasion. From trade in sea otter skins and commercial sealing to forestry and World War II, Makah tribal members were part of economic, political, and economic processes on a global scale.

For non-Makah observers, the clubs, community halls, and sewing circles probably appeared as evidence of tribal assimilation, and indeed, such developments did signal massive political, economic, and ideological changes. However, such gathering spaces and social formats also allowed the Makah people to carry on what they considered traditional customs and sensibilities. Perhaps most importantly, they enabled the Makah people to foster their sense of who they were as families and as a people. In an earlier discussion, we considered how solid-twine baskets represented both continuity and adaptation. Clubs and community hall gatherings (such as the Thanksgiving and furlough parties) are examples of how Makah cultural life remained rooted in or derived from the past yet bent or adapted to the strong currents of change. I return now to the Neah Bay public school to demonstrate the connection between the Ozette excavation and the MCRC and the long-standing efforts to preserve Makah culture.

Removing the "Iron Curtain" in the Schools

When I was in first grade, about 1946, the teacher asked the class if we knew where we came from. I raised my hand and said, "Yes, from the ocean." The teacher said, "Oh, how?" I told her how the earth once had been covered with water, and then I told her in detail the story of how we had come from the sea. Well, that was how my great-grandfather taught me how life began. She was mad. She said, "You little heathen. You pagan child!" She sent me home crying. I was living with great-grandma, but she didn't understand why I was crying, because I was speaking English. She got Isabelle [Ides]. I told Isabelle what happened, and she translated. Then she went home. That night she said, "Don't ever tell white people about what we taught you. They don't believe it. If you don't learn their ways, they'll take you away from me." You see, my great-grandma [Alice Anderson Kallappa] had a daughter, that would be my grandma. She was taken to boarding school. But Christianity was very prevalent in the schools in the 1940s and 1950s. (Wilkie 1995)

In her office at tribal council headquarters, Donna Wilkie shared with me her childhood experience with overt intolerance for Makah culture in the Neah Bay school system. As an adult in the 1960s, Wilkie become involved in a Head Start program for Neah Bay preschoolers. The shift in her lifetime — from school intolerance to tolerance for Makah culture — reflects increased Makah control over the curriculum, supported by liberal federal programs.

As we saw in a previous chapter, the relationship between the Makah community and formal educational institutions in Neah Bay began with James Swan's construction of the first schoolhouse nearly 150 years ago. From the missionary era to the public school era, some Makah parents trusted that the schools would take their children in the right direction, while others were extremely distrustful. There are a variety of reasons for the continuation of this distrust. In the first half of the twentieth century, few teachers were

Makah or even from the community of Neah Bay. Also, since World War II, when the Neah Bay schools were combined with the Clallam Bay schools into a public school district, the top-level administration was non-Makah and was based in a non-Makah community. During this time, Makah cultural perspectives and history were not only absent from the curriculum but often discouraged, even if a child brought them into the classroom. Incidents such as the one described above by Donna Wilkie reinforced the perception that the public school was more a continuation of the boarding school era than a break from it.

We can think of public schools in Neah Bay as another contact zone, or space where different ways of knowing have encountered one another under unequal power relations. Although Makah traditional knowledge was passed from generation to generation in many families, this set of knowledge was not reinforced in schools until the 1960s. By then, some substantive policy changes occurred that allowed the Makah community to begin reforming the education their children received.

Beginning in the 1960s, trends in educational theory and community economic development policies supported increased community involvement in setting goals and planning and implementing programs. The Community Action Program (CAP), for example, was developed by funds from JOM and the Office of Economic Opportunity (OEO). The community sought a way to pass on and reinforce traditional practices to counteract some of the dramatic changes in the transfer of traditional knowledge within family lines. The opportunity was at hand to reverse anti-Indian messages in the school and replace them with cultural preservation programs. For the first time, federal funds were being used to encourage rather than eradicate Makah culture. Hopes were that the school, like the clubs, would become an organization that could be adopted and reformed for the benefit of the community.

In 1964 CAP was brought to Neah Bay. Volunteers in Service to America VISTA volunteers, brought to Neah Bay by Bruce Wilkie (Makah), wrote successful grants to the OEO to acquire CAP.[5] Initially, CAP funded a summer program for work projects, classroom education, and arts and crafts instruction. The arts and crafts component of CAP included demonstration of basket weaving, and participation in the collection and preparation of bark with Virginia Holden, one of the women involved in the Arts and Crafts Store. The following year, the arts and crafts component of the summer program blossomed into a more comprehensive cultural unit that included making dance regalia for Makah Days and learning songs. By 1966, elders Nora Barker, Helen Peterson, Mabel Robertson, Dewey McGee, and Jack LaChester had become instructors for the program, spending three hours each day with the children teaching Makah language, dance, song, and creation of regalia.[6] Alec Greene, Luggie and Sebastian LaChester, Helen Peterson, and Nora Barker were among those who would gather in the community hall (which still exists today), stand in a circle, and practice singing.[7]

The considerable cultural activity that had been funneled through private homes, clubs, and public parties since the turn of the century began to reform the school curriculum in the 1960s. Cultural expressions that had been kept furtive or restricted to the home during the late nineteenth and early twentieth century had become public once again. A school play dramatized the fact that cultural traditions were open once again, and the *Makah Times* freely announced the community news and events. Using Foucault's terms, knowledge that had been once subjugated was being moved into the public school system, the realm typically associated with "official knowledge."

In the following decade, CAP would fund a range of community programs, including education, health, and social services. By 1965 the Head Start program for preschoolers began during summers, and by 1967 it had become year-round (Shirley Johnson 1995). The Head Start Program was an important part of healing the rift between school and community: "In 1967 I had my youngest child who was three years old in a Head Start Program. That's how I got involved. My job was to go out and get parents to come to parent-teacher meetings once a month. But it was hard because for all those years, the community wasn't allowed to be involved in the school. Innovative ways were used to encourage the parents to come and feel like they were part of the program. We had dessert parties and sent parents photos of their children in the program" (Wilkie 1995). Head

Start was one of the critical spaces where Makah culture and formal education were reunited. In 1969, Shirley Johnson began working for Head Start and tried to form a bridge between the traditional lifeways in her family and a more modern world in which children were being raised: "I wanted to teach the kids about what it means to be Makah. I thought it was important, especially in the midst of so much change. Many of the children's diets were getting away from the seafood. I grew up on seal meat, and my father was a fisherman. So my daily life went by the saying 'When the tide's out, the table is set.' But these children were more used to getting their food from the grocery store. I wanted them to know the different seafoods, be exposed to them. I wanted them to know how we lived from the sea" (1995).

The introduction of Makah culture into the curriculum provided an opportunity for more than passing on traditional knowledge. Perhaps more importantly, it passed on the traditional *means* of teaching, albeit in a modified format. Storytelling is one example. Elders who had grown up being told that their culture was "wrong" stepped forward to share stories with schoolchildren because they believed the stories taught values and provided a moral framework. The late Muzzie Claplanhoo was one of the several elders who taught in Head Start for many years. She was still working there when I interviewed her. "I tell them legends," she said, "Like when they're getting rough, I'll them the story about when the animals got together for a potlatch and they got rough and were jostling each other and stepping on the octopus's feet. I let them know the moral of the story and why I'm telling it, why they need to learn to respect each other" (Minerva Claplanhoo 1995). Irene Ward is another of these elders. She worked for Head Start for ten years and remembers translating Indian stories that Jessie McCarty told in qʷiˑqʷiˑdiččaq: "The kids were so interested. They learn fast at that age. I would [also] bring basketry and show them how to weave. Those little tots would learn and remember it later. Some of them weave now" (I. Ward 1995). Stories were an important means to convey both information and values.

Knowledge and values were also conveyed to children through song. Elders would come and sing dinner songs for the children, passing on a Makah manner of rejoicing and giving thanks for the abundance and sharing of food. Programs like Head Start extended a learning environment rich in Makah values and manner of showing respect from the home setting to the school. This means of transmitting knowledge allowed elders to extend their educational role beyond the children in their extended family to all of the children of the tribe.

Despite the apparent success of the Head Start program, some objected to the teaching of Makah culture. Muzzie Claplanhoo remembered:

Teaching culture in school wasn't done much before. Once I had a non-Makah mother who wrote me a real strong letter. She didn't want me teaching any of my culture to her child in Head Start. She said my culture was the work of the devil. People have said that, but it's not true. I saw the men bathe and pray at the stream. I saw the daily rituals of my relatives. They were always praying before they did things, and it was always to the One, The Great Spirit, and they always pointed up above. When I was in school, around six or seven years old, the teacher was hitting the hands of the children who spoke in Makah. Now I teach the children the names of body parts, animals, foods, things like that. . . . People have asked me why I want to pass on my culture to my children. And I say to them, "You have a culture, don't you want to pass yours on to them? Why shouldn't I want to? Why did people try to stop us?" (1995)

Facing accusations of doing devil's work or witchcraft was not uncommon, but Makah oral history frequently speaks of the way the community sustained respect for traditional religious practices during periods when they were strongly forbidden. Sadie Johnson's grandfather used to tell her: "Your grandfather brought you up this way, and it's not witchcraft." Remembering these words prompted Sadie to say: "my grandfather didn't read or write, but his words were the same [as spiritual and Godly] as those in the Bible" (Sadie Johnson 1995).

Makah cultural programming was expanded to the elementary and high school grades in the late 1960s, also by employing elders as

11. Makah youth learn the paddle dance at the Neah Bay school, May 1967. Drummers: Nora Barker, Sebastian LaChester, Mable Robertson. Photo by Ruth Kirk. Courtesy of the photographer.

teachers. Through CAP funding, in 1965 ten elders were employed to conduct classes in Makah culture; among these was Walter Green who taught traditional music (McDonald 1965). Adults who now dance the paddle dance remember learning this and other dances through the CAP program (figure 11). Many of the dancers taught in this way had been bequeathed to the tribe for use during Makah Days by Young Doctor (MCRC 1989). In the late 1960s JOM funds allowed Makah language to be offered for the first time as an elective in school. These classes were taught by fluent elders (see figure 12) and conducted orally since there was not yet a standard alphabet (MCRC 1991; Renker and Arnold 1988, 305). But not all elders chose to participate. Raised by her grandfather Francis Greene, Irene Ward was immersed in qʷiqʷidičč̓aq at home as a child. "That got me in trouble when I spoke Indian at school," she said, "They washed my mouth out with brown soap. That's why later, maybe it was the 1960s, when they invited me to teach language at the school, I said

12. Helen Peterson shares oral history with third graders in the Neah Bay school, May 1967. Photo by Ruth Kirk. Courtesy of the photographer.

no. I didn't want to teach it. I could still taste that brown soap in my mouth" (I. Ward 1995). In a fifty-year period she had gone from being punished for speaking qʷiʔqʷiʔdiččaq to being invited to teach the language.

Some parents and grandparents also chose not to teach the language at home. They feared the children would be punished, they believed it was of no use to the children in the future, or they felt the children had no interest in it (Cutler 1994; Colson 1953). Mary Greene's experience and that of her husband illustrate how choices were made differently in various households. Born in 1917, Mary's recollections refer to the 1920s: "I was young when the agency forbade the language. When I walked into the room, my father and mother would switch to English. I understood it clearly, but I never tried to speak. On the other hand, my husband lived with his grandfather, and he spoke it fluently. And his grandfather spoke Indian entirely so he wasn't going to let the BIA tell them what to do" (1995). In the 1960s, elders who had had contact with "speaking" households — those that decided to continue speaking the Makah language — were among those who could teach. Among this group, some felt that the schoolchildren were somewhat embarrassed to speak their own language (R. Claplanhoo 1995).

In 1971 Neah Bay was notified that it had been selected to participate in the Urban Rural School Development Program. After the U.S. Office of Education–funded program was presented to the community, it was accepted by community vote. Leveraged by the Education Profession Development Act, the program encouraged student retention programs, teacher training programs, and community involvement in decision-making projects. In 1970 an evaluation of the programming in Neah Bay concluded that "JOM and Urban, Rural, Racial and Disadvantaged funds have made it possible to introduce Indian personnel and Indian culture into the [Neah Bay] school and to dissolve the 'Iron Curtain' that has separated the school from the community that it serves. For the first time, the school and the community believe that meaningful change is possible."[8]

The philosophy of the new federal programs matched well with sentiments in Neah Bay. Lloyd Colfax (Makah), who eventually chaired the School Community Council (SCC), commented in 1975: "I found it hard to believe that the members of the society which put us in this spot would lead us out. I said if we are going to be led out, we are going to be led by ourselves. We are going to have our own leaders."[9] Finding homegrown leaders meant encouraging Makahs to become teachers who could "teach their own." The Teacher Training Program was perhaps one of the most important contributions of SCC since it addressed the need for Makah community members to become involved in the educational process on a permanent basis. Another means for the school to meet the needs of the community was to incorporate Makah history and culture into the curriculum.

The scc program sought to create an environment where children would be comfortable and would want to learn. The school initiated programs in Makah arts, crafts, legends, and language in order "to erode the mistrust and misunderstanding between school and community." This mistrust began nearly a century earlier. Makah student response to scc programming was positive, with 48.6 percent "very much interested" in these programs and another 23.8 percent "interested" or "slightly interested."[10] Other programming included the founding of a community radio station. CAP and scc represented windows of opportunity in government policy and educational theory that allowed the Makah community to influence the formal education of its own children. Not since the Treaty of Neah Bay had the Makah community been treated as valid guardians of their children's education.

By the late 1970s, the momentum of the various clubs and school programs converged with cultural programming from the new MCRC. By 1978 the scc Task Force had transferred its functions to the tribe's Health Education and Welfare program (HEW). The HEW staff—in conjunction with the school's culture coordinator, linguist Bill Leap, Dave Warren, and staff from the MCRC—developed a National Endowment for the Humanities proposal for a Makah language curriculum development project from preschool to adult. The International Phonetic Alphabet had just recently been applied to the Makah language so that oral history and curricula could be transcribed and written consistently; fluent elders could then be trained in the use of the orthography (MCRC 1991, Jacobsen 1979).

By 1978 "the Makah Language Program received official tribal approval of its three goals: the preservation of the Makah language; the restoration of the spoken language within the community living on the reservation; and the education of reservation children to produce scholars who can compete with non-Indian children while maintaining Tribal heritage and culture" (Renker and Arnold 1988, 305). As educational funding to support this curriculum in the school shrunk, Title IV-B Indian Education grants through the MCRC became increasingly important for funding Makah language instruction and curricula development from July 1, 1981, to July 31, 1990 (MCRC 1991).

With support from the National Endowment for the Humanities, team teaching between Makah elders and Makah instructors produced various curriculum units for a range covering preschool through adult (MCRC 1991). By 1984 all elementary grades and two levels of the tribal Head Start program were included (Renker and Arnold 1988, 306). Eventually, due to the passage of the Title I Native American Languages Act, Makah language was eligible for high school level foreign-language credit. This gave the Makah Language Program based at the museum the opportunity to teach in the high school (MCRC 1991).

Educational reforms like these were occurring in Native American communities around the country. Some communities fought battles over misrepresentation of their people in schoolbooks or other curricular materials. Formation of pan-tribal organizations, such as the National Indian Education Association (NIEA) and the American Indian Historical Society (of San Francisco), made it possible for relatively isolated, local efforts to join with others and communicate their message more effectively to the public and to policy makers. Makah teachers experienced this networking at NIEA meetings, where they were able to connect with Native American educators from other communities. This enabled Makah teachers to identify new educational programs, as well as the funding sources to achieve them (M. Hunter 1995). The American Indian Historical Society, for example, had as its primary mission to correct the misrepresentations and misinterpretations of American Indians on record, including in California's textbooks.[11] These efforts achieved some success when the State Department of Education agreed to work with the society and with publishers to review historical information in the text and illustrations.[12] The nationwide tribal struggles to call attention to stereotypes in textbooks was often contemporaneous with campaigns against stereotypes in advertisements.[13]

Makah demands for input into the educational system were part of a much broader effort to remember tribal history, protect and respect tribal identity, and uphold the right to self-manage natural and human tribal resources.[14] Not only did the Makah people seek to appropriate the public school system and reform it for their own purposes but they also had the opportunity to appropriate the anthropological discipline, including archaeology, cultural anthropology, and linguistics. In the winter of 1970, when a five-hundred-year-old longhouse began eroding from the embankment of the Ozette village site, the tribe turned to elements from the dominant society that would further its cultural survival. It entered into a massive archaeological project with Washington State University. One of the many outcomes of this decision was the creation of a cultural center on the reservation. This center would not only offer another gathering space and site for self-representation but it would also become nationally renowned.

Schools have been one of the many contact zones where different ways of knowing — Christian, non-Christian, formal, informal, official, subjugated — have encountered, influenced, and dialogued with one another under conditions of unequal power relations. The beginning of the Ozette excavation converged with and energized the school programs in a number of ways: by introducing a mini-museum in the school, by sparking Makah history–related school trips, and by fueling the movement to pass down Makah oral history to children. The school also began to incorporate programming related to the Ozette dig.

"This Is Your History That's Coming out of the Earth": Ozette

The beauty of the place called Ozette (*u·se·ʔit*) simply takes my breath away. Standing between the towering forest crowding up behind me, leaving a narrow band of grassy ground between myself and the rocky shoreline, I can look to Cannonball Island, down the beach to Ozette River, and beyond. The views are either shrouded in fog or mist or sparkling with spray pounded into the sunshine by surf. Hikers from the Olympic National Park would hardly know that this tip of Cape Alava was once a bustling Makah community. Nor would they suspect that in the mid-1970s more than sixty thousand visitors each year used to hike four miles each way to watch archaeologists excavate the remains of that community (Samuels and Daugherty 1991, 14). Today the sole signs of this excavation are two buildings: one is labeled the former archaeological field station; the other is best described as a lean-to that shelters a memorial to the people of Ozette.

In this lean-to, carvings, driftwood, and whale vertebrae are carefully hung over or leaned against a copper plaque, which reads:

OSETT MEMORIAL
FROM OSETT ENDINGS BECOME BEGINNINGS
AT OSETT COME NEW UNDERSTANDINGS

GENERATION TO GENERATION
OUR PEOPLE HAVE SHARED THE WEALTH
FROM THE LAND AND THE SEA
FROM THIS SITE WE HAVE GAINED
VERIFICATION OF THE WISDOM OF OUR FOREFATHERS
FROM THIS WE GAINED NEW STRENGTH
IN THEIR HONOR WE DEDICATE THIS MEMORIAL
THIS RICH CULTURE — OUR PROUD HERITAGE

THE MAKAH INDIAN NATION
OSETT • DIA'TH • WA'ATCH • TSOO-YESS • BA'ADAH
THE FIVE ORIGINAL VILLAGES
TREATY 1855

Cedar planks placed like benches along the wall of the lean-to are covered with smooth colorful shells and stones that hikers have placed there. A contemplative visitor might notice the way the rush and hiss of the waves echo in the lean-to like the sound of surf in a conch shell.

Few visit Ozette who are not touched by its spectacular location or moved by its sacredness to the Makah people. Perhaps the power of the place for so many people is what makes writing about it a daunting task. Ozette is not only a central reason for the creation of the MCRC, it is a charged site of memory for countless people both Makah and non-Native. The remains of Ozette village provide an unparalleled glimpse into precontact life on the Northwest Coast. Equally as important, however, is that rooted there are memories of Makah tribal history and of unprecedented collaborations between

Native Americans and anthropologists. I have relied upon a number of people — Makah and non-Native — to help me in describing what is important about this place.

Archaeologist Richard Daugherty shared his memories of how Ozette and the Makah people became an important part of his life and the lives of countless others in the Northwest Coast region. As part of a large survey he was conducting along the Olympic coastline in 1947, Daugherty located and mapped what archaeologists call a thick midden at the historic village site of Ozette (Daugherty 1995; Samuels and Daugherty 1991). Since Ozette had been vacated by permanent Makah residents only decades earlier, it had never been treated or explored as an archaeological site. It was not until 1966 that Daugherty was able to return to Ozette with funding from the National Science Foundation to dig trenches at Ozette and on nearby Cannonball Island. This preliminary work produced radiocarbon dates indicating that these sites had been occupied for twelve hundred and two thousand years, respectively (McKenzie 1974). At the end of this first field season a test pit struck a well-preserved buried longhouse. Daugherty was not able to return to Ozette the following summer because a critical salvage archaeology project came up elsewhere (Daugherty 1995), but a winter storm in 1970 would bring Daugherty back and bring the lives of many people together.

Daugherty will continue to help me tell this story, but I add to his reminiscences those of Makah tribal council members Edward "Ed" Claplanhoo and Mary Lou Denney. In the years following 1917, when Ozette was abandoned by the last permanent residents, many Makah families continued temporary and seasonal use of the village site. Many tribal members were aware that tourists were prone to pothunting the Ozette village site. Mary Lou Denney, a retired teacher and former board member of the MCRC, learned about pothunting from her late brother, Tye:

Every summer he [Tye] used to go down to Ozette and fish. . . . There were a lot of times he'd go down there and there would be people down there, before they [the archaeologists] started digging, and [the tourists] they'd be walking off with stuff.

He'd talk to them and tell them that they were taking things that didn't belong to them. . . . A lot of times he would say, "Why do you want this stuff?" "Just a souvenir." Well, there was glass beads there. They'd see these glass beads. Some of the glass beads were very nice beads. They knew their value because maybe they heard it from somebody else. They would be going down there and whatever they'd get they'd bring back to somebody that told them that stuff was very valuable. Basically it was maybe for monetary reasons. Maybe it was just for souvenirs. (Denney 1995)

In late summer or early fall 1969, an Olympic Park ranger notified the Makah Tribe of rumors that tourists were pothunting at Ozette at a location where stream erosion was removing artifacts from the village midden. Tribal council member Joseph Lawrence visited the site but was unable to confirm the report. He could see no artifacts where the stream cut into the midden, nor could he see any evidence of pothunting, such as digging (Lawrence 1995).

However, within months the tribal council heard more reports of pothunting. When I sat down with Makah elder Ed Claplanhoo in his living room to discuss Ozette, Claplanhoo remembered the day in 1970 that tribal council members went to Ozette in response to rumors of pothunting:

Next morning I went up to tribal council, and I told a council member, Gene Parker, who just passed away, and Hillary Irving, who passed away about ten to fifteen years ago. It just happened to be a very, very, very beautiful day. The Lord was looking after us, the gods were watching over us, and Mr. Parker had a brand new boat with a high horsepower engine on. He said, "Hillary, let's launch my boat and we'll go down. It's calm out there today. It's dead calm. We'll make it down." So they launched the boat and took off. The ocean was flat all the way down. All the way down. They got down there and true enough, there was a clump of earth about maybe half the height from here to the ceiling, and about ten or fifteen feet wide. (1994)

Upon investigation, they found that the erosion situation had worsened dramatically because an unusually violent winter storm had coincided with high tides. An entire section of the embankment had collapsed toward the ocean, exposing a longhouse structure and its well-preserved contents (E. Claplanhoo 1995).

The Ozette excavation became a subject for innumerable newspaper and popular magazine articles (e.g., Daugherty 1971; Daugherty and Kirk 1973, 1975; Gwynne 1977; Kirk 1980; Mauger 1982), dissertations, Washington Archaeological Research Center reports, and periodical articles (e.g., Huelsbeck 1988; Wessen 1988). Ed Claplanhoo contacted Daugherty and asked him if he could come and look at the site as soon as possible (Cutler 1994). Daugherty traveled from eastern Washington to the Olympic Peninsula and hiked out to the Ozette site. As Mary Lou Denney remembers, Daugherty and tribal members were astonished by what they found: "I guess they were absolutely flabbergasted at the stuff that was showing. Then they started talking to the [tribal] council people and telling them that 'this is your history that's coming out of the earth—you need to decide on what to do with it. If they were going to give us advice, they would say preserve it.' So when the news got down to the community, they felt, there was a lot of people that was really excited about it. Knowing that it was their history and that some of this stuff was dating back three thousand years ago . . . was really an exciting experience" (1995). Some community members hesitated at the mention of excavation, but pothunting threatened to remove sacred and historical objects treasured by families descended from Ozette and by the tribe as a whole. It wasn't long before the idea of a museum arose as a strategy for preserving the material. Daugherty described for me the dramatic evolution of the project:

> Well, you see, when we started out, we didn't know what we were going to find. We weren't prepared that we were going to find all these perishable items. As this went on, our first problem was, we've got to take care of these. We had to come up with some sort of preservation regimen, which we did with the polyethylene glycol treatment which stabilized things. . . . We started getting masses of material. We had the planks, we had

the baskets, we had everything, wooden boxes, everything, artwork. This started to accumulate. Now, obviously, I had a problem, "What's going to happen to this?" . . . So the next question was, "Where is it going to be? It's accumulating." At the same time, the Makahs themselves were much taken with all of this stuff. Particularly when we started getting clubs and the things like the whale saddle, these really important things that I'm sure that some of the elders had told their offspring about but they had heard of them and here they were all of a sudden. And that's when I got the first inquiry of, "What's going to happen to this?" And my immediate response to that is, "It's going to have to stay here." The University of Washington didn't have any place for it. And, at the same time, well we had had the Makah students working with us. . . . It wasn't just a bunch of scientists coming in and doing something. It was very much the involvement of the tribe, the young people who worked with us on the dig and were learning about how you go about doing this, as well as being informed a good deal about their past. And so a lot of these ideas begin to generate, and I think now, OK, if it's got to stay here, what are we going to do with it? which led to the idea of the museum or cultural center, whatever you want to call it, where they would have this material right there for their own enjoyment. It was their culture, why have it over in Pullman, Washington? And so, once we started thinking on those lines, then the question was . . . tribal elders are all for, let's get a cultural center. If that's what it's going to take, let's do it. (1995)

In the winter of 1970, the Makahs began to assert their rights to define parameters of the excavation in an agreement with the archaeologists. No artifacts would leave the physical jurisdiction of the tribe to be displayed, nor would prehistoric loss of life associated with the Ozette mudslide be mentioned publicly, if any were discovered.[15]

In order to care for the emerging possessions of their ancestors and in order to assert themselves as worthy guardians, the Makahs began to plan a museum. In Tribal Resolution No. 19-70, the Makah Tribal Council stated the ongoing historical and spiritual importance of Ozette for the Makah community and explained the community's intention to build a museum in Neah Bay. The museum was originally planned to care for the Ozette material and to display some pieces to the public. Greig Arnold and Ann Renker, the first and second directors of the museum, respectively, described the evolution of the project: "the goals for the Makah museum began to expand beyond the exhibit of artifacts for tourists. Old and young Makah people working to build the museum and identify artifacts started to include the Makah language, Makah photographs, and other Makah information in their plans to document Makah information and educate the community about ancestral Makah traditions" (1988, 304). The museum concept began to be influenced by a communitywide sentiment on the importance of remembering — remembering ancestors, remembering traditions, and remembering values.

The beginning of the Ozette excavation converged with and energized the school programs discussed previously in a number of ways: introducing a mini-museum in the school, sparking Makah history–related school trips, and fueling the movement to pass down Makah oral history to children.

The Neah Bay school system incorporated programming related to the Ozette dig. During the 1969–70 school year, a portion of JOM planning grant funds were used to build a display case, employ an "Indian curator," and pay for a coordinator to develop programs for the coming year.[16] School trips to Ozette exposed Makah children to the process of archaeological excavation and to the precontact Makah heritage uncovered there. Mary Lou Denney fondly recalled one of these trips (her perspective is especially valuable because she served as one of the few Makah teachers in the Neah Bay school system and as a board member of the MCRC):

I remember going down there one time with the class and we spent a whole day and the night. So the people that was digging down there, they fed us. Then that night they challenged the kids to *slahal* [bone gaming] and we had a really good time. We didn't realize that it was storming really bad. And it was just storming and lightning and everything. The parents got worried about their kids, you know, here. They knew we weren't going to come in until the next day. So what happened was that, by the time we got done *slahaling* and everybody went to sleep, the Ozette people had to get up at the regular time. And here comes Search and Rescue [laughter]. They sent some people in to see whether or not we were OK because of the terrible storms we had, which we didn't even realize because we were having so much fun (laughter). (1995)

Listening to stories of the Ozette excavation told by tribal members and non-Native archaeologists, I began to realize how the excavation of the Ozette village site had created yet another contact zone (figure 13). Both the Makahs and the anthropological community would be changed by this encounter in significant ways.

I turn now to archaeologist Jeff Mauger, whose life also changed course with the Ozette excavation. The many years he spent excavating at Ozette and working at the laboratory in Neah Bay and then in the MCRC collections provided him countless opportunities to witness the unique collaboration and interchange that surrounded the Ozette project. Mauger remembers that Makah youths and elders became involved in the excavation beginning in 1971:

Probably the one [Makah] person that spent the most consecutive summers down at the site was Lance Wilkie. . . . Lance was down there every summer from day one. . . . Some of the summer Makah people were paid on, I think, tribal program/federal funds — YOP [Youth Opportunity Program] type stuff. Some of them were paid to come down and work with us. Yes, my first field school summer was 1972, and they had already had 1971, and Makahs were involved then. Usually we didn't have Makahs spending the winter. . . . If not Lance then Greig Arnold was probably the first one to spend the winter down there as a winter crew member. . . . They were out there excavating. You

13. Lance Wilkie (Makah), Greg Colfax (Makah), and Richard Daugherty (WSU) crouch over the excavation of an Ozette longhouse designated as "House #2," ca. 1974. Photo by Ruth Kirk. Courtesy of the photographer.

go through the field notes, you'll see Bowechop names and different peoples'. . . .

Some people came down, I remember one summer when I was running things, Clifford Johnson and his wife, Hazel, — of course he's passed on — came down with their grandkids (like Chris that works in the store). That was pretty neat. Clifford was full of stories. I said, "Oh, would you talk to the field school, they'd really like it." He says, "Yeah." He gave a great talk, I taped it. He was talking about his family background and his interest in Ozette. And then Hazel got up and talked, and she was Skokomish. She was related to John Slocum who started the Shaker Church and so she told about the Shaker religion and how it all got started. The field school people, their mouths were on the floor. This was just great stuff. It was really neat. Clifford came in a couple times. (1994)

The Washington State University students who partook in the field school program at Ozette beginning in 1971 were able to integrate the study of archaeology with learning about a culture's history from the people themselves. While this teaching and research approach is considered more productive and ethical today, collaboration of this sort was still unique at that time (Spector 1993; Rice 1997).[17] Out of this collaboration two things began to happen: the respectful opening of the academic system to Native American ways of knowing and the increasing use of academic tools in Native American communities for creating autoethnographies. The Neah Bay school (and later the museum) became contact zones where these different ways of knowing and representing Native peoples came together and created something new.

Although the Washington State University archaeologists, field students, and Makah crew members laboriously removed the precontact possessions from heavy clay at Ozette, the elders breathed a kind of life into the objects for schoolchildren and others. Elders viewed objects in the lab in Neah Bay or at the site itself, when helicopter transportation was arranged to airlift them to Ozette (Cutler 1994). The sight, smell, and touch of those objects unlocked elders' memories; information about past lifeways and human relationships flooded anew into conversations (figure 14). Mary Lou Denney was one of many people who spoke to me about the crucial role of the elders' oral history in bringing the artifacts to life and connecting them to a sense of cultural self-esteem:

> It really jarred people's memories on how things were when they were growing up. It came like, "Oh, I remember when I was sent off to school" or, "I remember when the schools came to Neah Bay." So there was a lot of memory-jogging with the elders and even with the generation after the elders. . . . A lot of the things that came out [of Ozette], for instance, like some of the hooks that they used for fishing. My dad had the same kind of hooks. He had the same type of gear and stuff that they used when they would go fishing before they had the motorboats and the big engines. So he had a lot of stuff stored in a shed. I was really surprised, because I did a lot of comparison

14. Makah elders Harold Ides and Roger Colfax in the archaeology laboratory reminiscing over a harpoon point excavated from Ozette, ca. 1978. Photo by Ruth Kirk. Courtesy of the photographer.

to some of the stuff that he had to the stuff they were taking out to the museum. . . . They [the children] got really interested in learning about it and listening to people that know about it because we've never had that type of learning in the school. You never got to learn about our own people; we learned about a lot of other historic-type things, but not our own culture. (1995)

Many items removed from Ozette were still being produced in the late nineteenth and early twentieth centuries — within the memory of the elders living at the time of the excavation. Consequently, the fishhooks, dice, game paddles, adzes, spears, and so forth were immediately familiar to many. The Ozette artifacts illustrated and substantiated the ingenuity of Makah cultural achievements to which elders had testified throughout the twentieth century. After more than a century of being told to give up their lifeways in favor of American lifeways and values, these remarkably preserved artifacts from Ozette were an immense source of pride to the Makahs, a sentiment expressed on the Ozette memorial: "From this site we have gained verification of the wisdom of our forefathers; from this we gained new strength." Elders remembered how objects, such as adzes and halibut hooks, were used when they were children and thus linked the artifacts to moments they had spent with their parents, grandparents, and great-grandparents. The objects reminded elders of the oral histories that had been passed down to them — stories of whaling, fishing, and sealing adventures — and prompted them to recite family genealogies. The generation that was not yet elder at the time of the excavation remembered seeing some items pass out of use when they were young. Objects from Ozette were tangible reminders of how quickly lifeways were changing and of the urgent need to continue programming in the school, and in the museum/cultural center, that would educate Makah children about their heritage.

Ozette generated waves like those from a pebble as it hits a pond. The impact was felt not only in Neah Bay but in the anthropological community and the broader Northwest Coast public. The way the excavation, and the founding of the museum, was carried out collaboratively began to change how anthropologists and the public viewed the artifacts. Mauger offered a compelling description of how his views were affected by the Ozette excavation:

Digging Ozette was — comparing typical archaeological excavations to digging Ozette — as far as your relationship with those people who made these things, was sort of like talking over the phone long distance to somebody on the East Coast, as opposed to sitting at the table face-to-face like we are. It was that close. The slide was catastrophic. . . . It overwhelmed the houses. It smashed through the back walls of the houses and came under the roofs. We didn't recover much of the roofs at all. We recovered no rafter beams. They either floated on top or a lot of it was washed on out into the beach. Everything was maintained in water-logged state. This eliminated the bacterial action to only anaerobic bacteria. As a consequence, all the normal things we see in typical middens on the coast were preserved, which was stone, and hard organic materials such as bone and shell and antler. In addition, however, any plant — wood and plant fiber — was also preserved, very, very well. . . . Basically, everything from an archaeological point of view was remarkably intact. . . . Little scenes of things that happened. It was in your face, in-your-face archaeology that you didn't have that comfortable distance from the people who produced these materials. The lives that they were leading that you do in other excavations — like I say, it's the difference between like you're talking long distance and sitting there within two feet of a person and talking to them. We were that close. I don't think there was anybody who dug there that wasn't impacted in some way by the vignettes, really that we would find, literally in the excavation.

We'd find baskets but we would also find a pouch that was full of bark bundles — cedar bark bundles to be stripped and woven into baskets. Pouches . . . oh, one of the neatest things for me, it has always interested me — the technology — we'd find kits, like a sewing kit in a basket, the stuff for doing all their sewing or bark stripping. We found a basket that had a bunch of bark bundles in it, then we found another smaller basket and it had a bone awl and slate-bladed knife, and this is for slashing the cedar bark, slashing the tree. The awl was for prying the cedar bark up so you can get a grip on it and then stand back and pull it off. We didn't know what they slashed the tree with. We didn't know awls were involved in actually the gathering of cedar bark. So not only did we have these functional associations that you don't see in archaeological sites, they were all together in a basket. They were one person's things. That person had a name. We didn't know that name but we knew that person's things. A fishing kit that was the wonderful little pouch that unfolds and had all these wonderfully delicate, finely finished hooks in it and this little bundle of bone splinters and the stone for breaking them to make them into the barbs for the hooks. These little pieces of wood, just all stuck there. It's like being a voyeur. It was like eavesdropping or peeping through somebody's window. Imagine looking through somebody's window when they're not there but their dishes are out and their stuff is out on the table. There's food on the counter. There's toys on the floor. That's what we were doing.

The neat thing is that you'd be digging, standing beside a Makah and we're both sitting there with our mouths open. Neat, neat stuff. Incredible. (Mauger 1995)

Mauger's oral history is a vivid description of the collapse of the objective distance that social scientists, especially archaeologists, are accustomed to in their study of human cultures. The fact that this collapse of objective distance was experienced alongside the descendants of those who once occupied Ozette made it all the more remarkable. The Ozette excavation was just the beginning of the interaction between different ways of thinking about the Makah people and their history. It was a new contact zone. In contrast to the contact zones experienced by the Makah people throughout their history, this one would have a noticeably more equal distribution of power. The creation and operation of the MCRC has extended this opportunity to the present, a subject for greater discussion in the following chapters.

The anthropological community was not the only one to experience the pebble-in-the-pond effect from the Ozette excavation. The public, too, became involved and was challenged to think in new ways. Press coverage in the form of articles, films, and news shorts had been extensive from the early stages of the excavation. Reporters came to the site on a fairly regular basis, and consequently, the population around Seattle and all over the Olympic Peninsula was aware of the excavation. During the height of the summer tourist season, hundreds of people daily hiked the some four miles to the coastal site — school groups, boy scout groups, campers, and tourists. One of the tours given amid this five-tour-per-day schedule stood out in Mauger's memory:

I think one of the incidences that stick in my mind was some loggers that came in from Forks. They were kind of somewhat skeptical of this whole thing. There's not a whole lot of love lost between Forks loggers and Neah Bay Makahs. They saw us taking like a bench out. We're talking about a plank that's four feet wide, maybe twelve feet long. It suddenly hit them, here's this huge cedar plank and they didn't have chainsaws. Then they started asking questions: "How did they make that plank?" You could see it was. . . . I wouldn't go as far to say all their prejudices were lost, but they certainly understood something about Native Americans in terms that they knew. They worked in the woods all the time. You could see, not all their prejudice was buried, there was some respect that they had never had before. This was something they could relate to, and they were just blown away by these huge planks. They said, "How did they do this?" With wooden wedges. It was something they could relate to. It was stuff like that that was truly memorable. Everybody was just enthralled. (1995)

Gaining respect for Makah history and traditional lifeways was not easy. The removal of this massive cedar plank was a moment in which the prejudice that fueled often hostile politics surrounding natural resources was at least momentarily broken. This plank was joined by another artifact that made an even greater impact.

Since the 1950s, treaty-secured fishing rights have been highly contentious on the Northwest Coast. In the face of expanding fishing by non-Indian peoples and declining salmon populations, the state of Washington placed the brunt of conservation measures upon Native American communities, eroding their treaty right to fish in common with the non-Native population. Whether tribes would be allowed to use nets, as opposed to just hook and line, was just one of the many points of disagreement (Harmon 1998: 228–31). In the film *Gift from the Past*, Greig Arnold recounts how in the early 1970s the state was saying that fishing nets were a European-introduced good. The argument went that since the treaty secured traditional methods, Native Americans were precluded from using nets in modern times. A piece of fishing net that had been excavated from Ozette was mounted on Plexiglas and taken into court. Reflecting on the presentation of the net in court, Arnold said, "So here it is. We fished with nets. Our elders said we did. Now here it is, physical. No more. Couldn't argue. What could you say? End of story" (Cutler 1994).

In order to understand how Ozette, and subsequently the MCRC, relates to issues of cultural survival and self-determination, it is vital to acknowledge how the Ozette excavation communicated differently to different groups of people. To the public, to anthropologists, and to the courts, the scientific and archaeological investigation of Ozette generated a way of knowing Makah history that was acknowledged and could be considered "official" by the dominant society. Who would determine the outcome of the Ozette excavation? Who would keep or own the artifacts? Would they benefit a community that was building and trying out programs which would forward cultural survival? At the time of the winter storm in 1970, these questions had uncertain answers. The Makah Tribe was still engaged in a struggle to regain Ozette territory, a struggle that had been under way since 1944. Any discussion of Ozette and its recent, phenomenal role in Makah tribal history, must include how Ozette relates to an overall Makah tradition of defense of land, culture, and identity.

Ozette: National or Tribal History?

Largest and deepest shell midden on Washington Coast. Not excavated as yet. Should provide information on the cultural development of Northwest Coast maritime cultures. . . . A very good archaeological site — from historic on back. It should be preserved in the park.

NATIONAL PARK SERVICE STUDY, 1963

Our Makah people spent a lot of money fighting for Ozette — then the Good Lord took our side — made it rain — pushed the earth down and showed the world that Ozette belonged to the Makahs. Our heritage has been returned to us.

NORA BARKER, *Neah Bay*, 1972

Today the Olympic National Park has more than 900,000 acres of mostly mountainous terrain in the central and northern interior of the Olympic Peninsula. An exception to this is a fifty-two-mile stretch of undeveloped ocean beaches extending southward from Makah territory to the Quinault Reservation. This stretch of ocean beaches — called a jewel of the park—was added to park territory in 1940. This strip encircled but did not include the Ozette Indian Reservation. With the 1940 expansion of park boundaries, the Makah people and the National Park Service came into more frequent contact with one another. During and after the Ozette excavation, the relationship with the National Park Service was "very amiable" (Keller and Turek 1998, 95–96; 106–16). However, at times ambiguity over who owned Ozette made this terrain a contested ground.

Most historic and anthropological accounts have acknowledged the territorial and social complexity of the qʷidičča?atx̌, specifically their division into five distinct villages: Neah Bay (di·ya·), Ba'adah (bi?id?a), Wa'atch (wa?ač̣), Tsoo-yess (c'u·yas), and Ozette (u·se·?it̓) (Swan 1870; Densmore 1939; Taylor 1974). At the signing of the Treaty of Neah Bay, Governor Isaac Stevens designated a man from Ozette as the head chief of the Makah people. These five villages, which existed in precontact and historic times, were semiautonomous villages that shared language, kinship, and cultural traditions (Renker and Gunther 1990, 422). Remarkably, the 1855 Treaty of Neah Bay reservation boundaries excluded four of the five main villages; only the traditional village of di·ya· and a tiny portion of the northwestern corner of Cape Flattery were included. In 1860, Swan pointed out that widening the boundaries of the reservation would advance government policies that sought to make the Makah people into farmers. This was true, since all of the arable land was located outside of the reservation boundaries. Much later, Indian agents successfully argued that the original reservation boundaries were completely contrary to policy objectives (see figures 15 and 16). The civilization-through-farming policy provided ample motivation to include more of the traditional villages within the reservation because they were adjacent to land more suitable to farming. Thus on October 26, 1872, the reservation was expanded by Executive Order of Ulysses S. Grant (with Jan. 2, 1873, and Oct. 21, 1873, amendments)

15. This map drawn by James Swan represents minimal geographic and cultural
features on the landscape. The dotted line in the upper half of the map indicates
the boundary of the Makah reservation as set by the Treaty of Neah Bay. The
solid vertical and horizontal lines in the lower half of the map indicate Swan's
proposed reservation boundaries. Swan argued that extending the reservation
boundaries would include prairie lands suitable for farming. Makah Indian
Reservation, Washington Territory (J. G. Swan); map number 602, Records of the
Bureau of Indian Affairs, RG 75, National Archives at College Park, Maryland.

to include four Makah villages. However, the focus on the arable
waʔač prairie and Hobuck Beach on the reservation still left out the
southerly Ozette village.

Ozette land was brought into reservation status in 1893 by President Grover Cleveland. However, it was designated a *separate* reser-

16. This map, drawn by James Swan in 1862, details permanent and seasonal village sites, Makah place names, and the extent of forest and estuarine areas. By this point, Swan's proposal to extend the reservation boundaries has been approved by the superintendent. Map of Makah Indian Reservation, Washington Territory (J. G. Swan); map number 995, Records of the Bureau of Indian Affairs, RG 75, National Archives at College Park, Maryland.

vation, the Ozette Indian Reservation, rather than a portion of the Makah reservation. This 719-acre reservation was approximately six miles south of the Makah reservation border. As discussed previously, a variety of factors forced the residents of Ozette village to relocate to Neah Bay. Most notable was the mandatory schooling of children in Neah Bay. Others included the centralization of commerce with Euro-American peoples in Neah Bay's harbor. Eventually, only one resident, Elliot Anderson, remained, and he had no heirs. The bureaucratic distinction between "the Ozettes" and the Makah people would not be remedied until nearly eighty years later. By the late 1940s, when Elliot Anderson (the "last of the Ozettes") died, the popular impression that the Ozette Indian Reservation no longer had Indians was well entrenched. This perception of Anderson's death set in motion decades of jostling for the rights to Ozette by the Makah Tribe, the National Park Service, the Department of the Interior, members of Congress, and environmental groups (Keller and Turek 1998, 111–13).

During the 1940s and 1950s the Makah Tribe addressed a new government policy called Termination and Relocation, which promised various benefits in exchange for the elimination of federal ward status. It was a period for responding to the scrutiny of Court of Claims demands for proof that the Makah people descended from those who signed the Treaty of Neah Bay a century earlier. Land, ward status, and identity were simultaneously under fire.[18] In a comprehensive planning document from 1944, the Makahs outlined their intentions for Ozette as part of a large, traditional lands recuperation project:

Under the tribal Land Acquisition Plan, the tribe would like to take steps to acquire the now unused and deteriorated 720-acre Ozette Indian Reservation. . . . The Makah Tribe feels . . . a certain moral right to the ownership and control of the unused Ozette Reservation. The Indian people who originally lived at Ozette moved into, and were absorbed by, the Makah Indian community following the establishment of a government-building school at Neah Bay.[19]

By 1956, Makah claims on Ozette had not been settled, and a new threat to Makah jurisdiction over Ozette emerged. The Area Office of Indian Affairs notified the Makah Tribe that Ozette was going to be (1) turned over to the National Park Service, (2) turned over to the General Services Administration, or (3) declared open and unclaimed. On January 2, 1956, a special meeting was called between the Makah Tribal Council and the community to discuss Ozette. The tribe was given sixty days before one of the above actions would be taken. One Makah after another stood and stated that Ozette was part of the Makah Tribe and that they were forced to leave it in order to put their children in day school when the boarding school closed. People testified that Ozette was even cared for thereafter by families without children. They noted that Superintendent Bitney, who had cracked down on Makah cultural expressions, had strongly discouraged any return to Ozette. Tribal members were frustrated with the lack of support from the federal Bureau of Indian Affairs (BIA); opinions were expressed that the BIA should be supporting the tribe rather than undermining it. In 1956 Jack Westland submitted a petition on Ozette to the solicitor general in Washington DC.[20] In September 1956 the Makah Tribe made a personal plea to the Commissioner of Indian Affairs to resolve the dispute. In the climate of post–World War Indian policy that sought assimilation of Native peoples, Interior Deputy Solicitor Fritz reviewed the Ozette case and concluded that the Makahs had "no beneficial interest" in Ozette and recommended that it return to public domain.

Despite anthropological studies that substantiated their claims to the village site and its surrounding lands, by 1963 the Makah people had been denied a satisfactory conclusion to the Ozette case by the Department of the Interior and the BIA, the state of Washington, and Congress. As anthropologist Erna Gunther said, "the myth that Elliott Anderson was the last of the Ozettes is ridiculous" (Keller and Turek 1998, 111). The Makah Tribe appealed to then-president John F. Kennedy. Resolution did not come until October 21, 1970, when PL-91-489 declared that the Ozette reservation would be held by the U.S. government in trust for the Makah Tribe. By that time, the recent exposure of rich archaeological resources at Ozette was further heightening tension surrounding the future of Ozette.

Ozette: "our heritage" for some; "artifacts of Northwest Coast cultural development" for others. The final jurisdiction of the site and of the artifacts would determine which perception of Ozette had greater voice. Since the Antiquities Act of 1906, the federal government has been granted jurisdiction over historic and prehistoric Native American cultural resources on federal property (Thornton 1994, 543). In essence, this has made Native American cultural resources a significant component of *national* heritage and property.

The National Historic Preservation Act of 1966 authorized the secretary of the interior to expand and maintain a national register of places, structures, and objects of local, state, or national significance. The policy was structured so that the national historic landmarks on the registry would be reviewed for potential inclusion in the national park system. It is important to note that the majority of the eleven years of Ozette excavation were prior to the passage of the American Indian Religious Freedom Act. The Native American Graves and Repatriation Act would come much later. For a number of reasons, the path to national heritage, as opposed to tribal heritage, was a likely one.

The Washington State University archaeology project, which conducted the excavation at Ozette, was interested in collaborating with the Makah Tribe at all levels. The collaboration achieved over the eleven-year excavation period reached a level that today may be considered ahead of its time. Although today archaeologists' collaboration with tribes is common, if not mandated, that was less the case in the 1960s and 1970s when the Ozette excavation started. Looking back on the project, the archaeologist who directed the project, Richard Daugherty, felt strongly that the museum and artifacts should stay in Neah Bay for the benefit of those who descended from the original inhabitants of the territory. Yet he still conceived of the material as more than tribal heritage:

> I can understand in the history of what's happened to various groups that they would like to assert things [such as blocking excavations or demanding repatriation], but let's take that idea for a second. We have a nation that supposedly we take great pride in being a melting pot, that we have all kinds of racial groups, religious groups, whatever. Does this mean that every racial group or cultural group in the country can have its own,

can control its own history? Do we have black history controlled only by the blacks? . . . To me, the archaeology, I don't care whether its Colonial Williamsburg or Neah Bay, it's part of our national heritage. And it's not Native American heritage only. It's part of our national heritage. (Daugherty 1995)

It is precisely the question of who gets to control history — that is, write it, own it, interpret it — that made the Ozette land claims case so important to the development of the MCRC, which held the Ozette artifacts. Clear title to the artifacts established a firm foundation for the ability to create the MCRC as an autoethnography that could dialogue with other ways of knowing the Makah people.

As I argued previously, the view of tribal heritage as being national heritage is linked to the period when Swan was collecting Makah culture in the middle of the nineteenth century. Scientific discovery and investigation into the origin of America's indigenous peoples was associated, on logistical and ideological levels, with colonization of the continent. The intertwining of science with commerce and diplomacy in America had begun with large-scale military-economic expeditions that included scientific components and established a scientific reputation for the nation. They mapped established and new territories, and they established commercial and military transport, often in the name of defending national territory.

The melting pot ideal for American society continues to offer enticing promises of democracy and equal opportunity. Yet countless Native American communities remain embittered from being systematically excluded from participating in narrating their own history or authoring their future. Nonetheless, framing tribal histories as national patrimony can still be an immensely successful means to access federal and other granting sources.

The Ozette excavation and the development of the MCRC were part of a new era in the possibilities for remarkable collaboration between Native American peoples, academia, and museology. Both Ozette and the museum became new zones of contact, places where multiple ways of knowing and multiple strategies for representing that knowledge encountered one another. Although the power relations remained unequal at these new zones of encounter, tribal control over objects and self-representations was strengthened relative to other contact zones I have discussed here.

My presentation thus far has considered the complex origin of the MCRC. My interpretation has been that the subjectivity of the Makah museum and cultural center grew out of a long history of resistance and accommodation inherent to cultural survival. As is the case with autoethnographic processes, Makah self-representations appropriated elements of the dominant culture that were deemed acceptable. Makah autoethnography (in the form of the museum/cultural center) grew out of dialogue, in this case between the Makah Tribe and numerous academic and museum professionals. Without question, the growth of the MCRC stemmed directly from the Ozette excavation and the need to preserve those artifacts. However, the MCRC also stemmed indirectly from other contact zones, such as Swan's boarding school, the Makah Arts and Crafts Store, and a twentieth-century public school.

The following chapters continue the discussion of the subjectivity of the MCRC and its nature as a cultural self-portrait. Thus far I have emphasized the extent to which the MCRC has been shaped by specifically Makah memories of past colonial encounters. The following chapters shift our attention to exploring the degree to which Makah self-representations at the MCRC have been established through extensive collaboration with non-Native and Native professionals throughout the excavation of Ozette and the founding of the museum/cultural center. By working with members of the Smithsonian Institution, Washington State University, the Burke Museum, and the Royal British Columbia Museum, to name a few, the Makah people also influenced how people in these institutions listened to them and went about their daily business.

4 Voices of a Thousand People
The Nature of Autoethnography

Collaboration and the Subjectivity of the Makah Cultural and Research Center

"Like the hearts of the Makah, the doors of Ozette's longhouses in 1491 face the sea. The sounds are the wash of the surf, the sea gulls' chorus, a sea lion's bark, the sighing of hemlock, spruce, and cedar, and the voices of a thousand people" (Pascua 1991, 40). This quote from Maria Pascua's *National Geographic* article evokes for me the profound ties between the MCRC and a highly symbolic place in Makah collective memory: Ozette. The sounds that Pascua imagines characterized Ozette in the late 1400s — the time period explored by the archaeological excavation — are interpreted and reproduced for those who visit the MCRC. Sea lion barks echo outward from a gaping cavern that is a sea mammal diorama. A chorus of seagull cries is likely to send chills up the spines of visitors as they enter the darkened interior of a reconstructed Ozette longhouse. Once inside, the boom and hiss of ocean surf draw visitors to the seaward door of the longhouse. There, a diorama enables visitors to imagine themselves standing in the footsteps of an Ozette resident coming to the door first thing in the morning. Back over one's shoulder, one can hear the hushed voices of elders speaking in qʷi·qʷi·diččaq. The piped-in recording encourages visitors to imagine how elders might have gathered around the Ozette longhouse hearths, seated on cedar benches. Perhaps Pascua chose the phrase "the voices of a thousand people" to convey what must have been the bustling nature of the precontact community at Ozette, a premiere site for launching sea mammal hunts.

I have titled this book "Voices of a Thousand People" to invite readers to reflect on the phenomenon of museum subjectivity in this significant era in the history of museology. Throughout this book I have referred to the concepts of autoethnography, museum subjectivity, and contact zones. All three somewhat ungainly terms are simply tools to think with while attempting to understand the dramatic revolution underway in museology today. As I discussed previously, the subjectivity of any museum is nearly always shaped by many diverse and often conflicting voices, those of the founders, collectors, donors, staff members, board members, visitors, and surrounding community members. How were the collectors positioned relative to those whose artwork or material culture was collected? What was collected? What is communicated by the architecture and location of the building? All these factors significantly shape museums' subjectivity. Notably, various populations previously present more as *subjects* of exhibitions than *constituents* of a museum — such as Native American communities — are now active participants in museum and cultural institutions in unprecedented numbers. In other words, Native American voices are increasingly shaping museum representations as more museums accept the value and ethical imperative of creating open, diverse, and democratic institutions.

The oral histories I gathered about the MCRC forced me to consider the nature of autoethnography amid spaces of postcolonial encounters. My fascination is with the museum as a potential arena for counteracting social inequalities and stimulating social change. What happens when a Native American community adopts a Euro-American institution? Does the subjectivity of a tribal museum come to reflect the collective memory and sense of place of the community, or does it reflect Euro-American structures of knowledge and thought? My research suggests that "a thousand voices" have shaped the subjectivity of the MCRC. Through oral history, ancestral voices continue to make sense of and shape the sensibilities, traditions, and tastes of the Makah people. But so, too, do federal laws, professional standards, and popular music. As a creation of the Makah people, the MCRC reflects the heart and soul of a people at once connected to tradition yet thoroughly engaged with the modern world.

The subjectivity of the MCRC has also been shaped by countless non-Native peoples over the past hundred years, whether they were Indian agents, missionaries, amateur collectors, ethnographers, archaeologists, museologists, or linguists. In the following sections I explain how the MCRC embodies a Makah dialogue with dominant Euro-American culture, a cross-cultural dialogue that has resulted in a new form of institution — an indigenized museum, or rather a cultural center that makes sense to the Makah people and that strives to be relevant to them. This cross-cultural dialogue and exchange has not only shaped the community museum but also the disciplines of anthropology and museology.

This chapter and the one that follows describe examples of the collaboration between non-Native institutions and the MCRC. I will share my understanding of the MCRC's interaction with Native American programming in three mainstream museums — the Smithsonian Institution, the Thomas Burke Memorial Washington State Museum of the University of Washington–Seattle, and the Royal British Columbia Museum.

Historically, mainstream museums have conceived of themselves as the center of knowledge-making; in this vision Native American communities are left as the periphery or frontier of discovery (Clifford 1997, 192–93). I hope this book disrupts such expectations that would characterize the Makahs as simply passive victims, marginalized at the end of the world, and left in a kind of temporal backwater. While the concept of autoethnography celebrates human agency and creativity, it need not exoticize and isolate those whose voices were previously poorly heard. The time I spent in Neah Bay, Washington, and in Washington DC, persuaded me to pause and consider the Makah expression that they are at "the beginning [rather than the end] of the world." I have come to appreciate that the Makah community is a center of creativity thoroughly engaged with and influencing the world around it.

For the most part, museums in the nineteenth and early twentieth centuries structured Native Americans in museums as informants or subjects of study but rarely as enfranchised researchers. One notable exception is George Hunt, who worked closely with Franz Boas and many others (e.g., Cole 1985; Jonaitis 1991; Jonaitis and Inglis 1992). Despite this pattern, Native American peoples have not been merely passive subjects in the history of science. They have frequently cooperated with ethnographers, archaeologists, and folklorists attempting to nudge various studies in a direction beneficial for themselves or for their people (Deloria 1998). Yet, the development of *extensive* Native American participation in museum affairs in the latter half of the twentieth century has met with a mixed response from museum professionals. Some have welcomed it; others have been threatened by it.

In my conversations over the past ten years with non-Native museum professionals, I have found that many perceive the Native American museum movement with confusion and a sense of betrayal. Some have expressed their dismay in the following terms: "now we are being excluded from the process of telling Indian history"; "after caring for these objects for so many years, now we are accused of being racists"; or "after helping Indians to recover and learn about their own history, we are now judged to be inappropriate caretakers." Fortunately, museum professionals increasingly recognize that museums' historical ability to assemble these collections was made possible by their political and economic position in American society relative to indigenous peoples. Contemporary museum collections are inescapably palimpsests, entities whose surfaces have been inscribed repeatedly with meanings (Ames 1992, 141–42). It is true that Native American museum collections bear traces of former Native American lifeways and values. They also carry traces of the mentalities of scientists and collectors and traces of the colonial and national practices that disrupted Native cultures in an attempt to force Native American people toward Euro-American models of civilization. Collections, sometimes repatriated ones, now bear traces of Native American efforts at self-representation.

This history of a particular tribal museum and cultural center reveals how Native Americans have moved their position in the museum profession from relative *outsiders* to *insiders*. These spatial terms convey the changing popular and professional notions of who constitutes museum constituencies. "Moving inside" has meant more than gaining greater access to and influence over mainstream museums; it has meant becoming "speaking subjects" (Ames 1992, 6). We can recognize this when we see communities found their own museums. We can also recognize it with the shaping of the national museum, perhaps one of the most influential arenas for representing Native Americans. The Smithsonian Institution now includes the National Museum of the American Indian—a new museum that interprets Native American history and identity with an unprecedented degree of Native American participation and control.

As the Native American museum movement has increased its influence over the past two decades, various metaphors have emerged that express a tension associated with this change. One of these metaphors is the "Trojan horse," which suggests that once Native peoples are let in, they will take down the museum. Another, the "Indian shopping cart syndrome," has been used to refer to the impression that Native peoples would indiscriminately remove collections from museums, leaving their shelves empty. Subsequent sections of this chapter help to make sense of these metaphors and of the shifting position of Native American peoples relative to museology. I begin by exploring how and why the Smithsonian Institution was important to the earliest stages of the Native American museum movement, including the founding of the MCRC. The oral histories and writings of David Warren (Tewa), George Horse Capture (Gros Ventre), Herman Viola, and Meredith Heilman (Makah) will help me tell this story.

Trojan Horses and Shopping Carts at the Smithsonian Institution

The [American Indian Cultural Resources Training] program is not without its critics, however. The collections will be damaged or destroyed, some skeptics said. Others express the fear that militant groups will use the program as a Trojan horse, as an opportunity to discover objects to demand later for tribal museums.

HERMAN VIOLA, *Director of the American Indian Cultural Resource Training Program*

For newcomers to the Smithsonian Institution, getting from one monumental building to another can be an adventure, and a trying one at that. For the first three months of 1995 I resided at the Smithsonian as a graduate research fellow in the Office of Museum Programs (OMP) and in the Department of Anthropology in the National Museum of Natural History. I would take wrong turns when navigating my way to the more than twenty interviews I conducted with Smithsonian staff. I would get lost trying to reach the National Anthropological Archives (NAA) in the Natural History Building. I would go in circles trying to reach the Smithsonian Institution Archives in the Arts and Industries Building. The longer I was at the Smithsonian, however, the more boldly I took shortcuts down one corridor or another, up obscure elevators, through unmarked, heavy fire doors, and by security guards that I had not yet passed.

These explorations sometimes became as enlightening as my intentional research in archives and libraries. I discovered that the Natural History Museum contained corridors lined from ceiling to floor with storage drawers containing human remains. These were interrupted by little more than the entrances to curators' offices or laboratories. Before I understood the scale and complexity of the Smithsonian Institution, it surprised me that countless drawers containing controversial Native American human remains — exhibits dating back one hundred years — innovative Native American museum training programs, and a new NMAI could all coexist in one institution. If nothing else, my accidental meandering established physically what I came to understand theoretically — that the Smithsonian was an inscrutable bricolage of people, spaces, and things. It would take at least one entire volume to describe how these traces of past and present ideologies and practices have come to rest simultaneously in the nation's attic, a task that is beyond the scope of this book.[1] Instead, I share here my insights into how the museology discipline and its initiatives converged with the momentum of the Native American museum movement beginning in the 1970s, a process that profoundly changed both. Through discussing the early stages of this movement we can see how the extensive collaboration involved in conducting the Ozette excavation and forming the MCRC has shaped the subjectivity of the Makah Nation's museum/cultural center.

One of the interviews I conducted during my residence at the Smithsonian was with historian Herman Viola. We spoke at length by phone and in his office, surrounded by tall stacks of papers. Viola was one of several key individuals in the history of Native American training programs at the Smithsonian Institution, and his memories are very important to telling this story. So, too, are the archival documents that record the day-to-day operations of the Native American training programs. As Viola remembers, in 1972 Clifford Evans, then chair of the Smithsonian anthropology department, encouraged Viola to leave his position with the National Archives to direct the NAA. At that time, the NAA contained some 90,000 photographs and 3,500 cubic feet of documents, field notes, sound recordings, and personal papers, dating from 1847. These were once the archives of the former Bureau of American Ethnology. When Viola arrived in October, general public access to the archives had not been previously facilitated to any great degree. In our interview, he noted that stacks of correspondence from researchers had been left unanswered (Viola 1995). According to Viola, and to many other staff members whom I interviewed, the only Native Americans who had used the archives were those few who were professional Native scholars.

Viola remembers that within two weeks of starting his job, he was approached by a Santa Clara pueblo man, David Warren. At that time, Warren was the director of the Research and Cultural Studies Development (RCSD) section of the Institute of American Indian Arts of the BIA. Warren asked Viola, "Would you allow Indians to use the archives?" Having just come from the National Archives where freedom of information was foremost, Viola thought the question strange, but answered affirmatively (Viola 1995). In retrospect, the conversation between Viola and Warren can be recognized as an important moment in the history of the Native American museum movement. Warren — a Native American professional who was advocating for community-based cultural resource preservation projects — had just found a receptive entry point into a renowned institution that curated Native American heritage.

According to Viola, in the early 1970s, Native Americans were not using the NAA or the National Archives, in any great numbers. For the most part, tribes were hiring researchers or lawyers to investigate resources in defense of their Tribal Claims Act cases. Viola later discovered that Native Americans did not approach archival resources themselves because they felt alienated from the institutions. In an article reflecting on the history of Native American training programs at the Smithsonian, Viola wrote: "many seemed to think that the archives were closed to everyone except important scholars, an attitude expressed by several members of the Indian Community—Everett Burch and Eddie Box of the Southern Utes, David Warren, Director of the Research and Cultural Studies Section of the BIA, Joseph Medicine Crow, Chairman of the Crow Cultural Committee, Nelson Gorman of the Navajo Community College, and others who came to the archives" (Viola 1978, 143). Others, however, did approach the Smithsonian Institution with some rather delicate issues.

The Zuni, for example, asked the Smithsonian to close a mask exhibit case. William Sturtevant was able to close the exhibit, despite considerable opposition. This was the first time the museum had ever agreed to close an exhibit at the request of someone outside the museum. Regarding the repatriation of the masks, the Zunis faced arguments that (1) the masks under discussion included some that had been made specifically to take back to Washington; (2) removing the masks would set a precedent for outside groups to intervene in exhibits, particularly creationists and fundamentalists who wanted to withdraw exhibits on biological evolution; (3) the Smithsonian possessed the masks justifiably on legal, ethical, and scientific grounds; and (4) the Zunis had not sufficiently formalized their request (Merrill et al. 1993, 528–30). Seventeen years later, in 1987, the Zunis retrieved two century-old wooden images of the twin gods Ahayu:da.

During my fellowship at the Smithsonian, I spent many days in the Museum Reference Center of the OMP listening to archival tape recordings of panel sessions at the American Association of Museums (AAM) from the 1970s through the 1990s. Because Native and

non-Native museum professionals had referred to memorable annual meetings as turning points, crucial encounters, or moments
where new understandings were forged, I was moved to listen in on
these dialogues that had taken place at professional meetings. These
tape recordings revealed that when Native Americans began to participate fully in professional meetings in the 1970s, one of the commonly communicated messages was that museums had historically
been hostile or inaccessible to Native Americans.

It was this Native American reluctance to engage with museums
and other resource centers that inspired David Warren to launch a
project to facilitate tribal contact with federal resources. Warren
had joined the BIA in 1968 as the director of Curriculum and Instruction at the Institute of American Indian Arts. There, Warren observed that tribes wanted assistance in developing their cultural resources. Tribal communities nationwide wanted to strengthen and
revive Native languages and record their oral histories. Communities wanted to maintain traditional language and oral tradition to
counteract the historic repression of Native American knowledge
systems. In phone interviews Warren reflected with me on the challenges faced by the RCSD program. To Warren the central question
was: "How do we overcome tribal development strategies that have
previously been directed by a view of historical development based
on non-Native, academic theories?" (1995).

Throughout his career, Warren asserted that a paradigm predict-
ing inevitable Native American cultural extinction propelled conventional historiography and federal administrative policies (1974).
Following an alternative vision of Native American cultures as *living*,
Warren founded the RCSD program and attempted to establish tribally controlled educational, social, and economic development on
the reservations. This was an attempt to forward self-determination
from within the federal government, namely the BIA.

Warren set up the RCSD section of the BIA to identify and locate resource materials, to organize materials for community use, to develop new educational materials, and to decentralize and distribute
materials (Warren 1971, 2). What was one of the means for accom-
plishing these goals?—achieving Native American access to federally held resources or, to use the spatial terms discussed earlier, *get-*

ting inside institutions like museums. In effect, RCSD sought to transform federally centralized information and financial resources concerning Native Americans into locally disseminated resources for the benefit of tribal community programs. These objectives led Warren to approach Viola in 1972.

By June 1973 a pilot training program had been initiated in the NAA under Viola's direction — the American Indian Cultural Resources Training Program (AICRTP). If the program was successful, the plan was to approach Congress for more permanent funding. Word of the program spread quickly throughout "Indian Country." One of the first individuals to approach Viola with interest in the training program was George Capture, a Gros Ventre Indian (hereafter known as George Horse Capture). George Horse Capture has had a remarkable career, one documented in a memoir titled *From the Reservation to the Smithsonian via Alcatraz* (1994). Horse Capture's road from the reservation to the Smithsonian did not stop with his participation in AICRTP; his long career in museology has included directing the Plains Indian Museum at Cody, Wyoming, and working at the Bronx, New York, branch of the National Museum of the American Indian.

After receiving encouragement from David Warren, Horse Capture wrote to Viola in February 1973. At that time, Horse Capture was a University of California–Berkeley student who was researching and gathering Gros Ventre materials from his reservation and institutions nationwide. One of the most visible and well known set of incidents in twentieth-century Native activism, the occupation of Alcatraz, had set Horse Capture on a route that linked tribal self-determination with a museology career.[2] As he described it:

> I had climbed the white [Anglo] mountain, looked over its summit, and found nothing. We might have stayed there [in San Francisco] forever and eventually bought a house, but something [the occupation of Alcatraz Island] came up that changed my life and the Indian world. . . . Like a nova, its force and brilliance had exploded and reshaped the psyche of the Indian world, and the force generated is still being felt today. . . . I quit my job and enrolled in junior college full time to learn skills

that would be helpful to Indian communities. . . . One of the most interesting courses I took was bibliography. In order to make it meaningful to me, I focused on my tribe. . . . What started as a simple college course began to take over my life. (1994, 139–44)

As part of his bibliography course, Horse Capture started searching for primary and secondary materials about his tribe in libraries and museums nationwide. The project snowballed, and his community encouraged it.

I interviewed Horse Capture during my time at the Smithsonian. I traveled to the Bronx where he was a staff member of the former George Gustav Heye's Museum of the American Indian (founded in 1916 but not opened until 1922) whose collections, approximated at one million pieces, had become the basis for founding the NMAI at the Smithsonian Institution in 1989 (Kidwell 1999, 249). We sat and talked outside on a picnic bench within sight of the concrete tipis whose construction had been overseen by Mrs. Thea Heye (Kidwell 1999, 249). These must have been a significant source of ambiance for the grounds of a once popular museum now ringed with razor wire. In this interview Horse Capture shared that he found it very difficult to get a job after finishing at Berkeley and returning to the reservation. He decided against returning for a doctorate and chose another path. Viola's program at the NAA was one of the few available that combined training with tribal cultural projects (Horse Capture 1995).

In the course of our interview, Horse Capture linked his experience with a community cultural preservation project to the development of professional training programs for Native Americans: "During this period [of my Gros Ventre bibliographic study] museums were visited across the country and contacts were made with the museums, public and private, and they were asked if they would lend or give us some of their Gros Ventre materials. *The replies were positive, but conditional. They would lend or give us this material if we had a safe, secure place in which to house it staffed by trained personnel. . . .* There are no trained people in this field on our reservation. . . . It is a vital field; it is a good way to instill pride in our children" (1995).

Horse Capture's experience was common; Native American communities were encouraged to professionalize their community initiatives before collaboration with mainstream museums could begin. In archival documents and tapes, I repeatedly encountered statements that Native American communities were expected to achieve professional standards of cultural preservation before the decentralization of resources could begin. The training programs that emerged from the Smithsonian Institution became not only a means for tribes to identify and decentralize relevant information but also a way to validate their efforts in the eyes of the museum profession.

The professionalization of museums, which accelerated in the 1960s, has played both positive and negative roles in the relationships between museums and Native Americans. The movement to professionalize museums, in which Paul Perrot (assistant secretary for Museum Programs) played an instrumental role in the American Association of Museums, exposed to the public unethical museum practices, such as theft, trading, and sale of objects as well as the poor curation of objects. In the reform process, somewhat rigid procedures were established to prevent these practices. These hampered access to collections because control over objects became equated with professional behavior and was of great concern (Fuller 1995). On the other hand, this professionalization opened museums to public scrutiny and thus led to their democratization. As a result of the creation of the Institute of Museum Services, which was organized so that museums would have a support mechanism for providing operating expense funds and training and other services to the museum profession, it was expected that a museum would know what was in its collection. How many things were in the collection? How were they cared for? This accountability, however, led to an increased sensitization of the museum's debt to the public trust (Fuller 1995).

At times, the AICRTP did more than professionalize tribal museums or jumpstart careers; it also generated personal transformations. AICRTP offered participants the opportunity to reconnect with tribal and personal histories, partly by viewing photographs of relatives and touching family possessions they had never been seen be-

17. Lorraine Bizman and Augustine Smith, participants in the AICRTP, look over some of the photograph collections at the NAA, October 1973. Courtesy of the NAA, negative no. 73-8781-6.

fore (figure 17). Horse Capture told me he had always wondered why his grandmother had named him Spotted Otter. No one living in his family knew why. He discovered the answer through his participation in the AICRTP: "I found the answer in the tribal rolls of the National Archives. I found that my grandfather had a younger brother who had died young. His named was Spotted Otter. I had always carried that name with pride. And I knew that someday someone else would carry it with pride. But now I know where the name came from" (1995). Documentation of Native American interaction with museums and archives in the twentieth century is full of references to the unintended effects of training and educational programs. Native American scholars frequently discovered the devastating impact that the pressures to assimilate and the conventions of historiography have had on their tribe and on them, personally. These realizations seem to have released fresh opportunities for building self-esteem and changing the status quo (Silva 1975; Viola 1995; Bradbury 1995).[3]

The intertwining of professionalization, cultural preservation, and personal and tribal discovery were happening in Neah Bay, too, as part of the Ozette excavation and the early stages of the MCRC. Meredith Heilman—chairwoman of the board of trustees of the MCRC throughout my research—was one of the Makah youths personally affected by the process of moving inside the archaeology and museology disciplines. In an interview with me in her living room in Neah Bay, Heilman described the early stages of getting involved with Makah cultural preservation projects (figure 18):

Since I was a student at Evergreen College, I worked out a work-study project for the year, beginning in 1974. That was my first year at Ozette. After that year, I worked as an employee at the excavation, paid by the tribe. . . . Later, I worked in the lab down at Ozette. I loved working in the lab because of the opportunity to see and handle every object that came out of the excavation. There was a lot of pride seeing all of those things. Eventually, I worked in the lab up in Neah Bay. I remember one time my family was practicing our family songs, preparing for a graduation that was coming. So I brought my tape recorder into the lab where I was working so I could listen to the songs. It really struck me that there I was listening to my family's songs and working in the lab surrounded by all of those things from Ozette. I felt that connection. Many of those objects are still powerful. Some of them I never wanted to touch, probably because I wasn't supposed to. (1995)

18. The Ozette excavation and the development of the MCRC provided many Makah youths with experience in archaeology and museology and a wide variety of other cultural preservation initiatives. Meredith Flinn (now Heilman) was one of those who participated in Native American training programs at the Smithsonian Institution; she is shown here conserving Ozette basketry in the archaeological laboratory. Later in her career she served as the chairwoman of the MCRC's board of trustees. Photo by Ruth Kirk. Courtesy of the photographer.

The Makah Nation was one of the scores of tribes that participated in the AICRTP in its early years in the 1970s. Meredith Heilman (then Flinn) was one of the Makah youths sent by the tribe to locate and catalogue the vast quantity of Makah resources centralized in Washington DC. She was instructed to bring that catalogue and some of the materials back to Neah Bay.

Tribal governments nominated candidates and entrusted them with receiving training and bringing back copies of materials to the tribe. AICRTP participants also learned how to accession, curate, and exhibit archival materials. When I first worked in Neah Bay, I did not realize that Heilman had been an AICRTP participant, but when I went to Washington DC I encountered her file in the Smithsonian Archives. When I returned to Neah Bay I inquired about AICRTP, and she described for me how she entered the training program more than twenty years earlier, soon after it began:

> I learned about the Smithsonian archival training program when Herman Viola visited Ozette in the mid-1970s. I remember that Dr. Viola came to Ozette with Nan McNutt and her husband, who was the state historic preservation officer. Through him, I learned about the program, and with Nan's help — she was working at the Pacific Science Center — in acquiring support from the National Science Foundation, I had the funds to go to Washington. I believe I went in the fall of 1977 or 1978. . . . It was quite a culture shock. All the people, the heat, the noise. It was so different. I was there for maybe six weeks. Dr. Viola opened up everything to me and another person in the training program. We met with people from National Archives, Folklife Program, and Natural History. My job was to catalogue as much as I could about what they had on the Makahs. They were very open to us and treated us well. My commitment was to my people, to the Makah people. I remember that I was very grateful for the opportunity to document all of the information that they had which we didn't have on the reservation. (1995)

Through this program, Heilman was able to assemble copies of photographs, Indian Agency reports, and sound recordings that formed the nucleus of the Makah-managed historical archives at the MCRC. After the center opened, she continued to work with historical resources in the photo archives. Eventually, after her grandmother, Meredith Parker, passed away, Heilman took her grandmother's position on MCRC's board of trustees.

Soon after Heilman returned from Washington DC, the responsibilities of the AICRTP shifted to a different bureau of the Smithsonian and began one of several phases, or stages, in its evolution. Successors to the AICRTP have included the Native American Training Program in the OMP (which began in Feb. 1977 and was later renamed the Native American Museums Program [NAMP]) and the American Indian Museum Services (or AIMS) under the auspices of the new National Museum of the American Indian. Two other American Indian programs, one in the National Museum of Natural History and the other in the National Museum of American History, increased the venues through which Native American individuals and their worldviews could come inside and dialogue with members of the museum discipline. By 1980 the Native American Museum Program had conducted nine workshops reaching more than three hundred participants and placed thirty-three Native American museum employees in internships.[4]

The MCRC played an important role in the history of both programs that succeeded AICRTP: the Native American Museums Program (NAMP) and AIMS. Greig Arnold was instrumental in creating this new space for intertribal dialogue on cultural issues in museum settings. Arnold was one of the twenty leaders of cultural projects from around the country who attended the Native American Museum Directors' Workshop from October 30–November 3 in 1978 at the Smithsonian Institution, later becoming one of the organization's regional directors. Attending the workshop led to Arnold's role as a regional coordinator of the North American Indian Museums Association and host for its 1979 meeting. This association produced a newsletter published out of the Museum of the Cherokee Indian in North Carolina and funded by the Institute for Museum Services. Arnold later participated in a workshop on museum management, completed an internship in exhibition construction, and hosted an on-site, technical assistance evaluation. Other MCRC personnel completed internships under his directorship, such as Fran Bowechop in museum shop management and Keeley Parker in developing, managing, and maintaining collections.[5]

Despite the growing network of Native American museum professionals nationwide, the AICRTP had its critics. Many did not see programs such as these, and those that followed, in terms such as *community development, human rights,* or *self-determination.* Viola characterized the resistance in the following manner: "Curators at first feared that this initiative would be a Trojan horse used by Indians to gain access to the collections and to acquire information they needed to demand the return of specimens" (1990, 262). Others worried the program would increase the chances for damage to the collection. These notions prompted one AICRTP participant to state publicly at the Smithsonian: "We are not here to demand or destroy, but here to learn."[6] Some Native Americans openly speak of museums' fear for their collections—a shopping cart paranoia—wherein Native Americans pull up in front of the museum with their carts, select from the collections what they want, and empty museum shelves around the country. Mikle Taylor (Oglala) sketched this anecdote for museologists at a 1980 annual meeting of the AAM: "We know what specter of gleeful hoards of American Indians pushing shopping carts up to the doors of these museums mean to curators."[7]

These fears were expressed directly to me when a distressed Smithsonian collections manager queried: "Do you think they will come and take these baskets away? I am hearing now that even *moccasins* are sacred! What will it be *next*?" Former assistant secretary Perrot attributes these fears to what he calls *specimenitis*, a focus on the academic value of an object, its origin, and the particulars of its curation, at the expense of recognizing it as a work of art or as something having spiritual and emotional qualities (1995). One Native museum professional characterized it for me another way: "To hell with them! They don't have a passion for *living* culture." What some non-Native individuals, such as Perrot, and many Native American community members and professionals have shared, is a desire to shift institutional attention away from specimenitis and toward living culture. The Native American museum movement represents an effort to revolutionize museums to become a more proactive participant in community development and in empowering cross-cultural communication.

One of the other significant outcomes of establishing NAMP and organizing the Directors' Workshop was the founding of the American Indian Museum Association, later renamed North American Indian Museum Association (NAIMA) in May 1979 at a subsequent meeting in Denver, Colorado. More than eighty Native museums were represented at this meeting.[8] The Native American Museums Program coordinator supported NAIMA by acting as secretary and providing tools and services that would support the national network NAIMA was attempting to build. Rick Hill drew the parallel between this national Native American museum network and the historic phenomena of Indian confederations.[9] Native American regional representatives, appointed by NAIMA, were an important part of building a network of tribal cultural institutions nationwide and bridging between them and non-Native institutions. The same year that NAIMA was officially founded, the organization was invited to hold a panel at the AAM annual meeting. NAIMA members organized a panel titled "Native American Museums." Many of the panelists were among the original twenty directors who had attended the Smithsonian Institution meeting. At that AAM meeting, the new association presented itself to the museum discipline as a means to attribute credibility to Native spokespersons and raise ethical issues to the discipline and as a means to inform the museum profession about tribal cultural projects that seek to protect intergenerational transfer of identity.[10]

Coming on the heels of the passage of the American Indian Religious Freedom Act, this panel, and subsequent ones in 1980, generated considerable interest among museum professionals. Taylor interpreted this interest among some institutions as driven by what he called *subdued hysteria*. At the 1980 annual AAM meeting, Taylor named the kinds of foot-dragging and obstacles that Native Americans were receiving from museums. He pointed out that "there are those using uncertainty [of the effects of American Indian Religious Freedom Act] to their personal and institutional advantage" but that florid rhetoric was not the way to cooperate. He said that panic, sequestering of items, and sale abroad would not suffice in "the age of cooperation [that] is upon us."[11]

The annual meetings for the AAM provided a forum for extending the kind of dialogue between Native American and non-Native museum professionals that had flourished at the 1978 Native American Museum Directors' Workshop at the Smithsonian. The following two quotes are excerpts from statements made at AAM panels in the years immediately following the workshop. It was not uncommon for museologists to hear statements like these beginning in the late 1970s and early 1980s; the first is from Hill in 1979 and the second from Taylor in 1980:

> Native American communities have a very negative image of museums in general. Five years ago, a lot of people would have refused to come to this meeting. You used to represent the enemy to us. The things going on in museums created negative stereotypes. . . . It's that kind of image that's kept us out for a long time. We just didn't want to be involved. Now finally we say we have to, through self-determination, to take hold of these ideas and possibilities and develop them ourselves. It's as much our responsibility as yours.[12]

> It will be the supreme irony of this age if we Indians, still looked upon by some as benighted savages, are the people who drag museums, kicking and screaming, out of colonialism and into the twentieth century.[13]

In training sessions and annual meetings, museum professionals heard Native Americans state that museums were a non-Native format for knowledge (along with books and written laws) that communities should combine with traditional forms of knowledge in order to further their self-determination and survival goals. Furthermore, they heard the critique of museums' association with colonialism and that changing that historical relationship was part of a broad, Native agenda for social change.

In the summer of 1988, during a hiatus between receiving my master's degree and beginning work on my doctorate, I worked as a visiting professional in the Native American Museums Program at the Smithsonian Institution. Nancy Fuller was then directing NAMP through a difficult, two-year period when NAMP was effectively cut off from financial support due to shifts in the OMP's budget priorities. However, with the help of assistants, Fuller continued to act as a clearinghouse of information. She conducted research on tribal museums in order to produce a directory and a comprehensive summary of their structure and innovations. These materials became a valuable addition to the OMP's Reference Center, which is a library center for museum studies information. When the Native American Museums Program ended its decade of facilitation and advocacy, many of its objectives and techniques were reincarnated and expanded when the Smithsonian acquired the New York–based collection of the Heye Museum of the American Indian.

Years later, during my residence at the Smithsonian, I had the opportunity to observe how the successor program to NAMP—AIMS—encourages communities to indigenize, or adapt, the mainstream museum model. I participated in a workshop titled Collections Management for Tribal Museums, which was held in Cherokee, North Carolina, and hosted by the Museum of the Cherokee Indian. During her introductory remarks at the workshop, AIMS director Karen Cooper (Cherokee) encouraged participants to mold the information brought to them in order to help them run their museums "in an Indian way." The AIMS staff has recognized (as NAMP did before it) that Native American communities are not simply passive recipients of professional training provided by museum institutions and organizations, and it acknowledged that these communities would transform museology. One member of the Smithsonian Institution training staff articulated at the 1993 training session in Neah Bay that it's not just what the AAM has to offer to you, it's also what you have to offer it.

The MCRC is one of the institutions that has adapted traditional museum practices in order to fulfill the critical need for preserving living cultures. The MCRC has grappled with this issue by implementing archival, collections management, and educational policies that respond to both professional and Makah cultural standards. Native American and non-Native staff from MCRC have shared these experiences in regional, national, and international forums. At the 1994 AAM meeting, former MCRC director and non-Native linguist Ann Renker pointed to dual standards—*tribal* and *professional*—maintained by community museums in order to balance external policies and procedures that can be "subverting" and "unorthodox" to tribal cultures. In her presentation, she described how the Makah people place a high priority on the distinction between "public" and "private," or "family," knowledge. In response to the cultural distinction made between types of knowledge, she stated that the MCRC must work to prevent the erosion of the Makah processes that traditionally manage knowledge.[14] For example, traditional Makah knowledge and property (songs, dances, regalia, oral history, and so forth) can be owned by individuals, elders, or families and passed down following strict etiquette. Because of this, elders are allowed to designate beneficiaries for the oral histories that MCRC gathers. One implication of this is that not all information is available for research.

The AIMS program developed when the Smithsonian Institution founded the NMAI in 1990, a branch that would be required to have a presence both in New York City and on the Capital Mall in Washington DC. With NMAI funds, the recognition for the need of a Native American museum training program was rejuvenated, and the training initiative was again delegated to the OMP, which had previously hosted NAMP. The new program was named American Indian Museum Services, and Alyce Sadongei was hired in December 1990 as its first director. The appointment of a Native American director was one of the important changes that had occurred since the early 1970s. The other important change was a focus on indigenizing the mainstream museum model.

AIMS continued the tradition of responding to the training needs of Native cultural projects and providing intertribal and cross-cultural forums. Regional workshops using Native faculty and tribal museum hosting were important parts of AIMS's approach. On June 25, 1993, the MCRC hosted the first regional AIMS workshop. At this workshop, Sadongei commented how Native American museum professionals were still being caught between expectations to professionalize tribal museums and adhere to standard museum practices while at the same time maintain traditional knowledge systems and interpret objects in a new and respectful manner.

AIMS encouraged non-Smithsonian faculty to lead these workshops — especially Native American professionals who had by then had some twenty years of experience in their respective institutions. Facilitating the emergence of leadership from communities emphasized that community development should be addressed by more than top-down programs. When I interviewed Sadongei (who was by then the former director of AIMS) at the Smithsonian in 1995 she said that pulling faculty from communities avoided the "this is how we at the Smithsonian do it and how you should do it" approach. Instead, the approach has been to outline the literature, the techniques museum professionals are currently using, and then let communities decide what they want their institution to be. This philosophy that founded AIMS continues to the present.

AIMS workshops are a forum for Native American communities and professionals to share how they splice living traditions with conventional museum practices. For example, at the 1995 AIMS workshop in Cherokee, North Carolina, participants discussed issues such as "feeding" objects in the collection, blessings and purifications of collections in storage, and a variety of storage techniques necessary to maintain respect for living and powerful cultural objects. The AICRTP, the Native American Museum Program, and the AIMS — all based at the Smithsonian Institution — have involved many hundreds of Native American participants through workshops, internships, consultations, and publications over a twenty-year period, leaving few communities untouched. Between 1973 and 1981, more than 283 persons from 163 tribes were involved in AICRTP and NAMP (Merrill et al. 1993, 545). Between 1991 and 1994, more than 190 Native American professionals were participants in AIMS.[15]

The Makah community of Neah Bay is one of the tribal communities that significantly influenced these programs and which was also influenced by them. Neah Bay experienced the pattern of seeking federal resources for community and cultural resource development. Resources were sought on four fronts: (1) development of cultural curricula, (2) development of Makah language curricula, (3) excavation and stabilization of archaeological heritage, and (4) construction and development of a museum/cultural center. Throughout these initiatives, MCRC has set an example by engaging in collaborative projects wherein the Makah people have set the direction, and archaeological or museological experts have contributed advice, technical skill, and experience (André 1995, Quimby and Hanson 1995).

Since the 1970s, numerous MCRC staff members have participated in AICRTP, NAMP internships, workshops, and technical consultations. The MCRC has hosted regional NAIMA and AIMS meetings, and the current director, Janine Bowechop, has taught and published as faculty for AIMS programs. The MCRC has been involved in many aspects of running a tribal museums, including ethics, exhibit planning and construction, gift shop management, mission and governance, collections and archives management, and repatriation of human remains. The MCRC has participated fully in these programs by both benefiting from them and, through their participation and ideas, by having a part in reshaping the sponsoring institutions and professions.

The Thomas Burke Memorial Washington State Museum at the University of Washington in Seattle has had an instrumental role in shaping the subjectivity of the MCRC. Like the Smithsonian Institution, the faculty and staff of the University of Washington and the Burke Museum facilitated the shift of Makah people from outsiders to insiders relative to the museum profession. The University of Washington training program provided several Makah youth the opportunity to acquire professional skills that could be integrated into efforts to both preserve artifacts and reinvigorate a living, Makah culture.

Moving Inside through the Burke Museum

In the summer of 1975, young, non-Native artist Steve Brown found himself in Neah Bay carving a sealing canoe with four Makah students who were enrolled in the University of Washington's museology program. Greig Arnold, Joe McGimpsey, Scott Tyler, and Lance Wilkie worked with Brown to reproduce a sealing canoe for eventual exhibition in the MCRC. Throughout the summer and into the fall, in front of a storage building near the tribal center, the five men worked with eighteenth-century-style tools to transform a cedar log into a canoe.

Twenty years later, at the Seattle Art Museum in downtown Seattle, Brown hosted me in his office where he worked as assistant curator of Native American Art. Reminiscing about the MCRC project, Brown emphasized the truly collaborative effort required to construct a type of canoe that hadn't been carved in decades.

Brown's oral history told a story of how a log, eventually a canoe, became the focus point in the lives of many individuals — Makah and non-Makah:

[Makah elders] Harold Ides and Roger Colfax, in particular — they both said that they had never made or even worked on one [canoe] but that they saw it happen and were involved in using them all the time as younger men . . . having seen their fathers, grandfathers, uncles working on them. Like Harold said he had gone out whaling once but they didn't get a whale. Roger had been sealing, seal-hunting, a lot so he had a lot of interesting stories. Both of them in particular, more than anybody else, had a lot of interesting stories that had a bearing on what we did. I remember Harold, well, both Harold and Roger I think, talking about the platforms that get fitted in the end [of the canoe], particularly where the steersperson sits. Rather than just being a narrow thwart [it] was made as a board, a plank that went across and formed a seat in the tapering end of the canoe. He was very clear on the fact that it didn't want to be fastened in. It wanted to be set in there and supported, but it had to be able to come out because if the canoe swamped, you had to be able to push the water out through the stern. (1995)

While ethnographic documentation of canoe building was available to these novice canoe builders (such as T. T. Waterman's *Whaling Equipment of the Makah Indians*, 1922), the oral history and material evidence offered by community members provided valuable guidance.

The story of this sealing canoe illustrates the collaborative nature of not only artifact reproduction but of the forging of the subjectivity of the MCRC. Brown remembered that Ernest Cheeka Sr. was salvaging shake bolts in a clear-cut above the former village site of Archawat farther out on Cape Flattery. Cheeka found a number of trees that had been felled by burning and chiseling rather than by chainsaw. Brown related to me the impact this discovery had on their project:

So we went out to check that out and that was real interesting to see that evidence of real early technology, how big the tool was, the shape of the edge, the fact that you know you always hear about burning out the inside of a canoe or what have you, and it was real interesting to see how controlled, in the case of bucking that log, that burning was. That piece might still be around as far as I know. It was saved for the museum. It was about an eight- or nine-inch-wide channel that had been burned and chiseled about eighteen inches at least into the surface of the log, and there was no charring at all outside of that area. . . . It was very deliberate and obvious that this was a controlled burn. . . . All those little bits of evidence, or real aboriginal technology, not hearsay, not ethnographic accounts, not reconstruction in modern day from ethnographic accounts, but to see real aboriginal examples, and to hear people with either direct or indirect experience had a huge bearing on the relative success of the project. (1995)

The genuine interest of community members in their heritage supported the project in tangible ways.

Let's return to the institutional support that encouraged this collaborative project between Steve Brown and the four Makah canoe builders. In 1970 the dean of the college at the University of Washington appointed Dr. George Quimby at the Burke Museum chair of a committee to examine the potential of an American Indian Studies program at the University of Washington, Seattle. As a result of this committee, James Nason was recruited to a joint appointment in the anthropology department and the Burke Museum. While my research was based in Neah Bay, I traveled into Seattle and was fortunate to interview James Nason and George Quimby together in Quimby's home. They described how in 1972 Nason founded a museology degree at the University of Washington. Soon thereafter, Nason became director of a new American Indian Studies program. At the 1972 meeting of the AAM in Seattle, Nason was one of the early Native American speakers to publicly articulate to museologists the Native American discomfort with museum business as usual (Quimby and Nason 1995).

It was 1973 when the Ozette archaeological project converged with the new museology program at the University of Washington-Seattle. In 1973 Richard Daugherty (the director of the Ozette project and an archaeologist on the Washington State University-Pullman faculty) contacted the University of Washington to convey that the Makah Nation was interested in founding a museum to house the Ozette collection. Daugherty and the Makah Tribal Council traveled to Seattle to speak with Quimby and Nason. The council described their hope for Makah youths to receive training so the tribe could operate the museum itself. The following year the Museum Program of the National Endowment for the Arts funded a University of Washington training program. Five Makah tribal members participated in this training program (Quimby and Nason 1977). Nason and Quimby worked closely with the original Makah Museum Planning Committee on aspects of design, budget, governance, and exhibit, recommending designer Jean André as a consultant for the Makah museum project. It was through this museology program that Brown became involved as an artisan and project facilitator:

> I first heard about it through George Quimby and Bill Holm, that there were these Makah students at the Burke in the museology program, which I think was five at the time (including Cora Lee) and . . . they wanted a for-credit project that they could do in Neah Bay and still be advancing their course work, but they would spend the summer at home. Plus the idea of having a canoe that would end up in the museum was appealing to the people involved in organizing that. And so the idea was to go out there summer of '75 and work with the four which was Greig Arnold, Joe McGimpsey, Scott Tyler, and Lance Wilkie, and make one canoe. And we chose a seal-hunting canoe. . . . So many of the elders that were living in Neah Bay at that time had been involved in sealing. (Brown 1995)

Through the Burke Museum training program and the training programs at the Smithsonian Institution, Makah people were able to shift their position from outsiders to insiders relative to museology at the crucial time of the Ozette excavation and the planning stages of the MCRC. Consequently, Makah individuals, and thus their perspectives and sensibilities, had an opportunity to shape the subjectivity of the MCRC—who it was for, what it communicated, how it did its business. As a result, as I discuss further in the next chapter, the MCRC reflects the collective memory and sense of place of the Makah people, but the subjectivity of this tribal museum/cultural center reflects a thousand voices, including non-Native ones.

In the era of the Native American museum movement, tribal community museums/cultural centers embody a shift in previously unequal power relations. These institutions permit a nearly unprecedented degree of control over self-representation. This does not mean that institutions, such as the MCRC, have not borrowed heavily from the professional techniques and standards of museology, archaeology, and so forth. To a great degree, they were required to emulate mainstream museums to qualify for funding and academic respect.

Nonetheless, it is important to realize that in the process of adopting this Euro-American form of institution Native American peoples have indigenized it so that their museums are — to a significant degree — by them and for them. These modifications to the mainstream museum model have not remained at the local level; they have inspired significant changes in the disciplines of museology and anthropology nationwide and throughout the Western Hemisphere.

The emergence of the MCRC in the mid-twentieth century on the Makah reservation has provided a formal, institutional space (in addition to the public school) where tribal heritage and cultural resources can be claimed, honored, respected, and interpreted. Some of these cultural resources were physically brought back, such as the Frances Densmore collection of oral recordings, census rolls, photographic images, ethnographic documentation of stories and oral histories, human bodies, and other heritage of various types sometimes improperly removed from the Makah reservation.

The MCRC has not limited its definition of cultural resources to the material realm, however. It has also become a place for collecting and disseminating information on Makah language — knowledge encoded linguistically and carried by only a few remaining fluent elders. The Makah Language Program has established a formal curriculum, worked with a written alphabet, and established a research component of MCRC that documents vocabulary and syntax and develops language acquisition programs. The Makah Language Program has devoted itself to bringing back the right and ability to think and speak in qʷiqʷidiččaq.

In striving to achieve the community's hopes for it, the MCRC has become more than a museum. At the 1994 AAM meeting, Greig Arnold and Ann Renker compared MCRC to a grandparent. The MCRC, they said, is not simply a repository for artifacts; it is meant to be a living building, like a grandparent whose role is to teach at home and pass down information for many generations of Makah people to come.[16] Here the distinction between concepts of museum and cultural center is significant. The museum is often perceived in Native communities as a place to hold and exhibit things from the past, a place that implies that the culture is dead and gone. But as tribal chairman Joseph Lawrence Jr. once said, "The Makah people are not a fossil people; we are also a living people and the [Ozette] archaeological dig is unique in this respect also: it relates to a living Indian culture which goes on today."[17] The museum project became not only a place for storing and caring for the private and personal property of ancestors but a facility serving a living, thriving, growing culture through language preservation, oral history research and preservation, and educational programming.

The following chapter continues discussion of collaboration between the MCRC and non-Native institutions and professionals. In this chapter, the stories of the Smithsonian Institution and the Thomas Burke Memorial Washington State Museum have provoked us to think about the complex subjectivity of the MCRC and its participation in the Native American museum movement. In the following chapter, our discussion of the planning and construction of the museum will highlight how the development of a Makah curatorial voice and the incorporation of Makah sensibilities into the MCRC was facilitated by a representative from the Royal British Columbia Museum in Victoria, British Columbia.

5 Indigenizing the Museum

Subjectivity and the Makah Cultural and Research Center

with Kirk Wachendorf

Remembering How It Feels

All of this issue of values, this issue of collections management and or-
ganization by Makah language, by Makah categories . . . goes back to being
down at Ozette, out in the field with Makahs and non-Makahs, working to-
gether. We non-Makahs realized that these were not objects; these are not only
important to us as archaeologists, but they are much more important to the
descendants of the people who made these.

JEFFREY MAUGER, 1994

Every day during my year on the Makah reservation I walked from
my rented house in the center of Neah Bay to the MCRC at the eastern edge of the village. Splashing through the frequent puddles
along Front Street, I would pass the village gas station, then breathe
deeply as I came to the low building hosting the smoke shop, pizze-
ria, and the two gift shops. To pack a bag lunch, I would stop at
Washburn's store, the century-old grocery and general store that
was formerly the reservation's trading post. Sometimes I would get
delayed in the parking lot of the café across the street as I caught up
with residents who had become friends. Keeping the curved, harbor
beach off my left shoulder, I would eventually pass the Cape Motel,
from where the dull thud of RV doors sounded from the camp-
ground in the rear. Finally, taking a shortcut through tall grass and
barbed wire, I would reach the grounds of the MCRC.

Interpretation specialist Kirk Wachendorf usually greeted me as I entered the high-ceiling building. His workstation was to the left as I entered, in the midst of a gift shop burgeoning with masks, baskets, books, jewelry, and screenprints. It was here, between ringing phones and visitors' questions, that Kirk and I spent many hours discussing the history of the museum and the perceptions of the general public, who he encounters each year. As someone who has participated in the development of the MCRC since the early 1970s, Wachendorf's insights were invaluable to the shaping and editing of this chapter.

During the tape-recording of Wachendorf's oral history, the themes of collaboration and of reworking the mainstream museum model came to the forefront. When the Makah Tribe started planning for a museum in 1970, they began the long process of discovering and reworking the conventions of museum construction, exhibit design, and cultural interpretation. Like many other tribal members, Wachendorf commended non-Native exhibit designer Jean André for facilitating the collaborative creation of the Makah museum. André encouraged the Makah community to let their worldviews shape the identity, or subjectivity, of the Makah museum:

It seemed like at first the plans were just to hire an architect to design a fancy building with no thought of the kind of exhibit space or how to display things inside. Not much thought at all. And that idea just didn't go over well with everybody and so they threw those plans out even though it meant throwing away many thousands and thousands of dollars of some architect's work. But somehow the tribe and the museum committee got on a better road. . . . The tribe said Well, there's this person in Victoria — Jean André. . . . He was real excited about the project. A lot of people say Jean André designed the exhibit. Not necessarily. He came in and he had all the talent and all the ideas of how to present things, but he just didn't come in and tell people what to do. He offered very good suggestions and you could either accept them or not accept them. But we liked most of what he suggested. Things fell together really well, and we worked to design the museum. (Wachendorf 1995)

Later in our conversation, Wachendorf distinguished the term *museum* from *cultural center* as MCRC staff and board members often did in conversations with me. I asked him what the difference was between the two. He emphasized that the MCRC was a community-based institution with a dual purpose, hence, the need for the term *cultural center*:

Well, cultural and research center is a place where you are preserving a people's culture, and you are doing research to continue that and to preserve it and perpetuate it and that's why the language program is here. That's what our goals and purposes were to keep our artifacts and to take care of them, but then to also preserve the culture of the people and language and history.

The other side of it was to present it to the public that comes out here. . . . At the time, the tribe was just trying to do the best cultural research center and display and museum that they could do with the time and the money and the people that they had. They did spend a lot of time and money on the display that they had. It wasn't just a display just for Makahs. It is a display for the public. I think it's a good idea because without the public support and the public getting educated about what you really are it doesn't make it any easier to continue. So over the years [MCRC] has become fairly well known just because we did do a good job of putting it together and displaying it. (1995)

Because of the dual purpose — preserving living culture and educating the public — *cultural center* and *museum* were terms used interchangeably by MCRC staff, depending on the context.

The frequent mention of designer Jean André by Wachendorf and many others convinced me to arrange an interview with André at the office of his business, JJ André Associates, Ltd., in Victoria, British Columbia. This interview took me back to the 1970s when collaboration between the original Makah museum planning committee and a non-Native museum professional had a profound influence on the subjectivity of the MCRC.

André described how he was approached by the Makah Tribe in the mid-1970s when he was staff member at the Provincial Museum (now known as the Royal British Columbia Museum) in Victoria. At the time he was asked to review the plans for the Makah Museum storage area, he remembered that it was "a little round house" whose longest part was some eighteen feet long. When he asked about the artifacts to be stored there, he was told there were canoes of some twenty to thirty feet in length. Moved by the unmet potential of the design, André took a three-month leave of absence from the Provincial Museum to guide the planning and design stages for the MCRC (André 1995).

André encouraged the Makah Tribe to start with what he still considers to be the heart of the museum, the story:

> There's three things that you need to put an exhibit together — story, artifacts, and space. Simple. That's logical. So, the story, to me, is the most important thing. If the story is not good, you can have all the window dressing you want, it won't fly. It still will be a crummy story. That's typical of a large amount of motion picture where you have all the lights but there's no story at all. The day after you forget it, you don't know where you're at. So the story is crucial. My first visit there with the [Makah museum planning] group was OK. [I said], "I'll come back in five days—Victoria to Neah Bay. When I come back you get your storyline all ready." Then I came back five days later. They were drinking pop and looking at comic books. I say, "Where's my storyline?" . . . "Well, Jean, we don't know what you mean by storyline." There goes five days! "We can't do that, we have three months! That's all, to do the whole thing. Where are those five days?" Because nobody knew what I meant by storyline. "Storyline is what you want to say in the museum step-by-step. We go back where it began, to Ozette. And nobody leaves Ozette until we have the storyline. We stay there as long as it takes." (1995)

The museum needed to be more than a warehouse for artifacts. To determine what the museum would become as a concept, the museum planning committee and Jean André went and camped at Ozette for a few days. There, at the site of the historic qʷidičča?atx̌ village, they explored how to organize and respect vast meanings and memories associated with Ozette, tribal history, and family histories.

For days, they walked the beaches, looked at objects coming out of the village site, and reminisced. André encouraged the committee to ask themselves who the museum was for. In an interview with Shirley Johnson, one of the museum planning committee members who worked with André, she explained to me how at Ozette the vision of the museum project shifted crucially. The project shifted to include not only an artifact orientation but also an orientation to people, or living knowledge:

> When it came time for the storyline, we went to Ozette for three days. We camped out there, the whole committee. . . . We looked at pictures of some of the artifacts that came out of the site, and [Makah elder] Ham[ilton Greene] told stories about how those things reminded him of his experiences when he was young, the things that he knew about, how we lived from the sea. The younger members, like me, talked about the little bit that we could remember. Like I could just barely remember my dad using those same halibut hooks, just like the ones that came out of Ozette. We talked about how it was living from the sea, even though it was different in our lifetime. But when I compare what Ham knew with what I knew, he knew so much more. That made me want the knowledge to be passed on, not only to my generation but to the little ones. The museum was to be for the community to teach the youngest ones about what it means to be Makah, since there had been so much change. (Shirley Johnson 1995)

The desire for the community to continue remembering "what it means to be Makah" became a significant objective shaping the subjectivity of the MCRC. The museum was to be more than a display for the public. It was also for the Makah people.

The hopes were that a permanent installation of Ozette objects, placed amid the social space of Neah Bay, would trigger and reinforce memories of what it has meant to be Makah through the generations. "What it means to be Makah" is a lived experience, a feeling, a reality that is difficult to articulate. In some of my conversations with Makah people about tradition and identity, they would pause, stuck on how to express what their heritage meant to them. Then they would say: "I don't know how to explain it, but I know how it *feels*" or "In order for you to understand it, you must be here, live it, *experience* it with us." To try and represent identity in a museum, then, requires representing the unspoken, the feelings, the memories. How was a community museum to do this?

One of the themes to emerge from the conversations among members of the planning committee was that the museum/cultural center should be careful to preserve Ozette village possessions in a manner consistent with the memories and values that have grown out of the qʷidičča?atx̌ way of life. In other words, the museum should not only preserve a harpoon or a weaver's pouch but also the Makah etiquette that was associated with these activities and that is still valued today. It was felt that preserving the sensibilities and memories of Makah history was particularly critical given that the Makah ways of life were quickly changing (Shirley Johnson 1995).

With guidance from Makah elders, such as Hamilton Greene, the museum planning committee decided that the MCRC exhibit galleries should be structured around the seasons that had profoundly set the rhythm of qʷidičča?atx̌ social, economic, and spiritual activities. The committee decided to organize the museum as a walk through the seasons of one year: spring, summer, fall, and winter. Each seasonal exhibit highlighted the activities that predominated during those months, whether whaling, sealing, fishing, shellfish gathering, basketry, or storytelling. The challenge was to show not only how the qʷidičča?atx̌ made their living in a material and technological sense but also how they went about it emotionally and spiritually.

The MCRC shares a concern with other tribal museums/cultural centers about the connection between material artifacts and the emotional content of the past. In 1991 the MCRC hosted an AIMS workshop on Mission and Governance of Tribal Museums. At this Smithsonian-sponsored workshop, Rina Swintzell (Tewa-Santa Clara Pueblo) described what she considered a widespread challenge for Native American museums: "How do we remember some important things about who we have been in the past? And by remember, we began to talk about objects helping us to remember. But the primary thing was to remember a way of life. . . . It's about remembering feelings."[1] Like other Native American communities, the Makah Tribe was very concerned with finding a way to maintain respect for the spirit of their ancestors while inviting the public to look in and appreciate something about the Makah way of life.

Part of the solution was in challenging the convention of the single, objective, curatorial voice that speaks to gallery visitors, particularly through label text. Eliciting understanding in visitors through *feeling* or empathy is one technique for dispelling what Riegel (1996) has called visitor *distanciation* — the common phenomenon of museum visitors remaining passive and emotionally distanced while gazing at an object. Like other Native American communities, the MCRC began to experiment with the notion of voice. In this, they had the support of Jean André and several anthropologists, but the support was not unanimous.

André has been involved in a number of tribal museum projects since the MCRC project. In each he has advocated that in the museum "it is *their* [Native American] voice" that ought to be expressed. It is their story, their compelling historical experiences that ought to determine what visitors who attend the museum learn. Representing Native voices is one of the more recent developments in museology, one that has not been completely accomplished. While collaboration between museums and Native peoples over the past three decades has improved (Swidler et al. 1997; Zimmerman 1996), Native sentiments can still become muffled, even in their community museums.

In a variety of projects involving Native American material culture, André has witnessed the tendency for the scientific viewpoint of archaeological or anthropological consultants to dominate the planning process, particularly with respect to the exhibit text. As André explains it, this is a lost opportunity for the public to be touched by tribal perspectives (1995): "As a curator, if you've studied for many, many years, this is one viewpoint, this is what you can offer. I think it would be wise and excellent for the visitor to hear the other [Native American] voice. That doesn't threaten what we are doing with your [anthropological] research. That means one opinion, but let us also hear the other people. That's what the museum should be. . . . The museum should be a neutral ground where both voices can be heard. . . . Each one of us should have our voice. Let the people be the judge. Let the people speak their way — it's absolutely essential" (1995). This interest in multivocality, or in creating the space for multiple perspectives to coexist, is one of the collaborative innovations that has shaped the MCRC. One of the important ways to achieve it was to gather oral histories from Makah elders about the artifacts that were excavated from Ozette (Cutler 1994; Daugherty 1995, Wessen 1995). The other way was to allow these voices to coexist in the galleries with the analytical perspectives generated by archaeological analyses (Makah or non-Makah). In the tour of the MCRC galleries later in this chapter, I point out some of the effects of the Makah Tribe's commitment to multivocality.

Distressing the Canoe

In its early stages, the MCRC diverged from a model of staged Indianness that André called "Bring back the past, [make] it as a cute scene, or [get] all these guys they send in and cook bannock" (1995). André's point was that the representation was not just *about* Makah people but that it was predominately shaped *by* them.

Makah tribal members replicated a number of Ozette artifacts for the exhibition galleries, including baskets, canoe bailers, clubs, sealskin floats, cedar mats, and canoes for sealing, fishing, and whaling. As we saw in the previous chapter, canoe production was more than merely a technological process; it entailed extensive dialogue with elders who shared autobiographical memories and oral history about making canoes. It was also a spiritual process in that one prepared himself for the art of creating a seagoing craft that would safely navigate challenging waters.

In our interview, André discussed his realization that Makah artisans went beyond artifact replication:

They did the boats, the canoes, and one very special thing happened. I came to [Neah Bay to] look at the big canoe, it was one of the wooden canoes they did. It was all scratched and distressed nicely. That's what we do in exhibit. You know, when you do a table you want to make it old, you get the sandpaper and then you start to scratch it. [I said to them:]

"Not only did you do the canoe, but you distressed the canoe!"

"What do you mean distressed the canoe? We didn't distress the canoe."

"But it's all scratched!"

"We gave it its proper rights. We put it in the creek and literally baptized the canoe and then we paddled it to Canada and back."

And that was their attitude. And that shook me really in my shoes. I said, "My goodness, they paddled it as their forefathers would have done — to Vancouver Island and back so that that canoe can be exhibited. It's not a prop. It's a canoe." And that's the sort of thing which changed my attitude totally, I mean what these people were doing. And the aspect after that, what the museum was, it was quite unique because of that attention to the sensitivity and attention to detail that they put into it. (1995; cf. Cutler 1994)

The attention given to the complete *social process* of producing an object distinguishes the technological finesse of artifact replication from the reintroduction of a living object of Makah culture (figure 19).

Makah staff members went beyond artifact replication when they reconstructed an Ozette longhouse for the museum's winter gallery. The cedar plank longhouse was built outside while the museum

19. *From right to left:* Lance Wilkie, Bill Noel, Kirk Wachendorf, Mike Bowechop, and Scott Tyler or Joe McGimpsey test the canoe created for display in the MCRC. Photo by Ruth Kirk. Courtesy of the photographer.

was under construction. It weathered outside for about a year and hosted numerous parties and salmon bakes. Later, when the museum opened, the longhouse held graduation ceremonies, plays, and a wedding. Again, it was a longhouse, made to be used as a longhouse, not as a museum prop. The point is that the Makah people poured meaning, memory, and respect into the production of the museum. Visitors may perceive that difference in passing through its walls.

Most visitors to the MCRC will not physically encounter all of the ways the MCRC alters or indigenizes the mainstream museum model. Those few who tour the collections storage facility, however, will realize that collections management is another area where the MCRC commits itself to preserving and honoring ways of feeling and remembering. Conventional museums are often concerned with classifying objects under categories, such as tribal affiliation, age, social or technological function, or collector. The MCRC has, in addition to these, used qʷiˑqʷiˑdiččaq categories to shape classification systems and shelving organization.

In my interview with Jeffrey Mauger, he described how Makah and non-Makah staff collaborated to forge new ground: setting up culturally appropriate collections management systems for the Makah people. At least four Makah and non-Makah staff members worked together to carefully preserve Ozette village possessions in a manner consistent with the memories and values that grew out of the qʷidiččaʔaˑtx̌ way of life. These four were former director Ann Renker; former collections manager Jeffrey Mauger; Makah elder and cultural specialist Helma Ward; and Janine Bowechop (Makah), then-curator of collections. In our interview, Mauger recalled a critical transition in collections management philosophy that exemplifies the indigenization of the mainstream museum model.

Initially, Mauger thought the simplest way to physically access the collection would be to index and arrange it as material culture often is in an ethnography: sea mammal hunting gear, amusement games, and so on. At some point, however, he realized that these were English language cognitive categories:

So fifteen, twenty years ago I tried to impose some order and try to make some sense of the collection. I created a category of containers, a physical category and area and that's where I put all the containers — boxes and bowls. It was three or four years ago when I was taking classes in Makah and started to pick up the suffix for containers, which was *sac*, and one day I knew the word for box was *hax̌ʷiˑdukš*. One day it clicked that there was no *sac* on the end of that, meaning it was a container. So I went and asked Ann Renker who was director then, a linguist, "Where's the sac on hax̌ʷiˑdukš?" She said, "Gee, I don't know. I never thought about that." So then the two of us went out and she said, "Well, let's ask Helma Ward." . . . [That's what] led to the collections management approach that we have today where we realize that, in Makah, boxes were *not* containers.

Now, clearly, they were functionary. They [the Ozette villagers] knew they were containers; the point was that they were not classifying them cognitively as containers. . . . This light bulb went on, "Gee, what if we organized the collection based on Makah cognitive categories, rather than English categories?" (1995)

To explain the impact that shifting to Makah cognitive categories had on collections management policies and practices, Mauger described an experience that began with an effort to shelve wooden wedges:

Twenty years ago, canoe paddles were off with canoe gear, wedges were with wedges and maybe woodworking tools, and metal was floating around someplace else in the lab. There's no relation between those other than the fact that wedges and paddles are out of wood. There's no relation in English. . . . When Janine [Bowechop] and I were installing the collection, looking at names we noticed that a number of names are starting with ƛa (barred lambda a), and we physically collected canoe paddles, ƛataʼwačak, . . . Then we had wedges, which were ƛadit. . . . We had chisels, ƛačak, and metal, which is ƛayak. What that literally means is yak is a thing for something, and so metal is a thing for ƛa, whatever ƛa is. OK. We had to physically break out of our own English thinking. . . . Here was this group of tools that started with ƛa, and I could not see any relationship whatsoever between adzes, chisels, wedges, and canoe paddles. So we physically had to put them beside each other and — literally put them on the same range of shelving — and stand back, "What do these have in common?" What they had in common is the working surface is all perpendicular to the plane of the action. . . . A chisel is perpendicular to the action, a wedge is perpendicular to the action, an adze is perpendicular to the action, a canoe paddle is perpendicular to the action. So how did metal fit into that? Well, the metal, the prehistoric iron we found at Ozette was often used in chisels and so it's a thing for this action, and that's where the generic term for metal came from. That's the kind of insight, you see? (1994)

Makah conceptual categories became used not only for organizing the collection but also for stimulating reflection on Makah worldviews codified in their language. Mauger's account highlights the collaborative nature between research and the development of collections management policies.

The MCRC has fully adopted standard scientific archaeological collections management systems. Yet it has adapted these systems to meet a broader set of goals. The goals are not only to preserve the artifacts but also to preserve a living culture. Consequently, the management system is designed to preserve a range of values, including Makah conceptual categories, traditional property ownership values (such as ownership by house/extended family categories), and gender restrictions. This adaptation of the museum — akin to a shift from an object-orientation to a people-orientation — is indigenization of the mainstream museum model.

In our interview, Mauger described the process of transferring traditional values pertaining to gender restrictions to collections management policy:

I asked [Makah elder] Helma [Ward], "What about fishing gear?" She says, "Well, the woman can carry the fishing gear as long as it's kept in the pouch." There's a really neat little pouch. She says, "Oh, the woman can carry the guy's gear down to the canoe, that was no problem." But I said, "Can she handle the hooks and stuff?" Helma said, "No." How do we translate that into tribal collections management? Janine [Bowechop] can move a tray of hooks, but she can't arrange the hooks on that tray. Janine can't move a whaling shaft, a harpoon shaft. She can't move it, she can't touch it. So we'll translate this. Maybe in fifteen years or a hundred years, we survey the village and nobody has that value anymore. There's a new value or a different value that it's OK to do that, in which case we open it up. The point is that we respond; collections management should respond to values so long as they are (1) traditional and (2) held by somebody in the community; again, they don't have to be widespread. But if somebody holds a traditional value—our mission statement, our charter from the Makah Tribal Council is to preserve Makah culture—then we have to be in a position of responding to values rather than creating values. (1995)

MCRC staff members, such as Mauger and Bowechop, have served as faculty in the Smithsonian training programs I described in the previous chapter, supporting other tribes to consider this process of translating, or indigenizing, the mainstream museum model to meet their own needs. By allowing Makah knowledge and perceptions, as coded in language and social etiquette, to structure the Ozette collection, more than objects are preserved.

Preservation extends beyond specific types of knowledge to the structure of knowledge itself and what it reveals about Makah cosmology. The MCRC staff has asserted that curation abides by the philosophy that as long as there are still people subscribing to traditional values, the role of collections management in a tribal museum situation is to support those values rather than to indirectly erode them (Mauger and Bowechop 1995; Mauger 1994).

Other tribal museums and cultural centers have also incorporated curation policies appropriate to community values. The collections policy of the Kahnawake tribal museum, for example, insists that certain objects remain with the appropriate religious keeper on the reservation rather than in the museum. In doing so, the museum complements, rather than replaces, existing systems of traditional curation (Doxtator 1985, 25).

Because the MCRC policies intend to preserve values and sentiments of living Makah culture, they can sometimes disrupt the expectations of researchers and visitors. Public expectation of free and unlimited access to Native American material culture is frustrated by both curation practices that re-acknowledge the sacredness of objects and by the defense of intellectual property rights. Who decides what information is available, who owns it, and what can be done with it? Historically, Native American peoples have not had a large role in influencing the answers to these questions. Because Native

American museums/cultural centers are places where Native American worldviews are more likely to predominate, visitors and researchers can hit a wall in their understanding. Why are these material culture collections treated differently than ethnographic artifacts in other museums?

The writings of ethnomusicologist Frances Densmore record the complex nature of some of the meanings attributed to Makah material objects. As Densmore documented early in the twentieth century, carvings and paintings sometimes represented the spiritual power of the Makahs' creator. It was customary for a man to decorate his personal belongings with the image of an animal seen in his dream, although it might also be a fanciful design (Densmore 1939, 6, 24). Animal representations were often more than simply images of those animals; they could be representations of human ancestors who had transformed and taken the form of an animal (64). Originality and uniqueness of designs were important, too, in recognizing who owned a boat coming into harbor, or whose harpoon had killed a sea mammal (R. Claplanhoo 1995; H. Ward 1995).

Because of this relationship between spirituality, traditional knowledge, and material objects, knowledge has been carefully transmitted in Makah society. Songs and dances are performed carefully so as to respect the owner and the regulated manner of passing down or giving use-rights (H. Ward 1991). Past violations of these Makah protocols by non-Makahs has heightened contemporary tribal response and structured MCRC obligations to protect Makah cultural resources of all kinds. In the past, traditional stories have been published without any tribal permission. Songs have been recorded and entered the public domain without permission (H. Ward 1995). Photos of Ozette objects have been juxtaposed in publications with non-Makah legends. The potential for these kinds of incidents has increased with numerous non-Indian artisans flooding the market with "Indian art."

Certainly, the policing of boundaries between visitors and objects and the disciplining of visitors is common to nearly all museum institutions (Hooper-Greenhill 1991). The policies of the MCRC add another layer to general museum visitor disciplining. MCRC policies embody Makah perspectives that may counter visitors' perceptions of objects as ethnographic artifacts.

Historically, Native American material culture has been treated by mainstream museums as artifacts, or art, which may have had spiritual significance. They were not, however, handled as though they were living objects or gifts from a sacred realm. Hence, the MCRC protocols demand another kind of respect from its visitors. Although a visitor may learn that the Makah people attribute successful carving and other accomplishments to spirit power received through dreams and visions or that the Makahs consider the pre-contact material to be "personal possessions of our ancestors," he or she still might not understand that these values have not left been behind in the past.

The challenge comes in teaching the public that Makah material culture items or traditional knowledge forms must still be cared for with respect due to traditional patterns of ownership.[2] At these moments, conventional views of objects as strictly artifacts or perhaps works of art does not capture the full range of meanings attributed to them by the Makah people. Given that the MCRC straddles both traditional and modern systems of property ownership, the responsibility of the tribal institution is not always clear. Not infrequently, tension arises over the degree to which the MCRC should limit or facilitate access to cultural resources, even to tribal members. As Ann Tweedie has written:

Although all community members and approved outside researchers are permitted to view Ozette artifacts in storage, few Makah tribal members avail themselves of the opportunity and the MCRC makes little attempt to actively promote such community interest and use. It seems that this position stems in part from feelings of some staff that since family affiliation is unknown for these [Ozette] artifacts, no one should be permitted to view them lest design elements or other knowledge be utilized by inappropriate individuals. Thus, the MCRC as an institution must walk a fine line between service to the entire community and adherence to traditional patterns of ownership and control of personal objects and private knowledge. (1999, 191)

Maintaining traditional structures of Makah intellectual property rights, in addition to sacredness, has been a struggle not only within the community but also in the face of popular conceptions of Native American culture. The transmission of songs, stories, oral history, artistic designs, fishing techniques, herbal remedies, and other traditional knowledge is often highly regulated along lines of gender, age, family, village, and tribal lines. These regulations are critical given the spiritual nature of Makah artistic composition.

The MCRC becomes a kind of gateway operating on behalf of the Makah Tribal Council to ensure the Makah Tribe exerts some kind of influence over cross-cultural understandings of knowledge transmission. For example, researchers and scholars are made aware of the special relationship between the Makah Nation and the U.S. federal government when they apply through the MCRC board to conduct research. An "MCRC Statement on Payment and Professional Responsibility Code" makes researchers "cognizant of the implications research can have in the matter of the tribe's relationship with both the federal government and the government of the State of Washington." This professional code is based on the Indian Religious Freedom Act (PL 95-341); the National Historic Preservation Act (PL 96-515), and the Indian Self-Determination Act (PL 93-638). In accordance with the intentions of these laws to protect Native religious, intellectual, and cultural rights, the board requires that any "material published or produced must be reviewed for accuracy by the Board before publication or release."

Tribal museums/cultural centers have emerged as significant mechanisms for demanding respect for intellectual property rights.[3] Through experiencing research restrictions on the collections, archaeologists and others are exposed to knowledge systems that contextualize the artifacts, information not normally available in association with archaeological collections in museums. As such, the protocols are valuable contributions. Because the archaeological materials are considered ancestral possessions, they are cared for with policies appropriate to Makah standards. Consequently, by Makah Tribal Council policy, researchers must apply to the MCRC Board of Trustees before conducting any cultural projects on the reservation, whether they have ethnographic or archaeological focus. For some film directors, anthropologists, archaeologists, and others, such reviews are perceived as constituting obstruction of free access, or the dissemination of knowledge. But the MCRC maintains that "scientists who work with the Ozette materials are constrained by the same value system as the ancestors who created those materials five hundred years ago" (Mauger and Bowechop 1995, 4).

"The Ozette Houses Are Canoes": The MCRC Galleries

It may seem remarkable to many readers that I have not described the exhibition galleries in any detail until this late in the book, the very detail that often comes to mind first when one thinks of a museum. This is, however, altogether intentional. One could begin and end with a detailed description and interpretive analysis of the galleries at the MCRC. This would mean "reading" the labels, floor plans, and object arrangements of the exhibit galleries almost as though they were the text of a book. These analyses, however, are sometimes labeled "closer to travel writing than to ethnography or historical research" (Clifford 1992, 214). Like other scholars, however, I find this approach invites the saying, You can't judge a book by its cover.[4] In other words, no matter what museum you look at, the exhibition galleries are only one expression of the institution's identity. More often than not, museum staff members never get to accomplish their ideal plans for the galleries. One needs to know the history of the surrounding community, the collections, the staff, and the mission statement in order to understand how the museum sees itself and is seen by others.

The analysis of museum subjectivity must look *through* the museum, using the museum as a window onto various historical issues and cultural processes. In the case of the MCRC, if we were to focus solely on the exhibition galleries, we would not recognize its cultural center aspect, its role as a significant site of remembering and adaptation.

Nonetheless, the exhibition galleries are primarily what off-reservation visitors to the MCRC see. The important question remains: When Native American peoples adopt a Western institution, like the museum, what happens to it? How and what does the MCRC communicate? Does the incorporation of Native voices alter stereotypical representations of Native Americans in museums, somehow changing what non-Native peoples see and hear in tribal community museums? In the remaining portion of this chapter, I encourage readers to connect their reading of the MCRC's galleries to all the historical issues and cultural processes that have been described in previous chapters.

The introductory gallery is the permanent gallery that has changed the most over the past twenty years. The original design for the introductory gallery has only been implemented since 1995. Before that time, the galleries did not explain how Ozette was related to the creation of the museum. As Wachendorf explained to me, that placed a significant interpretive burden on the Makah staff and on one or two videos that were made available to visitors. In 1995, however, the introductory gallery was renovated, and later dedicated at a community dinner. There, the contributions of Jean André, and many other long-standing friends of the MCRC were honored.

Beginning with the spring gallery and continuing through the summer, fall, and winter galleries, the MCRC attempts to disrupt visitor distanciation, or emotional distance, by placing artifacts and visitors in simulated cultural and natural contexts. Some of the techniques for doing this are appropriated from largely conventional natural history museum exhibits.

Let us begin a tour where visitors are always encouraged to begin, in the introductory gallery next to the gift shop. There, visitors may read the following text panel: "The Ozette houses are canoes carrying scientists into a world that respects the oral history of our people. The Ozette houses are war clubs against ignorance and hostility. The Ozette houses are thunder and lightning for Makahs, voices from the past illuminating our heritage." When visitors begin their walk through the permanent galleries, then, they are introduced to a distinctly Makah metaphor for entering their way of seeing the world: getting into their canoe. Reference to the canoe offers the visitor an invitation to understand the Makah people, on the Makahs' terms. The museum galleries frame objects as what social scientists would call precontact Makah artifacts. But they are also presented as possessions of their ancestors from one of the traditional villages, Ozette. In establishing this sense of affiliation and continuity between Ozette ancestors and contemporary Makahs, the Makah cultural center and community museum begins to redirect and refocus the Euro-American lens that frames the image of their people.

In the curved and low-ceilinged introductory corridor, critical juxtapositions immediately occur. Reproductions of late-eighteenth-century artist renderings and late-nineteenth- and early-twentieth-century photographs — what visitors are probably accustomed to seeing — are placed side-by-side with contemporary photos of elders and labels sharing excerpts of oral history. These ways of knowing Ozette and its importance to contemporary Makah identity are presented alongside descriptions of archaeological methods and interpretations of Ozette. The completion of MCRC's narrative through its new introductory gallery, with its multivocality, has been essential.

From the MCRC's introductory section, the galleries dramatically open up into the broad and high-ceilinged spring gallery, the first in the seasonally organized galleries. The focal point of this gallery is an enormous reproduction of the famous historic photograph by Asahel Curtis documenting a Makah whaler poised before thrusting his harpoon into a whale (see figure 9). Enlarged to some twenty feet high, this photograph provides a dramatic backdrop to a collection of artifact replicas gathered at its base. This collection includes full-scale whaling and sealing canoes outfitted with woven, cedar mats, sealskin floats, harpoons, bailers, and a variety of other traditional sea-mammal hunting tools that visitors may handle and inspect. As described in the previous chapter, these replicas were produced by contemporary Makah community members, sometimes in collaboration with non-Makah artists or anthropologists.

To either side of this dramatic focal point, tall glass exhibit cases incorporate Makah voices to interpret the late precontact era traditions of whale and seal-hunting. Through the inclusion of first-person voice and oral historical style exhibit text, Makah staff have provided visitors with the opportunity to become aware of contemporary Makah presence, to think about how oral tradition has passed down memories from previous generations. The seal-hunting case, for example, contains the following exhibit text:

> Some Makahs were whalers, some were fishermen and some were seal hunters like me. I was always fascinated by that long slender sealing spear. Throwing this spear with a harpoon attached called for added finesse rather than the brute strength of the whale hunter. I liked the smaller canoe and the fast thrashing action of an enraged seal that had just been harpooned. I considered all of my prey as food and clothing for the family. Tonight we will have fresh seal meat. Tomorrow my wife and grandmother will render the fat to make seal oil. This winter we will enjoy smoked seal meat as a result of our hunting today. I will never tire of this calling that requires in return that I be physically and spiritually prepared to face the ocean and overcome the seal in his own environment.

This inclusion of a transcribed oral historical narrative continues the possibility begun in the introductory gallery for visitors to rethink Ozette artifacts as family possessions and to think about how they relate to Makah humanity, memories, and values.

The visitor response to the presence of Makah voices in the MCRC galleries has been very positive over the past twenty years. After visiting the MCRC in 1991, a forestry service archaeologist specifically mentioned the aspect of voice when asked to describe his experience in a survey: "It is so interesting to read the interpretation of a peoples [sic] heritage. From their point of view. As an archaeologist I am used to giving a scientific interpretation which is only part of the story. You, the people, provide the other part — the poetry and spirit of that life. Thank you." According to Kirk Wachendorf, visitors respond favorably to this type of narrative in the galleries. Yet they still rely heavily upon Makah interpreters or tour guides to answer questions. Often, these questions reveal that the tribal museum/community center is a badly needed forum for dialogue. Such a forum opens the possibility for dissolution of stereotypic ways of thinking about Native peoples.

In my conversations with Wachendorf I realized that visitors expect representations of Native Americans as part of past national or natural heritage. Most visitors expect that representations will be distinctly separate from their own personal, non-Native history. But the MCRC has created the opportunity for non-Native visitors to encounter living Native peoples and to see something of themselves in representations of Native American history. It can be a place for a new understanding of one's own (non-Native history). Wachendorf told me about one of the many times this occurred:

Visitors ask [me], "This is Ozette, but what's happened between then and now?" They may be surprised, uncomfortable, or horrified to hear about what happened. I had a lady come in and we talked about this. She had never heard anything about the boarding schools and stuff like that. I recommended some things for her to read. She left, and apparently dug into it. She came back and actually apologized. She said, "I'm sorry for what my people have done to you." She was almost crying. Some people have left here crying. I don't mean for that to happen. It makes me very uncomfortable. I know they weren't the ones that did it. Other people have a real hard time believing that what I'm saying is true. They say, "This really happened to you guys?" Do they think that I'm kidding? Most people are embarrassed to learn about this part of their history. They just don't know. (1995)

Elements in the permanent exhibition galleries are likely to stimulate provocative questions from visitors and lead to discussions of difficult historical issues. One of these elements is the presence of Makah language on the exhibit labeling.

The sealing exhibition in the spring gallery contains bilingual label text. In the mid-1990s, the MCRC began to accomplish a long-term goal of making exhibit text bilingual. Sharing the Makah names for objects perpetuates the original and appropriate names of the objects and educates Makah and non-Makah peoples about the original meaning of the term. The sealing exhibit case contains bilingual labels that identify Ozette sealing gear:

čapxtuˑp seal harpoon insert blade (mussel shell)
　čapxtuˑp
skim along surface-stem intensifier
thing that intensively skims along the surface

ƛataˑwačak paddle (yew)
　ƛataˑwačak
go along-epenthetic-device for
"device for going along"

Bilingual labels such as these communicate the qʷiˑqʷiˑdiččaq name, English name, morphemic analysis, morpheme-by-morpheme translation of the qʷiˑqʷiˑdiččaq name, and the free translation of the morphemic analysis. Although the Makah people were historically discouraged from speaking qʷiˑqʷiˑdiččaq, MCRC incorporates the language into as many aspects of the institution as possible. In this way, intellectual dimensions of Makah history and worldview are incorporated into the cultural center and presented to the public and the community. As Wachendorf related to me, bilingual labels can also generate questions about the state of the spoken language today. In turn, this opens the opportunity to discuss the Makahs' experiences with government-supported schools and language restrictions described in earlier chapters.

Innovations, such as bilingual labeling, are not present throughout, however. In the spring gallery, as in other exhibits, large black and white photomurals are prominent. These photomurals are reproductions of E. S. Curtis's staged representations of Native peoples, such as of the seal hunter. Although these photos may encourage visitors to shift their focus from the Ozette items on display to the people who used them in precontact times, the MCRC did not take advantage of the opportunity to discuss the history of the staging of these photographs.[5] The summer and fall galleries also contain cases that suggest little substantial modification of conventional exhibit technologies. The Wood Technology, Tools, and Woodworking cases all follow the predictable archaeological focus on how natural materials are employed in toolmaking and what various technological processes — such as kerfing and halibut hook or wedge construction — look like. Following this, in the Plant Gathering section, three photomurals depict women dressed in cedar bark gathering shellfish, bark, and other materials. Some remarkable Ozette artifacts, such as a pouch containing cattails, twig bundles, and cherry bark bundles, illustrate the diversity of plant life harvested by women. Again, the photomurals potentially shift visitors' object-focus to the Ozette village residents.

As visitors approach the next case, Stone Technology, the contextualizing strategies intensify through exhibit labeling, dioramas, and simulated village environments. The exhibit labeling once again overtly shifts to the oral historical style: "I was told that often times on sealing expeditions a shark would follow closely behind the canoe. Since the sharks were so huge and unpredictable, a method of diversion was developed using a fairly large rock. When the shark swam close by, the rock was dropped from the canoe. The shark would follow the rock down never to return." As in the Sealing case in the spring gallery, the individual identity of the speaker is not given, although the voice clearly encourages visitors to consider the richness of Makah oral tradition. To the visitors' left, a painted diorama offers an uncanny representation of the beach area just north of Ozette, looking toward Shi Shi Beach. At the foot of the painting, shells, driftwood, campfire remnants, and a cutaway of a dune prepare visitors for a transition from representations of the natural environment to a simulated longhouse village environment.

A ramp of wooden planks invites visitors to walk along a slanted, earthen slope and continue to the next gallery. To either side of the ramp hand-split cedar planks are tied to posts, simulating the walls of an Ozette longhouse. On the earthen slope, whalebones have been arranged in a linear pattern to simulate an Ozette village drainage feature discovered by archaeologists.[6] When visitors reach the top of this ramp the exhibit cases of the winter gallery and the entrance to the reconstructed Ozette longhouse awaits them on their right (figure 5).

Inside the reconstructed longhouse, visitors are free to walk throughout the darkened interior.[7] Each of the living areas, reconstructed to house the several families that inhabit the longhouse, contain furnishings for visitors to explore. These replicated Ozette artifacts include broad, cedar plank benches, woven cedar bark mats, fire hearths, and weaving, spinning, or carving projects that were interrupted and left as they were. Visitors also hear the voices of elders singing or storytelling in qʷiqʷidiččaq. Freshly smoked salmon scents the longhouse from its rafters. A longhouse door opens onto a painted diorama simulating the Ozette beach, where a partly carved canoe awaits completion.

These features seem designed to draw from the visitor an appreciation for the aesthetics of a way of life. In one of MCRC's surveys, a visitor was moved to comment on his response: "One of the best museums and presentations I have ever seen in my life — museum helps one enter spirit, vision, way-of-life of Makahs. One hears sound of surf . . . smells saltiness of sea . . . recognizes significance and symbolism of whales, seals, salmon, etc. . . . the blessing of earth, sky, and water. Thank you."

The permanent galleries end with a long series of exhibit cases in the winter gallery representing significant social activities and material technologies. These showcase some of the most remarkable Ozette artifacts, including carved planks and an impressive ceremonial whale saddle decorated with hundreds of sea mammal teeth (see figure 20). In the wealth of symbolism case, the labeling touches upon the spiritual importance of ceremonials: "Much of the Makahs' expression came in songs and dances and were usually presented at large ceremonies which were mostly held during the winter months. In addition, carvings from the artists, success of the hunters and fishermen were all attributed to the spiritual power which individuals received through dreams, visions, and sometimes after one has been seriously ill." Makah interpretive guides frequently develop various issues in the contemporary community related to the content of this exhibit case, issues such as the ceremonial role of chiefs, or heads of family, and traditional patterns of owning ceremonial privileges, or *tupaat*.[8] Other Northwest Coast tribal museums also prompt questions about property ownership—for example, the Kwagiulth Museum and Cultural Center in Cape Mudge Village, British Columbia (Clifford 1992, 226–27).

Before completing the preferred circular path back to the gift shop, visitors walk through the final exhibition space, a relatively small sunroom used as a temporary exhibition gallery. This space is intended to host visitors who have questions that Makah interpreters, such as Wachendorf, deal with on a daily basis: What happened after Ozette? In the original plan there was a main gallery devoted to the representation of recent historic and contemporary Makah life; however, lack of funds at the time the MCRC was built prevented the execution of what André has called "from five hundred years old until tomorrow," or the "missing page" (1995)—a classic example of the disparity between the ideal, planned museum/cultural center and the real, accomplished one.

Without the temporary exhibition gallery, the MCRC would be limited to a representation of Ozette life in the precontact past. Without the content presented by exhibitions in the temporary gallery, a large gap would be left between the institution's mission and the content of its galleries. Without the more reflexive style of the bookends—the introductory and temporary galleries—the permanent galleries would tend toward the reproduction of a genre of the ethnographic present, a timeless, authentic, and distant cultural space in the past (Fabian 1983).

In an effort to counteract stereotypes and educate the public about late historic and contemporary Makah presence, the MCRC has produced a series of temporary exhibits that address this shortcoming. The MCRC has mixed historical and aesthetic exhibition styles to create temporary exhibits, such as *Portrait in Time: Photographs of the Makah by Samuel Morse, 1896–1903* (Marr 1987); *Riding in His Canoe: The Continuing Legacy of Young Doctor*; and *In Honor Of Our Weavers: Makah Cultural and Research Center's Twentieth Anniversary*. Collectively, these exhibits have documented missionary influence, effects of tourist trade and cash economy, and processes of cultural adaptation and crisis.

As I have described in greater detail elsewhere (Erikson 1999), temporary exhibits such as *Riding in His Canoe* advance the efforts of the permanent Ozette galleries to incorporate Makah oral history, worldviews, and first-person voice in shaping a distinctly Makah representation of Makah history and contemporary identity.

In this chapter I have described my understanding of how the MCRC has indigenized the model of the mainstream museum. The Makah people have modified the conventions of museology as they have balanced two needs: (1) cultural preservation and education of their own community and (2) negotiating the standards of professionalism set by disciplines of museology, archaeology, and linguistic anthropology. This process of appropriating the museum and translating it to other cultural idioms is by no means limited to the Neah Bay community; rather, it is widespread among indigenous communities throughout the Western Hemisphere, as well as throughout Third World populations globally.[9]

More than twenty years ago, Edward P. Alexander noted a trend among museums, a movement toward becoming cultural centers (1979, 215–29). He noted that in order to reach out to wider audiences, many mainstream museums in the late twentieth century had begun to adopt a broad range of cultural programming. This meant hosting performances in music, drama, and dance; it also meant serving as an attractive setting for cocktail and dinner parties. Alexander used *cultural center* as an umbrella term to cover the shift in museums toward activities generally associated with theaters, art schools, and so on (Alexander 1979, 228). Because I find there is often still a lack of understanding about the difference between expanding styles of programming and forwarding the preservation of living cultures, I pause here on Alexander's use of the term *cultural center*.

In his discussion of the cultural center trend, Alexander also noted that relatively marginalized communities in American society were becoming hosts for a type of institution that had not historically served them. He called these "neighborhood museums" and cited El Museo del Barrio in New York City, the Anacostia Neighborhood Museum in Washington DC, the Pueblo Cultural Center in

Albuquerque, New Mexico, and Daybreak Star in Seattle, Washington, as examples. Alexander astutely observed that these are good examples of both the Native American museum/cultural center movement and its corollary in several historically marginalized (in his article, African American and Puerto Rican) groups in the United States. Asian American populations, too, have been appropriating the museum and translating it to their community needs for collaboratively producing knowledge and exploring the meanings of their own past (Wei Tchen 1992).

Mainstream museums diversifying their programming due to fiscal crisis, cultural irrelevancy, or political pressure is not the same as socially marginalized communities founding and altering museums for the purpose of cultural survival of their people. As Topper Carew once said, "Community museums have always existed in the black community, on street corners, in backyards, on stoops. It's just that it's a living museum" (in Alexander 1979, 227). In other words, the type of cultural center that is the topic of this book has been emanating from communities whose populations have been under stress to assimilate but who still want to continue their ways of knowing, their values, their cultural distinctiveness. None of this, of course, precludes accommodating the standards of the surrounding society. As Clifford has noted, tribal museums are locally based but must participate in national and global arenas. They appropriate at the same time that they must adapt to and oppose museum conventions (Clifford 1992, 226). While cultural centers certainly entail reconstructions and rediscoveries of sometimes forgotten pasts, the processes of research, interpretation, representation, and narration are based on living communities intent upon perpetuating themselves.

Conclusion

Exhibiting Whaling

In the summer of 1997 my family and I took a detour in our annual trip to Seattle and the Makah reservation to see *Whales: The Enduring Legacy*, a temporary exhibit at the Royal British Columbia Museum (RBCM). The opening of this exhibit was a topic of much discussion by the MCRC staff because Ozette artifacts had been lent to the RBCM for the exhibit. Overall, the staff seemed pretty pleased with the presentation of Makah materials. I was intrigued. It was extremely rare for Ozette materials to leave the reservation on loan. I knew that the Makah relationship with the RBCM staff had been a long one and that the RBCM's exhibit designer, Jean André, had contributed to the subjectivity of the MCRC.

The RBCM exhibit provided an opportunity to reflect on another aspect of the Native American museum movement. Has the collaborative production of Makah autoethnographies, or self-portraits, in the MCRC had any impact on representations at mainstream institutions, such as the RBCM and the Seattle Art Museum? Do institutions like the MCRC successfully translate indigenous perspectives cross-culturally and modify the subjectivity of other museums?

When I entered *Whales: The Enduring Legacy* at the RBCM, I first focused on the light dappling the darkened walls and ceiling. I later learned this was meant to create an underwater effect, simulating a marine environment for the apparent centerpiece of the gallery. This centerpiece was an installation called the superpod — an eclectic clustering of a whale skeleton suspended from the ceiling, several ceremonial masks representing whales, a large dugout canoe, and a six-thousand-pound cannon for harpooning whales.

Competing for my attention to the superpod were recordings of whale voices, slide projections of other marine mammals, and historic film footage of whaling. After an initial struggle with where to begin my circuit through the exhibit, I noticed that banners suspended from the ceiling marked portions of the gallery that had been developed by different departments of the museum. The sections titled Ritual, Myth, and Legend; Evolution and Biology; The Hunt (including an aboriginal whaling section); and Images and Products of the Whale embodied a rare effort on the part of the RBCM to prepare an interdisciplinary exhibit that integrated historical, biological, and anthropological approaches.

Not surprisingly, Ozette artifacts were incorporated in the *Whales* exhibit to represent the history of aboriginal whale hunting. What was remarkable was how the presentation of the Ozette artifacts differed from the rest of the exhibit. In a telephone conversation with Peter McNair, one of the curators of *Whales*, he described the various ways the RBCM collaborated with Native American peoples of the Northwest Coast to produce the exhibit. The RBCM consulted with many tribes, including the Nuuchahnulth, Makah, Kwakwaka'wakw, and Gitskan peoples. Ceremonial masks were borrowed from U'Mista Cultural Center and the Campbell River Museum; whaling artifacts were borrowed from the Nuuchahnulth people; Native language consultants provided ceremonial names for different whale species; and descendants of families who owned and loaned ritual property were consulted as to how particular pieces should be exhibited.

McNair explained to me that in planning the interdisciplinary exhibit the RBCM wanted to represent the ancient history of whale-human relations through archaeology. This led McNair to get in touch with the MCRC and to appear before the Makah Whaling Commission. Standing in the aboriginal whaling section, The Hunt, I could see how the staff of the MCRC had influenced the exhibit. Several exhibit cases featured Ozette whaling artifacts. Most distinctive was the shift in curatorial voice. In no other section did I witness a shift to a first-person voice and to a personal, conversational, or experiential perspective. The text accompanying a whale-bone club, for example, read "This club was used to enforce the law of our people and to protect our families and properties." The text accompanying a canoe paddle read, "Paddles are very personal tools. Your measurements are used to make a paddle that will fit you perfectly. Many hours went into shaping this paddle from yew wood." The distinctive, yet still anonymous curatorial voice of this section was signaled by red-on-black exhibit text, in contrast to the white-on-black used elsewhere. Similar to some of the recent modifications to galleries at the MCRC, Makah language and conceptual categories were used to identify the materials in the cases.

According to McNair, the extremely short preparation time of this temporary exhibit precluded any extensive Native American consultation. Yet in the context of a unique interdisciplinary endeavor with an extremely short preparation time, it is impressive that Native American communities had any impact on the *Whales* exhibition. Unlike the rest of the exhibit, the portion featuring Ozette materials shifted curatorial voice and employed Makah conceptual categories. It appeared that collaborations between the MCRC and the RBCM have done more than influence the tribal museum/cultural center. Some of the autoethnographic strategies that attempt to humanize Native American peoples are being translated across institutional boundaries. Mainstream museums are listening. Their subjectivities are being affected, opening possibilities for visitors to hear different voices, to listen differently through exposure to a multivocal curatorial voice.

The RBCM is not the only mainstream museum that is listening, collaborating, and restructuring how knowledge is presented to the public through their relationship with the MCRC. The Seattle Art Museum also is. In the 1970s Steve Brown was working with the Burke Museum at the University of Washington–Seattle. By the time I interviewed him in 1995, he was curating Native American collections at the Seattle Art Museum. His earlier relationship with the Makah people in setting up their own museum/cultural center (in addition to his extensive experience with other Native American tribes and artisans) paved the way for Makah and other Native American sensibilities to influence the representations at the Seattle Art Museum.

In a tour through the Native American art galleries, Brown pointed out for me all of the ways that the members of a Native American advisory council—including Kirk Wachendorf—had modified the Seattle Art Museum's way of doing business. As in the MCRC galleries, historic photographs had been incorporated in installations of Northwest Coast art objects. Using photographs to provide art with context or its historic social significance is more unusual for an art museum. Brown explained to me how it came about: "It was the motivation of the Native advisory council as a group that established . . . the amount of historic and contemporary contextualizing photography that's in the exhibit. . . . What they were trying to accomplish by that was to show visitors to the museum that these weren't just isolated objects of art in the sense that art is an isolated object in American culture. . . . Part of the motivation was to get [visitors to recognize] Native peoples interacting with the objects in the exhibit in the form of photography" (1995). The Native American advisory council was translating an autoethnographic strategy into the galleries of the Seattle Art Museum. This strategy brought *people* — not just the objects — to the public's attention to counteract what Cruikshank has called a Western aesthetic dominated by fetishized objects (1992, 7). Including photographs of living or deceased individuals whose *names* could be identified was one of the means to accomplish this.

In an effort to incorporate Native American sensibilities into the Seattle Art Museum's representations, the Native advisory council also concerned itself with the issue of voice. Brown described how this affected the exhibit technologies and content:

But [the advisory council] also felt that it was important not only to get images of people, but as often as possible the direct words of people. So that, as much as anything, is the reason why there are a lot of quotes — either from Native speakers historically or historians contemporarily — accompanying the objects. In some cases, it is a Native voice quoted and identified by name

and tribal affiliation and date that showed or introduces an object or introduces the importance of an object or the historical
background of an object in the permanent installation. . . .

Some people on the Native advisory council felt very
strongly that to have not only the written words of Native
peoples speaking about the objects but also to be able to hear
the languages, not just to have the names — native terms for
the objects on the labels which also comes from this same motivation — but to have the sound of it in the space. For one
thing, in a spiritual sense, to comfort the spirits that accompany the objects into that space so that they can hear the sound
of their own voices, the sound of their own language in the
space from time to time and so that other people can be exposed to the beauty of the sound of the languages, the beauty
of the melodies of the songs, the beauty of the rhythm of the
speech-making and the storytelling. (1995)

Following this advice, the permanent Northwest Coast art installation in the Hauberg Gallery included tribal song recordings. Conventional curatorial voice was further disrupted by another Makah
tribal member, Greg Colfax. Colfax's open letters, written in first-
person voice to his ancestors made up some of the interpretive
labeling. In these letters Colfax explored the multiple meanings attributed to objects on display, including his own very personal memories associated with them. Brown reported that many visitors were
touched by the poignancy of this exhibit labeling and had requested
copies of the letters.

According to Brown, the Native American advisory council moved
the subjectivity of the Seattle Art Museum toward an awareness of
living Native American peoples and away from the paradigm of art
objects devoid of social relationships. The advisory council encouraged the Seattle Art museum to think about the objects not only as
authentic and precious artworks but as living objects, or extensions
of human encounters with a spiritual realm.

Both of these brief examples point toward how the subjectivities of mainstream museums are slowly, albeit sometimes inconsis-

tently, undergoing transformation through collaboration with Native American peoples.

Hunting Whales

Whale hunting was once a significant spiritual, social, and economic practice for the qʷidičča?a·tx̌, and they were adamant about securing the right to it in their 1855 treaty with the U.S. government. Although the Makah people still enjoy occasional meals of salmon, halibut, sea urchin, gooseneck barnacles, and many other sea creatures, gray whale has not been a part of their diet since they stopped whale hunting early in the twentieth century. By the 1920s, the whale population, decimated by commercial hunting, could no longer support this tradition (Pascua 1991).

In 1995 the Makah Tribe announced its intention to resume hunting the gray whale because this species had recently been removed from the endangered species list. This announcement generated considerable commotion internationally among anti-whaling activists and effectively launched the Makah people into the international news arena—a place already familiar because of the Ozette excavation.

Journalists and TV crews traveled from as far away as Norway and Japan to feature the Makahs and their territory on the northwestern tip of the Olympic Peninsula. These nations were particularly interested in the Makahs' intention to resume whaling as they have historically challenged the international ban on whaling and sought loopholes in it. As an anthropologist researching how tribal museums articulate community history and contemporary self-determination, I felt privileged to witness how the MCRC became an arena for international dialogue. For me, the whaling controversy highlighted the way tribal museums become critical points of encounter for processes of knowledge-making and remembering.

With the advent of the whaling controversy, the museum became a kind of pilgrimage site for media. Reporters and television crews were drawn to the museum by the historical photographs, linguistic and oral historical documentation, and precontact material culture from the Ozette archaeological site. All of these document traditional Makah lifeways, including the longevity, intensity, and nature of the whaling tradition. The museum exhibits also represent Makah whaling practices.

For those who visit the MCRC's representations of lifeways during Ozette and subsequent time periods, it is obvious that whaling remains significant to contemporary Makah identity. In addition to the whale motifs on the sign outside the MCRC, an artistic assemblage of whalebones in the introductory gallery initially alerts visitors to the presence of whales in Makah historical experience. Next, the permanent galleries — organized by season and featuring their associated subsistence activities — begin with an explanation of springtime whaling and sealing traditions. The text of the first exhibit case in the main gallery explains the importance of whaling:

While the Makah were noted for their ability as fishermen and seal hunters, they were probably most noted for their exploits as whale hunters. More than anything else, whale hunting utilized almost every technical skill possessed by the Makahs, from the building of the canoes to the development of the equipment, the intense physical training, the fulfillment of spiritual preparations for the hunt, and extraordinary knowledge of the ocean. The whaling canoe holds a crew of eight men with each man having a specific task to perform throughout the entire whale hunt. Once the whale was harpooned, float bags made of hair seal skins were attached to the harpoon line and were thrown into the water as a means of tiring the whale. The actual killing of the whale was done by a special lance. Once this was done, a man dove into the water and sewed the whale's mouth shut to help prevent the whale from sinking after he was dead. The whale was then towed ashore and was divided among the people of the village. More than anything else, the whale hunt represented the ultimate in both physical and spiritual preparedness and the wealth of the Makah Indian culture.

The media has been drawn not only to these narrations of the history and technology of whale hunting but also to the dramatic centerpiece of this spring season gallery—reproductions of whaling and sealing canoes and their equipment. Visitors may walk around and touch these canoes, carved from cedar trees. On the wall behind the canoe, a photographic image attributed to Asahel Curtis — enlarged to some twenty feet high — documents a Makah whaler hurling a lance into the back of a whale (see figure 1).

By way of curating their exhibits and archives, the MCRC has become one of the possible stages for projecting Makah voice(s), for projecting Makah interpretations of why recuperating whaling matters to many community members. Narrations of Makah history draw from the museum's library and the collection of Ozette artifacts. A staff member can point out passages in several ethnographies, including, for example, Densmore's *Nootka and Quileute Music* (1939), which detail the significant presence of whaling in Makah ceremonial life early in the twentieth century. Densmore detailed how Makah Wilson Parker described potlatches organized by successful whalers. In these potlatches, special dancers wore prayer garb, imitated the motions of a whale, and shook a whaler's rattle of elk horn.

According to oral history gathered by Densmore (1939) and James Gilcrest Swan (1870), the area around the dorsal fin of the whale was ceremonially significant. When whale meat was distributed on the beach, the dorsal fin area, or whale saddle, was hung, decorated, and treated ceremonially for days. Apparently, whaling-related ceremonies took place in the presence of the whale's saddle or in the presence of a wooden effigy of the saddle (Swan 1870, 21–22). One of these wooden effigies — inlaid with more than seven hundred sea mammal teeth — was excavated at Ozette and is now on exhibit at the MCRC (figure 20). Remarkable artifacts, such as the wooden effigy of the whale saddle, are available for staff members or other interpretive guides to point out as they explain the history of Makah whaling.

In the wake of save-the-whales campaigns — the *Free Willy* and *Free Willy II* movies and the saga of repatriating the whale, Keiko, to his

20. Ceremonial whale "saddle" or effigy — excavated from Ozette — inlaid with hundreds of sea mammal teeth, each tooth representing a successful whale hunt. Photo by Eric Long and Keely Parker. Courtesy of the MCRC.

original homeland in Iceland — the Makah people have faced considerable anti-whaling sentiment. The Sea Shepherd Society and P.A.W.S. (Progressive Animal Welfare Society) have led very high profile campaigns against the Makahs' intention to whale. Some of the more intense elements of this anti-whaling strategy have included threats to destroy Makah whaling vessels, blockading the Neah Bay harbor, and swamping the annual Makah Days gathering with protestors (Mapes 1998b). Not all animal rights organizations have made the same choice, however. Greenpeace, for example, has maintained a low profile, choosing not to challenge indigenous rights secured by treaty (Tizon 1998) and citing that other factors pose a greater threat to whale populations (Tizon 1999).

In the early morning of May 17, 1999, Makah whalers paddled their thirty-two-foot hand-carved cedar canoe, the Hummingbird, off the coast of Point of Arches. Anti-whaling protestors were absent because days before the U.S. Coast Guard had confiscated their boats.

For months, the media had shadowed the movements of the cedar canoe and its crew, prompting one *Seattle Times* television critic to describe the whale hunting controversy as "this region's own CNN-style epoch" (Verhovek 1999). Despite this, on the morning of the successful hunt, the U.S. Coast Guard and National Marine Fisheries Service observers looked on without the protestors. Motorized Makah support boats stood ready. In her home, Makah elder Helma Ward lay motionless in bed following the belief that female relatives must observe certain taboos to ensure the success of the hunt (Gunther 1942, 67–68).

Pulling up alongside a thirty-foot juvenile female gray whale, harpooner Theron Parker stabbed the whale with his harpoon. With the whale towing the canoe by the harpoon line, the motorized chase boat pulled alongside and shot the whale in the vicinity of the brain with two bullets from a .50 caliber rifle. With the help of two fishing boats, the whalers refloated the sinking whale and towed it to Neah Bay harbor where a crowd of tribal members had spent hours waiting for their arrival. As they approached the harbor with an accompaniment of four other canoes from neighboring tribes, the whalers detached the whale from the fishing boat and pulled it to shore with their canoe. After a jubilant landing and a ceremonial dusting of the crew and carcass with eagle down, tribal members hauled the whale — hand over hand — onto the beach with the towline. Over a span of several days, the Makah people butchered the whale, cooked the meat, rendered its oil, and hosted a parade and large potlatch celebration for hundreds in the high school gym.

The *Seattle Times* received hundreds of phone calls, letters, faxes, and e-mails — many of them laced with hateful or racist remarks. Communications from protestors outnumbered those from supporters at a 10 to 1 ratio (Tizon 1999). As one journalist characterized it, "Blood has spilled, and a door has opened to all manner of incivilities. The public discussion has become a free-for-all. Political correctness, for better or worse, has gone out the window" (Tizon 1999).

One of the main objections to Makah recuperation of their whaling tradition, especially by the Sea Shepherd Society (perhaps the most visible opponent to Makah whaling) is based on the conviction that the Makah people are opening a Pandora's box on commercial whaling (Watson 1999a, 1999b). The fear is that if the Makah Tribe successfully uses *cultural necessity* as justification for hunting, others will be emboldened to cite cultural necessity, such as other Northwest Coast aboriginal groups in the United States and Canada, as well as in Norway, Japan, and Iceland.

As has happened elsewhere, the process of asserting *animal* rights, has brought *human* rights and cultural survival issues under attack (Wenzel 1991). Although the Makah right to hunt whale is secured by their 1855 treaty with the U.S. government, the specifications of the International Whaling Commission (IWC) are shaping the debate. One of the exceptions to the worldwide ban on whaling is *aboriginal subsistence*, an exception that requires demonstration of a continuing tradition of hunting and eating whales (Blow 1998). The Makah people have negotiated this stipulation with arguments such as the following: "Many of our tribal members feel that our health problems result from the loss of our traditional seafood and sea-mammal diet. We would like to restore the meat of the whale to that diet. We also believe that the problems that are troubling our young people stem from lack of discipline and pride and we hope that the restoration of whaling will help restore that. But we also want to fulfill the legacy of our forefathers and restore a part of our culture that was taken from us" (Johnson 1998). Anti-whaling activists seek to undermine these cultural arguments by highlighting the modernity of the Makah people (for example, the use of modern technology in the hunt). As Paul Watson of the Sea Shepherd Society stated on the NBC Today Show following the successful hunt, "This is the most expensive whale hunt in history, and for what? Fun. . . . We don't see any tradition in this" (Watson 1999b).

Some of the submissions to the *Seattle Times* reveal how the whaling issue has unraveled some fragile seams holding back general, anti-Indian sentiments:

These peoples want to rekindle their traditional way of life by killing an animal that has probably twice the mental capacity they have. These idiots need to use what little brains they have to do something productive besides getting drunk and spending federal funds to live on. (Tizon 1999)

Hey, I think we should also be able to take their land if they can take our whales. Publish this article but don't use our last names. We wouldn't want to lose our scalps. (Tizon 1999)

I am anxious to know where I may apply for a license to kill Indians. My forefathers helped settle the West and it was their tradition to kill every Redskin they saw. "The only good Indian is a dead Indian," they believed. I also want to keep faith with my ancestors. (Tizon 1999.)

Such are the racial hatreds, drawing from pan-Indian stereotypes, directed at the Makah people.

Part of what fuels this debate is the conceptual separation of Makah whaling from its history and the insinuation of the disingenuity of Makah cultural needs. This skepticism has been compounded by accusations that any intentions to sell the whale meat would strip whaling of its aboriginality (Tizon 1998). The underlying assumption here is that traditional Native American culture was and should be separate from economic trade. Striking a middle ground, some critics have suggested that rather than kill whales the Makah people should spiritually count coup, that is, simply touch them. Some have also suggested that if such encounters were reenacted for ecotourists, it could help revitalize the reservation economy (Johnson 1998; Peterson 1996, 1998).

Opposition to whaling has not come from strictly non-Makah sources. Some members of the Makah community feel that the Makahs "know who we are" and don't need whaling to prove "Makahness." Others fear for the lives of the whalers. Significantly fewer Makah individuals share animal rights activists' sentiments that whale hunting constitutes a wrongful abuse of animal rights (Hogan 1996; Mapes 1998a, Verhovek 1998). Still others, while indifferent to the prospect of resuming whale hunting, maintain the legitimacy of their right secured by treaty.

From my perspective, at the heart of this whaling controversy are the processes of authenticating and discrediting Makah identity in the twentieth and twenty-first centuries. Who gets to control the expression of Makah identity — both its legitimacy and legality? Who gets to decide what is "cultural," "traditional," or "necessary"? Here, the identity politics and politics of representation inherent to the whaling controversy articulate with my own research on the evolving relationship between museums and Native peoples in the Western Hemisphere.

In the ongoing dialogue between non-Native and Native peoples regarding who Indians are and how they should live, tribal museums/cultural centers become a critical tool for negotiating the significant gap between the dominant constructions of Indianness and self-perceptions by Native peoples. As a prominent member of a Makah whaling family has said, "We've got to get the story out. . . . If we didn't we'd be these horrible, dirty savages, the killers of the whales. It's just not that way" (Johnson in Verhovek 1998).

Museums have always been highly complex zones where contact between indigenous and nonindigenous peoples takes place (Clifford 1997). However, in an era characterized by abundant tribal museums and charged by the politics of treaty rights and repatriation, the nature of this contact has recently become significantly different. To a greater degree, Native American and mainstream museums offer opportunities to Native American peoples to present self-portraits to the public in the hope of sensitizing the public to sensibilities and perspectives other than its own.

Rooting and Bending

I began this book with a discussion of Makah solid-twine basketry. Attempting to describe the way this distinctive basketry style represented to me a continuation of tradition and an adaptation to new economic needs and consumer tastes, I employed swamp grass as a metaphor. Swamp grass, a commonly used element in solid-twine basketry, is firmly rooted, yet it bends with the currents of water or air. My point was that identity, like swamp grass, roots itself and bends. Both the rooting and bending are important means to survival.

Through portraying a museum/cultural center and its relationship to a community, this museum ethnography has shown how the identity of the Makah people and the identity of their museum/ cultural center are interwoven. The identity, or subjectivity, of the MCRC is one manifestation of the identity of the Makah people. The identity of the Makah people, or any other people for that matter, does not exist independently from or in isolation from the identity of other peoples. Identities are forged through our relations with one another. As Donna Haraway has stated, identity is a relational category, a "set of effects which develop from the collision of history. It is not an abstraction. It's an extraordinarily complex kind of sedimentation" (Bhavnani and Haraway 1994, 21). The MCRC reveals the sedimentary layers deposited by the collision of histories. The *collisions*, or encounters, explored here are those between multiple ways of knowing — for example, between Euro-American and Native American ways of knowing — that have struggled with one another and reached some kind of accommodation. One could also choose to look at how the MCRC reveals encounters between different Makah families and their different ways of experiencing sacred and mundane worlds (Tweedie 1999).

The MCRC is one of many spaces in Makah social life that is imprinted with memories. As this ethnography has explored, memories are rooted to gathering places, such as Tatoosh Island, Bowman Beach, or places where lodges, homes, clubs, and halls once stood. Memories of conflict and survival are also rooted to places, such as the place where the Spanish Fort tried and failed to establish a presence, the places where Indian Affairs established its schoolhouses, the place called Ozette where a village used to be. All of these marked places on the Makah landscape trigger memories of gathering, teaching, laughing, celebrating, dying, and surviving. These places are traces of former social milieus, yet they are still part of the contemporary, lived experience. The places resonate with ongoing cultural practices. Historic struggles over how the Makah people would relate to American society have profoundly shaped Makah identity and the nature of the MCRC. The interweaving of Makah and MCRC identity does not stop there.

This tribal museum/cultural center is more than a product of an encounter, more than a reflection of cross-cultural or interfamilial dialogues. The identity of the Makah people is negotiated, defined, and preserved through the MCRC. The Makah adaptation of a Western type of institution is also a means for continuing to adapt and persist as a people. Like Makah solid-twine baskets and like Makah community halls and other modified, postcontact gathering spaces, the museum/cultural center is a means for simultaneous rooting and bending. It is a means for making compromises and accommodations, but it is also a means to define oneself on one's own terms, to the degree to which that is possible. The MCRC is a Western cultural element — the museum — that has been indigenized to a different cultural logic. The MCRC attempts to support "being Makah" in meaningful and appropriate ways.

Mainstream museums historically have been zones of contact where primarily Euro-American ways of seeing the world have driven the study and representation of Native American peoples. Native American museums/cultural centers, on the other hand, are relatively new zones of contact that attempt to address and counter unequal relations of power between Native American and Euro-American societies. They are creating autoethnographies, representations of themselves that engage with dominant cultural systems yet still have a degree of local control. Tribal museums have emerged as a new gathering space where the community can continue remembering, albeit in new ways. It is one of the places where memory can resonate with contemporary life, leaving both enriched through this resonance.

Notes

Introduction

1. Throughout the book I will use *precontact* rather than *prehistoric*. Although the latter term has extensive use in archaeology and pertains to the Ozette materials discussed here, I prefer the term that delineates a time period prior to European contact over the term that suggests that history, or civilization in its broadest sense, begins upon European arrival.

2. C. A. Huntington, August 25, 1875, U.S. Office of Indian Affairs (hereafter USOIA) 1875, 864–66.

3. The Smithsonian Building, known today as the Arts and Industries Building, was erected in 1878 to hold the collections displayed at the exposition. (The collections were later transferred to the Smithsonian collections.) The Arts and Industries Building is a close copy of the government building that housed the displays in Philadelphia (Viola 1985, 2; Zegas 1976, 163).

4. Swan to Baird, June 6, 1883, Smithsonian Institution Archives (SIA), Acc. 1326.

5. Daniel Dorchester, USOIA 1893, 392–93.

6. Those institutions that were counted are accessible to the public and have public exhibitions or programs (with only about half charging admissions). Most combine public services with more private services for the tribe, sometimes in a separate facility. These numbers include urban centers governed/managed by Native Americans, as well as some reservation centers that may have nontribal funding sources (e.g., churches) but that are still tribally governed. These numbers do not include facilities such as the BIA

arts and crafts centers (American Indian Museum Studies Program [1996]; Karen Cooper, personal communication).

7. I use the term *longhouse* to refer to what anthropologists have formerly called Northwest Coast shed houses, or to what tribal people indigenous to the region have called big houses and potlatch houses (Suttles 1991).

8. See Erikson (1996a, 302–9) for a review of tribal museums founded in the nineteenth century and pre–World War II twentieth century and Simpson (1996, 136–49) for an account of the history of the Museum of the Cherokee Indian in Cherokee, North Carolina.

9. In 1861 Swan warned the Makah people of the danger of contacting smallpox by wearing clothes acquired from shipwrecks (Swan 1971, 113).

10. Michael Ames articulates these two levels of analysis while reflecting upon papers by Virginia Dominguez and Ira Jacknis. Ames sat on a panel with them ("The Objects of Culture") at the November 1988 AAA meeting in Phoenix (Ames 1992, 141n. 173).

11. See Phillips (1998, 16–17) for a discussion of Ortiz's writing and how it influenced Pratt.

12. My definition of transnational (as opposed to international) follows that put forth by Basch (1994, 4–7). Transnational phenomena are the lived experiences and cultural practices stretched across national borders that stand outside formal and official politico-economic structures (although they may subsequently be authorized, legitimized, and appropriated by official entities).

13. The Office of Repatriation in the National Museum of Natural History has completed a transnational Iroquois repatriation. The repatriation was to the Iroquois–Six Nations Reserve in Brantford, Ontario, through the Onondaga in New York. The NMAI is also negotiating repatriation with tribes that straddle international boundaries (Chuck Smythe, personal communication, 1996).

14. I am indebted to Small (1997) for calling attention to this term. See also Prosler for discussion of the generalization of cultural forms around the world, followed by their particularization (1996).

1. Anthropologists in Neah Bay

1. Swan to Baird, Jan. 9, 1863. SIA, Record Unit (RU) 305, Office of the Registrar (OR), 1834–1958 (accretions to 1976), Box 13, Acc. 269.

2. This point was also made by Cole (1985, 4).

3. Swan to Baird, June 9, 1863, SIA, RU 305, OR, 1834–1958, Box 13, Acc. 269.

4. Swan to Baird, Feb. 27, 1864, SIA, RU 305, OR, 1834–1958, Box 13, Acc. 418.

5. Swan's diary, Mar. 5, 1862, Mar. 21, 1862, University of Washington Special Collections, Manuscripts and University Archives (UWSC); Swan 1870.

6. Swan to Baird, July 10, 1864, SIA, RU 305, OR, 1834–1958, Box 13, Acc. 494.

7. Swan to Baird, Mar. 13, 1863, SIA, RU 305, OR, 1834–1958, Box 13, Acc. 418.

8. Swan to Baird, Jan. 29, 1863, SIA, RU 305, OR, 1834–1958, Box 13, Acc. 244.

9. Swan to Baird, Feb. 27, 1864, SIA, RU 305, OR, 1834–1958, Box 13, Acc. 418.

10. Swan, June 30, 1865, USOIA 1875, 262.

11. Swan to Baird, June 9, 1863, SIA, RU 305, OR, 1834–1958, Box 13, Acc. 269.

12. Swan's diary, Sept. 25, 1862, UWSC.

13. Swan's diary, Sept. 25, 1862, UWSC.

14. Swan's diary, July 19, 1862, UWSC.

15. Swan's diary, July 3, 1863, UWSC.

16. Swan's diary, Sept. 23, 1866, UWSC.

17. Swan's diary, Sept. 22, 1863, UWSC.

18. Swan to Baird, June 9, 1863, July 6, 1863, SIA, RU 305, OR, 1834–1958, Box 13, Acc. 269.

19. Swan's diary, Jan. 17, 1862, Dec. 11, 1863, UWSC.

20. Swan to Baird, n.d., 1864, SIA, RU 305, OR, 1834–1958, Box 13, Acc. 494.

21. Swan to Baird, Oct. 13, 1863, SIA, RU 305, OR, 1834–1958, Box 13, Acc. 295.

22. Swan to Baird, Oct. 13, 1863, SIA, RU 305, OR, 1834–1958, Box 13, Acc. 295.

23. My observation here resonates with Robinson (1981) and with Westerman's work (1994, 178–79) on Central American refugee testimonies.

2. Redefining Civilization

1. Swan's diary, Oct. 15, 1862, UWSC.

2. Swan's diary, Nov. 10, 1864, UWSC.

3. Swan's diary, Nov. 14, 1864, UWSC. Following is an entry from Nov. 15, 1864: "John and Old Doctor came in this afternoon and expressed themselves pleased with the school. John said that the Indians were very desirous of having good feelings toward us and more particularly since they now saw that I was in earnest in taking care of and teaching their children."

4. Swan's diary, Nov. 18, 1864.

5. E. M. Gibson, Sept. 1, 1873, USOIA 1873, 674–67.

6. Willoughby, Aug. 5, 1878, USOIA 1878, 628.

7. W. L. Powell, Aug. 15, 1887, USOIA, 1887, 293.

8. Gibson, Sept. 1, 1872, USOIA 1872, 735.

9. Huntington, Aug. 18, 1877, USOIA 1877, 583.

10. Powell, Aug. 11, 1888, USOIA 1888, 226.

11. Huntington, Aug. 25, 1875, USOIA 1875, 865.

12. USOIA 1895.

13. Minutes of Special Meeting of School Board of District #58, Aug. 3, 1931, Greg Colfax personal archives; Superintendent Bitney to commissioner of Indian Affairs, Aug. 14, 1931, Greg Colfax personal archives.

14. Superintendent Raymond Bitney to commissioner of Indian Affairs, Jan. 4, 1933. Greg Colfax personal archives.

15. H. A. Webster, June 30, 1865, USOIA 1865, 259.

16. USOIA 1863, 1865, 1870, 1871, 1873.

17. Gibson, Sept. 1, 1873, USOIA 1873, 676.

18. Willoughby, Aug. 7, 1879, USOIA 1879, 251–52.

19. Huntington, Aug. 18, 1877, USOIA, 1877, 583.

20. Willoughby, Aug. 5, 1878, USOIA 1878, 627.

21. Willoughby, Aug. 26, 1882, USOIA 1885, 216.

22. O. Wood, Aug. 13, 1885, USOIA 1885, 413–15.

23. Powell, Aug. 15, 1887, USOIA 1887, 292.

24. Powell, Aug. 11, 1888, USOIA 1888, 225.

25. These included the *Deeahks, J. G. Swan, Amature, Emmet Felix, Puritan, Mary Parker*, and the *August*. Wilbur Claplanhoo remembers that Jongie Claplanhoo's schooners include the *Deeah,* the *Fisher Brothers, and the Perkins* (Claplanhoo 1995).

26. Willoughby, Aug. 17, 1880, USOIA 1880, and J. McGlinn, Aug. 17, 1891 USOIA 1891; Frank Smith 1995

27. McGlinn, Aug. 19, 1892, USOIA 1892, 495.

28. S. Morse, July 21, 1899, USOIA 1899, 356.

29. S. Morse, July 21, 1899, USOIA 1899, 356. The commercial halibut industry collapsed and became regulated in 1923 when the United States and Canada established the International Fisheries Commission (IFC), which regulated seasons and catch quotas. Young Doctor is recorded in the 1930s as saying that two hundred 30- and 40-foot sloops (and later larger ones) belonging to white commercial fishermen overwhelmed Neah Bay in the 1890s. He said that when the fish were gone the boats went away and the Makah people were left without food (Brombach 1995).

30. Powell, Aug. 17, 1886, USOIA 1886, 453; Powell, Aug. 9, 1894, USOIA 1894, 317; I. Ides 1995. For more on hop fields see Ruby and Brown 1992 and Tollefson 1994. For logging camps see USOIA 1894, 317; and R. Claplanhoo 1995. For strawberry picking see Bates 1987, 247–81.

31. Wood, Aug. 11, 1884, USOIA 1884, 207.

32. Powell, Aug. 6, 1894, USOIA 1894, 317.

33. Willoughby, Aug. 26, 1882, USOIA 1882, 216.

34. As Willoughby reported in 1879, he was monitoring the way several young Makah people who could read English were "eagerly perus[ing]" the weekly papers. He noted that they were aware of the "hostiles [Indian uprisings] in Oregon" the previous year but bragged that their loyalty remained firm to the U.S. government (Willoughby, Aug. 7, 1879, USOIA 1879, 253).

35. Swan's diary, Nov. 17, 1878, Nov. 21, 1878, UWSC; Frank Smith (1995).

36. R. Bitney, Aug. 21, 1931, Report of the Secretary of the Interior, 1931, 9, Greg Colfax personal archives.

37. Willoughby, Aug. 26, 1882, USOIA 1882, 217.

38. Swan's diary, Sept. 23, 1866, UWSC.

39. Bitney, Aug. 21, 1931, Report of the Secretary of the Interior, 1931, 7, Greg Colfax personal archives.

40. Swan's diary, Dec. 19, 1878, UWSC.

41. Swan's diary, Dec. 3, 1878, Dec. 4, 1878, UWSC.

42. Willoughby, Aug. 17, 1880, USOIA 1880, 278; Willoughby, Aug. 26, 1882, USOIA 1882, 217.

43. Willoughby, Aug. 18, 1881, USOIA 1881. Organized policing, at least that involving Indian labor, began as early as 1879. Willoughby appointed five members of each village to act as elders or headmen to judge petty offenses. Punishment was subject, however, to Willoughby's final approval. Willoughby is silent on how this system worked in tandem with any prior

intervillage disciplinary system. In 1882 it is reported that a jail building has been constructed and that an Indian police force, consisting of seven sergeants and privates, is led by the agency physician (as chief of police) and by the interpreter (as captain) (Willoughby, Aug. 26, 1882, USOIA 1882, 218.) By 1883 the "Indian court" is said to have "failed" since "suitable Indians" were unwilling to serve (Wood, Aug. 15, 1883, USOIA 1883, 202). It is not explained what suitable means. Thus the agent and the physician are the ones rendering judgments, the punishment for which is mentioned as jail and hard labor.

44. McGlinn, Aug. 14, 1890, USOIA 1890, 224.

45. Willoughby, Aug. 18, 1881, USOIA 1881, 54.

46. Swan's diary, Aug. 5, 1864, UWSC.

47. Wilbur Claplanhoo added to this transcript that his mother, Lizzie, was bedridden for more than eighteen years.

48. *Report of the Secretary of the Interior*, June 31, 1924, Greg Colfax personal archives.

49. *Report of the Secretary of the Interior*, 1929, "Law and Order" section, Greg Colfax personal archives.

50. Quoted in Goodman 1991, 233; here Bitney distinguishes himself from members of the early-twentieth-century reformist movement that proposed slower, less forceful, and more indirect forms of supporting development of Indian communities.

51. Bitney, Aug. 21, 1931, *Report of the Secretary of the Interior*, 1931, 10–11, Greg Colfax personal archives.

52. *Report of the Secretary of the Interior*, 1931, 10–11, Greg Colfax personal archives.

53. Willoughby, Aug. 18, 1881, USOIA 1881, 54.

54. Here I find that my analysis converges with that of Gerald Sider (1993), who described how the "imposed elements of history" are experienced in Indian communities; hence my language is borrowed from his terminology.

3. Many Gifts from the Past

1. Makah Tribal Council minutes, Jan. 10, 1956, Folder 064, Box 269, Record group (RG) 75, National Archives and Records Administration, Pacific Alaska Region (hereafter cited as NARA–Pacific Alaska).

2. By 1949 a youth group had also been interested in language and tradition classes and had petitioned the tribal council to use the community hall (Miller 1952, 270).

3. Makah Tribal Council minutes, June 21, 1951, Folder 060.064, Box 268, Tribal files (TF) 1919–68, RG 75, NARA–Pacific Alaska; Makah Tribal Council Minutes, Aug. 3, 1959, Erna Gunther Papers, University of Washington Manuscript Collections; Makah Tribal Council Minutes, Aug. 17, 1960, Folder 060, Box 0009, TF1919–68, RG75, NARA–Pacific Alaska.

4. The Slahal Club organized bone games and fund-raisers, too, so it could pay for holiday gatherings (I. Ward 1995).

5. In 1965 OEO funded twenty-nine out of one hundred tribal proposals submitted (BIA Report in *Indian Historian* 2[2]:18).

6. Classroom instruction, arts and crafts, recreation, social enrichment, and camps were also funded through BIA and tribal support. Preteens and teenagers were included (Makah-Summer Program (M-SP) 1964, 1965, 1966, Educational Summer Program case files, 1962–66, Box 331, RG 75, NARA–Pacific Alaska).

7. Sandy Johnson Osawa, personal communication, 1995.

8. Neah Bay Exemplary Project, 1970. Neah Bay Evaluation Report. Washington State Johnson-O'Malley Indian Education Annual Report, 1970–1971, Olympia, Washington, 46.

9. Greg Colfax in Beverly Vorpahl, Makahs "Positive" Educator. *Seattle Times*, Apr. 13, 1975, 11.

10. Student Opinion Poll, Neah Bay School (grades 7–12), Mar. 1972, 7, 24, Greg Colfax personal archives.

11. *Indian Historian* 1(1):7; 2(8):14.

12. *Indian Historian* 3(8):3.

13. For an example, see Chippewas Tame GE on "Wild Indian" Ad in *Indian Voices* Dec.–Jan. 1966–67, 3.

14. This statement is based on the following archival materials:
J. Duane Vance to Makah Tribal Council on Hoko Case, Dec. 4, 1951, Folder 064.6, "Makah 1952," Box 268, RG 75, NARA–Pacific Alaska; Minutes of Annual General Meeting of the Makah Indians of the Makah Reservation, Jan. 3, 1952, Folder 064.6, "Makah 1952," Box 268, TF 1919–68, RG 75, NARA–Pacific Alaska; Minutes of Special Tribal Meeting on Hoko Fishing, Jan. 22, 1952, Folder 064.6, "Makah 1952," Box 268, TF 1919–68, RG75, NARA–Pacific

Alaska; Minutes of the Special Meeting of the Makah Tribal Council, Apr. 1, 1952, Folder 064.6, "Makah 1952," Box 268, TF 1919–68, RG 75, NARA–Pacific Alaska; Superintendent Bitney to Charles E. Peterson, chairman Makah Tribal Council, June 17, 1952, Folder 064.6, "Makah 1952," Box 268, TF 1919–68, RG 75, NARA–Pacific Alaska; Minutes of Regular Meeting of the Makah Tribal Indian Council, July 11, 1952, Folder 064.6, "Makah 1952," Box 268, TF 1919–68, RG 75, NARA–Pacific Alaska; Special Meeting of the Makah Tribal Indian Council, Sept. 5, 1952, Folder 064.6, "Makah 1952," Box 268, TF 1919–68, RG 75, NARA–Pacific Alaska; Minutes of Regular Meeting of the Makah Tribal Indian Council, Oct. 5, 1952, Folder 064.6, "Makah 1952," Box 268, TF 1919–68, RG 75, NARA–Pacific Alaska; Minutes of Special Meeting of the Makah Tribal Indian Council, Oct. 23, 1952, Folder 064.6, "Makah 1952," Box 268, TF 1919–68, RG 75, NARA–Pacific Alaska; H.R. 7981, A Bill to Provide for the Termination of Federal Supervision over the Property of the Makah Indian Tribe, Feb. 18, 1954, Folder 103.3, "Makah Withdrawal Program," TF 1919–68, Box 271, RG 75, NARA–Pacific Alaska; H.R. 7981, Termination of Federal Supervision over Certain Tribes of Indians, Feb. 25, 1954, Folder 103.3, Box 271, TF 1919–68, RG 75, NARA–Pacific Alaska; General Meeting of the Makah Tribe and Council, Mar. 29, 1956, Folder 064, "Makah Minutes of Meetings 1955–56," TF 1919–68, Box 269, RG 75, NARA–Pacific Alaska; Richard Balsiger, BIA Portland Area Office, to Western Washington Agency on Acculturation, May 11, 1963, Folder 024.1, "Acculturation Reports May 1, 1963, Lummi, Makah, Muckleshoot, Quinalt, and Swinomish Reservations," Box 0006, "General Correspondence, 1952–68," RG 75, NARA–Pacific Alaska; A Report on the Student Summer Program, Aug. 2–27, 1965 (Sept. 3, 1965) from Sandra Johnson to BIA, M-SP 1965, Box 331, "Education Summer Program case files, 1962–66, RG 75, NARA–Pacific Alaska.

15. Gerald Grosso to Dr. Richard Daugherty, May 3, 1976. Daugherty's personal archives document that the tribal council rejected a request to display highly decorated Ozette artifacts at a Northwest Coast Studies conference.

16. Supt. of Public Instruction, Indian Education Annual Report, 1969–1970, Olympia, Washington, 10. Mary Hunter personal files.

17. Rice (1997, 218) names the Ozette excavation and a burial relocation program on the Snake River as exceptional cases in the 1970s where contact with Native Americans was an integral part of project planning and studies. He goes so far as to say that "Apart from these exceptions, things only began

to change with the legislative requirement for tribal consultation." See Spector (1993) for her attempts to integrate tribal oral history with archaeological excavation and teaching in the 1980s and 1990s.

18. Indian Claims Commission Act (60 Stat 1050) section 2 limited land claim eligibility to American Indians who were an identifiable group and who were descendants from the treaty negotiators.

19. Taholah Indian Agency Jurisdiction Ten-Year Planning Program by the Makah Indians for the Makah Reservation, Washington, Mar. 1944, Folder 060.064, "Makah," Box 271, Records of the Western Washington Indian Agency, 1950–65, RG 75, NARA–Pacific Alaska.

20. Makah Tribal Council meeting minutes, July 12, 1956, Folder 064, "Makah Minutes of Meetings 1955–56," Box 269, TF 1919–68, RG 75, NARA–Pacific Alaska.

4. Voices of a Thousand People

1. My dissertation (Erikson 1996a) contains more of my analysis that excavates the subjectivity of the Smithsonian Institution. See Hinsley (1994) for a wonderful account of primarily nineteenth-century research at the Smithsonian Institution pertaining to Native American peoples.

2. When the group United Indians of All Tribes seized Alcatraz in 1969, one of its demands was the means to establish its own American Indian cultural and educational center (Cooper 1996, 4; DeLuca 1983; Fuller and Fabricius 1992, 226). The first Alcatraz occupation spawned other Native American center projects. For example, the Alcatraz occupation inspired one thousand Native Americans living in the Puget Sound area to organize and acquire Fort Lawton in Seattle. The fort's 290 acres was about to be declared surplus by the U.S. Army. After organizing as the United Indians of All Tribes Foundation (UIATF), the group negotiated with the city of Seattle and acquired a ninety-nine-year lease on 17 acres at Fort Lawton. With $500,000 of municipal funds and $312,000 of Economic Development Administration EDA funds, the Daybreak Star Center opened in 1977 (Biddle 1977, 41–42). The founding of other cultural and educational centers was linked to the Alcatraz occupation (Deganawidah-Quetzalcoatl University near Davis, California [Jack Forbes, 1995, personal communication]); Fuller and Fabricius 1992, 226).

3. Merlee Markishtum, 1979, "Native American Museums." AAM an-

nual meeting, tape recording, American Association of Museums; George Abrams, 1977, AAM annual meeting, tape recording, American Association of Museums.

4. Native American Museum Program Annual Report, 1980. SIA RU 631, OMP Records, ca. 1974–89.

5. James Hanson Apr. 1, 1981, to Jane Glaser. Native American Museums Program Monthly Report, SIA RU 631, OMP Records, ca. 1974–89; Roger J. Contor to Paul Perrot, Feb. 11, 1980, SIA RU 631, OMP, ca. 1974–89,; Untitled, 1980, SIA RU 631, OMP Records, ca. 1974–89; Nancy J. Fuller to John Fleckner, Nov. 14, 1984. Acc. 90–094, SIA, OMP Records, Box 4.

6. David Fanman (Southern Cheyenne of Oklahoma) at the Smithsonian Institution after participating in the AICRTP. Quoted in Native American Training Program, OMP, Smithsonian Institution, by James Hanson, 1977, SIA RU 631, OMP Records, ca. 1974–89.

7. Mikle Taylor (Native American Advisory Council, Denver Museum of Natural History), 1980, "American Indian Legal Issues and Cultural Institutions," AAM annual meeting, tape recording, American Association of Museums.

8. Hill, 1979, AAM annual meeting, tape recording, American Association of Museums.

9. Hill, 1979, AAM annual meeting.

10. Hill, 1979, AAM annual meeting.

11. Hill, 1979, AAM annual meeting.

12. Hill, 1979, AAM annual meeting.

13. Taylor, 1980, AAM annual meeting.

14. Ann Renker, 1994, "The Presentation and Representation of Native Peoples in Museums," AAM annual meeting, tape recording, American Association of Museums.

15. Karen Cooper, director of AIMS, personal communication, Feb. 1995.

16. "The Presentation and Representation of Native Peoples in Museums," AAM annual meeting, tape recording, American Association of Museums.

17. Statement of Makah Tribal Council to Interior and Related Agencies Sub-Committee on Appropriations Concerning the Proposed Makah-Ozette Museum, 1972, MCRC Archives.

5. Indigenizing the Museum

1. Apr. 8, 1991, Smithsonian Institution Mission and Governance of Tribal Museums Workshop, Neah Bay, Washington, videotape, MCRC Archives.

2. Dialogue between the MCRC and non-Makah people is not restricted to exhibits, research, curation protocols, and interpretations. Through the development of curricular materials and educational activities for grades K–12, the MCRC contributes to reformation of public education curriculum on and off the reservation. MCRC cultural programming, which started in the schools in the 1960s, has contributed to the development of language, culture, and history curricula and has offered qualified Makah staff employment as part-time teachers. In addition, staff resources are available within the museum for school tours and special activities, often with the assistance of an elder from the community. For example, MCRC recently developed a traveling Makah curriculum unit. It included detailed models of a longhouse, a canoe, and cedar bark clothing, as well as a wide array of background and explanatory materials for K–12 teachers to use in designing discussions and activities on Makah customs and history. In effect, MCRC acts as a center for the production of alternative curriculum materials that can be disseminated to public schools. Collectively, exhibit structures and educational materials and activities serve to disrupt Indian stereotypes and remake the imagery so that Makah people can at least recognize themselves in it.

3. See Jocks (1996) for a discussion of the various arguments used to protect intellectual property rights.

4. See Sharon MacDonald's discussion (1996, 5–6) about the need for theory that distinguishes museums from texts while still acknowledging their commonalities.

5. See Lyman (1982) and Holm and Quimby (1980) for discussion of the romantic photographic legacy of Native Americans produced by the Curtis family.

6. See Huelsbeck (1988) for an account of the role of whale blubber, meat, and bones in daily Makah life.

7. This longhouse exhibit shares several qualities with the reconstructed chief's house at the RBCM in Victoria, British Columbia, which partly inspired it (André 1995).

8. For a rich collection of oral historical narratives and photographs regarding chiefly privileges, or *tupaat*, see Black (1999).

9. See chapter 1 of this volume for a fuller discussion of this widespread phenomenon. See also Simpson (1996, 135–69) for an interesting account of several Native American museums/cultural centers nationwide. Macdonald (1996, 2) and Prosler (1996, 40) discuss the processes of appropriating and translating the museum that are occurring globally.

Glossary

čiˑbap	swamp grass for making baskets
qʷiˑqʷiˑdiččaq	the Makah language
qʷidiččaʔaˑtx̌	People Who Live by the Rocks and Seagulls
babałids	House over the Water People; whites
c'aˑyiq	healing ceremony
huhuʔaq'it	an old saying and teaching from way back
ƛuˑkʷaˑliˑ	Kloqually dance or wolf ritual
hax̌ʷiˑdukš	box
ƛadit	wedge
ƛayak	metal, iron
ƛataˑwačak	canoe paddles
ƛačak	chisel
čapxtuˑp	seal harpoon insert blade

References

ABRAMS, GEORGE H. J.

1990   Dialogue. *Smithsonian Runner* 90(6):2.

1994   The Case for Wampum: Repatriation from the Museum of the American Indian to the Six Nations Confederacy, Brantford, Ontario, Canada. In *Museums and the Making of "Ourselves": The Role of Objects in National Identity*, ed. F. E. S. Kaplan, 351–84, London: Leicester University Press.

ABU-LUGHOD, LILA

1990   The Romance of Resistance: Tracing Transformations of Power through Bedouin Women. *American Ethnologist* 17(1): 41–55.

1993   *Writing Women's Worlds: Bedouin Stories*. Berkeley: University of California Press.

ALCOFF, LINDA

1997   Cultural Feminism versus Post-Structuralism: The Identity Crisis in Feminist Theory. In *The Second Wave: A Reader in Feminist Theory*, ed. Linda Nicholson, 330–55. New York: Routledge.

ALEXANDER, EDWARD P.

1979   *Museums in Motion: An Introduction to the History and Functions of Museums*. Nashville: American Association for State and Local History.

1983   *Museum Masters: Their Museums and Their Influences*. Nashville: Association for State and Local History.

AMERICAN INDIAN MUSEUM STUDIES PROGRAM

1996 *Directory of North American Tribal Museums.* Washington DC: Center for Museum Studies.

AMES, MICHAEL M.

1986 *Museums, The Public and Anthropology: A Study in the Anthropology of Anthropology.* Vancouver: University of British Columbia Press.

1987 Free Indians from Their Ethnological Fate: The Emergence of the Indian Point of View in Exhibitions of Indians. *Muse* 5(2): 14–29.

1988 Boycott the Politics of Suppression: Museums and Politics: The Spirit Sings and the Lubicon Boycott. *Muse* 11(3).

1991 Biculturalism in Exhibitions. *Museum Anthropology* 15(2):7–15.

1992 *Cannibal Tours and Glass Boxes: The Anthropology of Museums.* Vancouver: University of British Columbia Press.

1994 The Politics of Difference: Other Voices in a Non Yet Post-Colonial World. *Museum Anthropology* 18(3):9–17.

ANDERSON, BENEDICT

1991 *Imagined Communities: Reflections on the Origin and Spread of Nationalism.* London: Verso.

ANDRÉ, JEAN

1995 Oral history transcription from interview by Patricia P. Erikson, Victoria, British Columbia. MCRC Archives.

ANONYMOUS

1913 The Rodman Wanamaker Expedition of Citizenship to the North American Indian. Address of the President of the United States and Other Messages. Summer 1913. N.p.: Rodman Wanamaker.

APPADURAI, ARJUN

1986 Introduction: Commodities and the Politics and Value. In *The Social Life of Things: Commodities in Cultural Perspective*, ed. A. Appadurai, 3–63. Cambridge: Cambridge University Press.

1988 Putting Hierarchy in Its Place. *Cultural Anthropology* 3:36–49.

APPADURAI, ARJUN, ED.

1986 *The Social Life of Things: Commodities in Cultural Perspective.* Cambridge: Cambridge University Press.

1990 Disjunctures and Difference in the Global Cultural Economy. *Public Culture* 2(2):1–24.

ARIMA, EUGENE Y.

1983   *The West Coast People: The Nootka of Vancouver Island and Cape Flattery.*
        Victoria: British Columbia Provincial Museum.

ARNOLDI, MARY JO

1992   A Distorted Mirror: The Exhibition of the Herbert Ward Collection
        of Africana. In *Museums and Communities: The Politics of Public Culture,*
        ed. I. Karp, C. Kreamer, and S. Lavine, 428–57. Washington DC:
        Smithsonian Institution Press.

ASAD, TALAL

1986   The Concept of Cultural Translation in British Social Anthropology.
        In *Writing Culture: The Poetics and Politics of Ethnography,* ed. J. Clifford
        and G. Marcus, 141–64. Berkeley: University of California Press.

ASAD, TALAL, ED.

1973   *Anthropology and the Colonial Encounter.* London: Ithaca Press.

ASSEMBLY OF FIRST NATIONS AND THE CANADIAN MUSEUMS
ASSOCIATION

1992   Task Force Report on Museums and First Peoples. *Museum Anthropol-
        ogy* 16(2):12–20.

BASCH, LINDA G., NINA GLICK SCHILLER, ET AL.

1994   *Nations Unbound: Transnational Projects, Postcolonial Predicaments, and
        Deterritorialized Nation-States.* Amsterdam: Gordon and Breach.

BATES, ANN M.

1987   Affiliation and Differentiation: Intertribal Interactions among the
        Makah and Ditidaht Indians. Ph.D. diss., Indiana University.

BENEDICT, BURTON

1981   World's Fairs and Anthropology. *Council for Museum Anthropology
        Newsletter* 5(2):2–7.

1983   *The Anthropology of World's Fairs.* London: Lowie Museum of Anthro-
        pology and Scholar Press.

BERLO, JANET CATHERINE, AND RUTH B. PHILLIPS

1992   "Vitalizing the Things of the Past": Museum Representations
        of Native North American Art in the 1990s. *Museum Anthropology*
        16(1):29–43.

BHAVNANI, KUM-KUM, AND DONNA HARAWAY

1994   Shifting the Subject: A Conversation between Kum-Kum Bhavnani
        and Donna Haraway, April 12, 1993, Santa Cruz, California. *Femi-
        nism and Psychology* 4(1):19–39.

BIDDLE, LUCY

1977   Keeping Tradition Alive. *Museum News* (May–June): 35–42.

BIEDER, ROBERT E.

1986   *Science Encounters the Indian, 1820–1880: The Early Years of American Ethnology*. Norman: University of Oklahoma Press.

BIRD, GLORIA

1992   Search for Evidence of Colonialism at Work: A Reading of Louis[e] Erdrich's "Tracks." *Wicazo Sa Review* 8(2):40–47.

BLACK, MARTHA

1999   *Out of the Mist: Treasures of the Nuu-chah-nulth Chiefs*. Victoria: Royal British Columbia Museum.

BLOW, RICHARD

1998   The Great American Whale Hunt. *Mother Jones* 23(5):49.

BOCK, PAULA

1995   The Accidental Whale. *Pacific Magazine*, November 26, 1–32.

BOONE, ELIZABETH H., ED.

1993   *Collecting the Pre-Columbian Past*. Washington DC: Dumbarton Oaks Research Library.

BOURDIEU, P., A. DARBEL, ET AL.

1991   *The Love of Art: European Art Museums and Their Public*. Stanford: Stanford University Press.

BOWEN, BLAIR

1979a American Indians vs. American Museums: A Matter of Religious Freedom, part 1. *American Indian Journal* (May): 13–21.

1979b American Indians vs. American Museums: A Matter of Religious Freedom, part 2. *American Indian Journal* (June): 2–6.

BRACKEN, CHRISTOPHER

1997   *The Potlatch Papers*. Chicago: University of Chicago Press.

BRADBURY, DIETER

1995   "What Does It Mean To Be an American?" *Maine Sunday Telegram*, October 8, 1995, 1C–2C.

BRAY, TAMARA L., JAVIER URCID, AND GARY P. ARONSEN

1994   Inventory and Assessment of Human Remains from Clallam County, Washington, in the National Museum of Natural History. March 7, 1994. Washington DC: Repatriation Office, Smithsonian Institution.

BROMBACH, DAVID

1995　We Shall Always Claim That Bank. *Strait History: Journal of Clallam County History Society, Port Angeles, Washington.* 9(1).

BROWN, STEVE

1995　Oral history transcription from interview by Patricia P. Erikson, Seattle. MCRC Archives.

BRUNER, EDWARD

1986　Ethnography as Narrative. In *The Anthropology of Experience*, ed. V. Turner and E. Bruner, 139–55, Urbana: University of Illinois Press.

BUIKSTRA, J. E.

1983　Reburial: How We All Lose, An Archaeologist's Opinion. *Council of Museum Anthropology Newsletter* 7:2–5.

BURKE, CHARLTON

1937　The New Iroquois. *Museum Service* 10(8).

BURKE, PETER

1991　Overture: The New History, Its Past and Its Future. In *New Perspectives on Historical Writing*, ed. P. Burke, 1–23. Cambridge: Polity.

BUTLER, SHELLEY

1999　*Contested Representations: Revisiting "Into the Heart of Africa."* Amsterdam: Gordon and Breach.

CAMERON, DUNCAN

1972　The Museum: A Temple or the Forum. *Journal of World History* 14(1):197, 201.

CANNADINE, D.

1983　The Context, Performance and Meaning of Ritual: The British Monarchy and the "Invention of Tradition," c. 1820–1977. In *The Invention of Tradition*, ed. E. Hobsbawm and T. Ranger, 101–64. Cambridge: Cambridge University Press.

CANNIZZO, JEANNE

1989　*Into the Heart of Africa.* Toronto: Royal Ontario Museum.

CHAMPE, J. L., D. S. BYERS, ET AL.

1961　Four Statements for Archaeology. *American Antiquities* 27:137–38.

CLAPLANHOO, EDWARD

1994　Oral history transcription from interview by Patricia P. Erikson, Neah Bay, Washington. MCRC Archives.

CLAPLANHOO, MUZZIE

1995   Field notes from an interview by Patricia P. Erikson, Neah Bay, Washington. Erikson personal files.

CLAPLANHOO, RUTH ALLABUSH

1995   Field notes from an interview by Patricia P. Erikson, Neah Bay, Washington. MCRC Archives.

CLAPLANHOO, WILBUR

1995   Field notes from an interview by Patricia P. Erikson, Neah Bay, Washington. Erikson personal files.

CLIFFORD, JAMES

1987   Of Other Peoples: Beyond the "Salvage" Paradigm. In *Dia Art Foundations Discussions in Contemporary Culture*, ed. Hal Foster. Seattle: Bay Press.

1988   *Predicament of Culture: Twentieth-Century Ethnography, Literature, and Art*. Cambridge: Harvard University Press.

1992   Four Northwest Coast Museums. In *Exhibiting Cultures: The Poetics and Politics of Museum Display*, ed. I. Karp and S. D. Lavine, 212–54, Washington DC: Smithsonian Institution Press.

1997   Museums as Contact Zones. In *Routes: Travel and Translation in the Late Twentieth Century*, 188–219. Cambridge: Harvard University Press.

CLIFFORD, JAMES, AND GEORGE E. MARCUS, EDS.

1986   *Writing Culture: The Poetics and Politics of Ethnography*. Berkeley: University of California Press.

COHEN, FAY G.

1986   Fishing the Columbia: Can Negotiation Replace Litigation? In *Treaties on Trial: The Continuing Controversy over Northwest Indian Fishing Rights*, 118–36. Seattle: University of Washington Press.

COLE, DOUGLAS

1982   Tricks of the Trade: Northwest Coast Artifact Collecting, 1875–1925. *Canadian Historical Review* 63(4):439–60.

1985   *Captured Heritage: The Scramble for Northwest Coast Artifacts*. Vancouver: Douglas and MacIntyre.

COLFAX, GREG

1995   Field notes from an interview by Patricia P. Erikson, Neah Bay, Washington. Erikson personal files.

COLSON, ELIZABETH

1953   *The Makah Indians: A Study of an Indian Tribe in Modern American Society*. Minneapolis: University of Minnesota Press.

COOMBE, ROSEMARY J.

1995   The Cultural Life of Things: Globalization and Anthropological Approaches to Commodification. *American University Journal of International Law and Policy* 10 (winter): 791–835.

COOPER, KAREN

1996   American Indian Protests of Museum Exhibition Policies and Practices. Master's thesis, University of Oklahoma.

CRANMER WEBSTER, GLORIA

1991   The Contemporary Potlatch. In *Chiefly Feasts: The Enduring Kwakiutl Potlatch*, ed. Aldona Jonaitis, 227–50. Seattle: University of Washington Press.

CROES, DALE R., AND ERIC BLINMAN, EDS.

1980   *Hoko River Archaeological Project: A 2,500 Year Old Fishing Camp on the Northwest Coast of North America*. Vol. 1, Office of Archaeology and Historic Preservation, Washington State.

CRUIKSHANK, JULIE, WITH ANGELA SIDNEY, KITTY SMITH, AND ANNIE NED

1990   *Life Lived like a Story: Life Stories of Three Yukon Elders*. Lincoln: University of Nebraska Press.

1992   Oral Tradition and Material Culture: Multiplying Meanings of "Words" and "Things." *Anthropology Today* 8(3):5–9.

CURTIS, MIMI WASHBURN

1995   Field notes from an interview by Patricia P. Erikson, Tacoma. Erikson personal files.

CUTLER, ROBIN

1994   *A Gift from the Past*. Indian America series. Videocassette. 60 mins. Washington DC, Media Resource Associates.

DAUGHERTY, RICHARD D.

1971   At Cape Alava: A Time Capsule Unsealed. *Pacific Search* 5(8):1–3.

1995   Oral history transcription from interview by Patricia P. Erikson, Lacey, Washington. MCRC Archives.

DAUGHERTY, RICHARD D., AND RUTH KIRK

1976   Ancient Indian Village Where Time Stood Still. *Smithsonian* 7(2): 68–75.

DAVIS, MARY B., ED.

1994   *Native America in the Twentieth Century: An Encyclopedia.* New York: Garland.

DEAN RUNYAN AND ASSOCIATES

1995   *Tourism Market Analysis and Development Plan, Makah Indian Reservation: A Preliminary Report.* Portland OR: Dean Runyan and Associates.

DEFERT, DANIEL

1982   The Collection of the World: Accounts of Voyages from the Sixteenth to the Eighteenth Centuries. *Dialectical Anthropology* 7:29–35.

DELACRUZ, J.

1989   From Self-Determination to Self-Government. In *Indian Self-Governance: Perspectives on the Political Status of Indian Nations in the United States of America,* ed. Carol J. Minugh et al.: Kenmore, U.S.A.: Center for World Indigenous Studies.

DELORIA, PHILIP J.

1998   *Playing Indian.* New Haven: Yale University Press.

DELORIA, VINE

1969   Custer Died For Your Sins. *Playboy,* August, 131–32, 172–75.

DE LUCA, RICHARD

1983   We Hold the Rock, The Indian Attempt to Reclaim Alcatraz Island. *California History* 62(1):2–23.

DENNEY, MARY LOU

1995   Oral history transcription from interview by Patricia P. Erikson, Neah Bay, Washington. MCRC Archives.

DENSMORE, FRANCES

1939   *Nootka and Quileute Music.* Smithsonian Institution Bureau of American Ethnology, Bulletin 124. Washington DC: Government Printing Office.

DIXON, JOSEPH K.

1913   *The Vanishing Race: The Last Great Indian Council.* Garden City NY: Doubleday, Page and Company.

DIXON, SUSAN R.

1992a   Indians, Cowboys, and the Language of Museums. *Akwe:kon Journal* 4(1):16–27.

1992b   Reclaiming Interpretation: An Interview with W. Richard West Jr. *Akwe:kon Journal* 9(4):4–10.

DOMINGUEZ, VIRGINIA

1990   The Politics of Heritage in Contemporary Israel. In *Nationalist Ideolo-gies and the Production of National Culture*, ed. Richard G. Fox, 130–47. Washington: American Anthropological Association.

DOXTATOR, DEBORAH

1985   The Idea of the Indian and the Development of Iroquoian Muse-ums. *Museum Quarterly* (summer): 20–26.

DREYFUS, HUBERT L., AND PAUL RABINOW

1982   *Michel Foucault: Beyond Structuralism and Hermeneutics.* Chicago: University of Chicago Press.

DRUCKER, PHILIP

1951   *The Northern and Central Nootkan Tribes.* Bureau of American Ethnol-ogy, Bulletin 144. Washington DC: Smithsonian Institution.

DUNCAN, CAROL

1991   Art Museums and the Ritual of Citizenship. In *Exhibiting Cultures: The Poetics and Politics of Museum Display*, ed. Ivan Karp and Steven Levine, 88–103. Washington DC: Smithsonian Institution Press.

ECHO-HAWK, WALTER

1985   Sacred Material and the Law. Presentation at The Concept of Sacred Materials and Their Place in The World. Plains Indian Museum's Ninth Annual Plains Indian Seminar, September 1985. Buffalo Bill Historic Center's Plains Indian Museum.

1992   Nebraska's Landmark Reburial Act. *Arizona State Law Journal* 24(1).

ERIKSON, PATRICIA P.

1995   "Community Museums, Cultural Patrimony, and Grassroots De-velopment of Indigenous Pueblos in Oaxaca, Mexico," Grassroots Development Report. Virginia: Inter-American Foundation.

1996a   Encounters in the Nation's Attic: Native American Community Museums/Cultural Centers, the Smithsonian Institution, and the Politics of Knowledge-Making. Ph.D. diss., University of California, Davis.

1996b   "So My Children Can Stay in the Pueblo": Indigenous Community Museums and Self-Determination in Oaxaca, Mexico. *Museum Anthropology* 19(3):37–46.

1996c   Resistance through Representation: Transnational Currents in Indigenous Museos Comunitarios. *First Nations-Pueblos Originarios*

1(2):11–25. Davis: Indigenous Research Center of the Americas, University of California, Davis.

1998   Spirit Helpers and Cash: A Century of Makah People Honoring Identity and Surviving Political Economy. Paper presented at the Annual Meeting of the American Society for Ethnohistory, Minneapolis, November 12.

1999   A-Whaling We Will Go: Encounters of Knowledge and Memory at the Makah Museum. *Cultural Anthropology* 14(4):556–83.

2000   Exhibit Review of Mashantucket Pequot Museum and Research Center. *Museum Anthropology* 23(2):46–53.

ERNST, ALICE

1952   *The Wolf Ritual of the Northwest Coast.* Eugene: University of Oregon.

EWERS, JOHN C.

1952   Museos Para Indios en Los Estados Unidos de America. *Educación fundamental boletín trimestral* 4(1):3–9.

1958   A Century of American Indian Exhibits in the Smithsonian Institution. In *Annual Report of the Board of Regents of the Smithsonian Institution*, 513–25, Publication 4354. Washington DC: Government Printing Office.

1964   The Emergence of the Plains Indian as the Symbol of the North American Indian. *Annual Report of the Board of Regents of the Smithsonian Institution*, 531–44. Publication 4613. Washington DC: Government Printing Office.

1978   Richard Sanderville, Blackfoot Indian Interpreter. In *American Indian Intellectuals*, ed. Margot Liberty, 116–26. St. Paul: West Publishing.

1995   Field notes from an interview by Patricia P. Erikson, Washington DC. Erikson personal files.

FABIAN, JOHANNES

1983   *Time and the Other: How Anthropology Makes Its Object.* New York: Columbia University Press.

FARMER, GARY

1994   Going beyond Indian: The Art of James Luna. *Aboriginal Voices* 1(4):19–23.

FITZHUGH, WILLIAM

1995   Field notes from an interview by Patricia P. Erikson, Washington DC. Erikson personal files.

FOUCAULT, MICHEL

1970   *The Order of Things: An Archaeology of the Human Sciences.* New York: Pantheon.

1974   *The Archaeology of Knowledge.* London: Tavistock.

FRIEDLANDER, PETER

1996   Theory, Method and Oral History. In *Oral History: An Interdisciplinary Anthology*, ed. David K. Dunaway and Willa K. Baum, 150–60. Walnut Creek CA: Altamira.

FULLER, NANCY

1992   The Museum as a Vehicle for Community Empowerment: The Ak-Chin Indian Community Ecomuseum Project. In *Museums and Communities: The Politics of Public Culture*, ed. Ivan Karp, Christine Kreamer, and Steven Lavine. 327–66. Washington DC: Smithsonian Institution Press.

1993   Staff Development and Training Opportunities for Native Americans at the Smithsonian Institution: A Brief Overview. *ICOM News* 46:9–10.

1995   Field notes from an interview by Patricia P. Erikson, Washington DC, Erikson personal files.

FULLER, NANCY, AND SUZANNE FABRICIUS

1994   Tribal Museums. In *Native American in the Twentieth Century: An Encyclopedia*, 655–57. New York: Garland.

1996   Historical Overview and Current Issues. *Zeitschrift für Ethnologie* 117:223–37.

FUSCO, COCO, AND PAUL HEREDIA

1993   *The Couple in the Cage: A Guatinaui Odyssey.* Videocassette. 32 mins. New York: Third World Newsreel.

GEERTZ, CLIFFORD

1973a   *The Interpretation of Cultures: Selected Essays by Clifford Geertz.* New York: Basic.

1973b   Thick Description: Toward an Interpretive Theory of Culture. In *The Interpretation of Cultures*, 3–30. New York: Basic.

GENDRON, V.

1958   *Behind the Zuni Masks.* New York: Longmans, Green.

GIBBS, GEORGE

1855   *Report of Mr. George Gibbs to Captain Mc'Clellan, on the Indian Tribes of the Territory of Washington.* Washington DC: U.S. War Department.

1855   Treaty of Neah Bay [Transcript of Journal Proceedings]. U.S. National Archives, Records Relating to the Negotiation of Ratified and Unratified Treaties with Various Tribes of Indians, 1801–1869. Microcopy no. T-494, roll 5.

1863   Instructions for Research Relative to the Ethnology and Philology of America. *Smithsonian Miscellaneous Collections* 160. Washington DC: Smithsonian Institution.

GLASER, JANE

1995   Field notes from an interview by Patricia P. Erikson, Washington DC. Erikson personal files.

GLASSBERG, DAVID

1990   *American Historical Pageantry: The Uses of Tradition in the Early Twentieth Century.* Chapel Hill: University of North Carolina Press.

GLICK SCHILLER, N., L. BASCH, ET AL.

1992   *The Transnationalization of Migration: Perspectives on Ethnicity and Race.* New York: Gordon and Breach.

GOODMAN, LINDA J.

1978   This Is My Song: The Role of Song as Symbol in Makah Life. Ph.D. Diss., Washington State University, Pullman.

1991   Traditional Music in Makah Life. *A Time of Gathering: Native Heritage in Washington State*, ed. R. K. Wright, 223–33. Singapore: Times Publishing Group.

GREEN, RAYNA

1988a The Indian in Popular American Culture. In *Indian-White Relations*, ed. W. E. Washburn. Vol. 4 of *Handbook of North American Indians*, ed. William C. Sturtevant. Washington DC: Smithsonian Institution.

1988b The Tribe Called Wannabee: Playing Indian in America and Europe. *Folklore* 99(1):30–50.

1995   Field notes from an interview by Patricia P. Erikson, Washington DC, Erikson personal files.

GREENE, MARY

1995   Field notes from an interview by Patricia P. Erikson, Neah Bay, Washington. Erikson personal files.

GREY, ZANE

1925   *The Vanishing American.* New York: Harper and Brothers.

GUNTHER, ERNA

1942   Reminiscences of a Whaler's Wife. *Pacific Northwest Quarterly* 33: 65–69.

1972   *Indian Life on the Northwest Coast of North America: As Seen by the Early Explorers and Fur Traders during the Last Decades of the Eighteenth Century.* Chicago: University of Chicago Press.

GWYNNE, PETER

1977   Indian Pompeii. *Newsweek*, September 5: 81–82.

HALBWACHS, MAURICE

1950   [1980] *The Collective Memory.* New York: Harper and Row.

HANCOCK, SAMUEL

1927   *The Narrative of Samuel Hancock, 1845–1860.* Intro. Arthur D. Howden Smith. New York: Robert M. McBride.

HANDLER, RICHARD

1985   On Having a Culture: Nationalism and the Preservation of Quebec's Patrimoine. In *Objects and Others: Essays on Museums and Material Culture,* ed. G. W. Stocking Jr., 192–217. Madison: University of Wisconsin Press.

1988   *Nationalism and Politics of Culture in Quebec.* Madison: University of Wisconsin Press.

1992   On the Valuing of Museum Objects. *Museum Anthropology* 16(1): 21–28.

HANSON, JAMES A.

1980   The Reappearing Vanishing American. *Museum News* 59(2):44–51.

HARAWAY, DONNA

1989   Teddy Bear Patriarchy: Taxidermy in the Garden of Eden, New York City, 1908–1936. In *Primate Visions: Gender, Race, and Nature in the World of Modern Science,* 26–58. New York: Routledge.

1991   Situated Knowledges: The Science Question in Feminism and the Privilege of Partial Perspective. In *Simians, Cyborgs, and Women: The Reinvention of Nature,* 183–202, New York: Routledge.

HARMON, ALEXANDRA

1999   *Indians in the Making: Ethnic Relations and Indian Identities around Puget Sound.* Berkeley: University of California Press.

HARRISON, JULIA D.

1987   *The Spirit Sings: Artistic Traditions of Canada's First Peoples.* Toronto: Glenbow Museum.

1988   The Spirit Sings and the Future of Anthropology. *Anthropology Today* 4(6):6–9.

HARTMAN, RUSSELL P.

1983   The Navajo Tribal Museum: Bridging the Past and the Present. *American Indian Art Magazine* 9(1):30–36.

HARTMAN, RUSSELL P., AND DAVID E. DOYEL

1982   Preserving a Native People's Heritage: A History of the Navajo Tribal Museum. *Kiva* 47(4):239–55.

HAYES, DEREK

1999   *Historical Atlas of the Pacific Northwest: Maps of Exploration and Discovery.* Seattle: Sasquatch.

HEILMAN, MEREDITH FLINN

1995   Field notes from an interview by Patricia P. Erikson, Neah Bay, Washington. Erikson personal files.

HILL, RICHARD (RICK)

1995   Field notes from an interview by Patricia P. Erikson, Washington DC. Erikson personal files.

HILL, TOM, AND RICHARD W. HILL SR., EDS.

1994   *Creation's Journey: Native American Identity and Belief.* Washington DC: Smithsonian Institution Press.

HINSLEY, CURTIS M.

1981   [1994] *The Smithsonian and the American Indian: Making a Moral Anthropology in Victorian America.* Washington DC: Smithsonian Institution Press.

1989   Zunis and Brahmins: Cultural Ambivalence in the Gilded Age. In *Romantic Motives: Essays on Anthropological Sensibility,* ed. G. W. Stocking, 169–207. Madison: University of Wisconsin Press.

1990   Authoring Authenticity. *Journal of the Southwest* 32(4):462–78.

1992   Collecting Cultures and Cultures of Collecting: The Lure of the American Southwest, 1880–1915. *Museum Anthropology* 16(1):12–20.

1993   In Search of the New World Classical. In *Collecting the Pre-Columbian Past: A Symposium at Dumbarton Oaks, 6th and 7th October 1990,* ed. E. H. Boone, 105–21. Washington DC: Dumbarton Oaks Research Library.

HINSLEY, CURTIS M., JR., AND B. HOLM

1976   A Cannibal in the National Museum: The Early Career of Franz Boas in America. *American Anthropologist* 78:306–16.

HOBSBAWM, ERIC

1983   Introduction to *The Invention of Tradition,* ed. E. Hobsbawm and T. Ranger. New York: Cambridge University Press.

HOBSBAWM, ERIC, AND TERENCE RANGER, EDS.

1983   *The Invention of Tradition.* Cambridge: Cambridge University Press.

HODGE, FREDERICK W., ED.

1907–10 *Handbook of American Indians.* Smithsonian Institution Bureau of American Ethnology Bulletin 30. Washington DC: Government Printing Office.

HOGAN, LINDA

1996   Silencing Tribal Grandmothers. *Seattle Times,* December 15, B8.

HOLM, BILL, AND GEORGE IRVING QUIMBY

1980   *Edward S. Curtis in the Land of the War Canoe: Pioneer Cinematographer in the Pacific Northwest.* Seattle: University of Washington Press.

HOOPER-GREENHILL, EILEAN

1989   The Museum in the Disciplinary Society. In *Museum Studies in Material Culture,* ed. S. M. Pearce, 61–72. London: Leicester University Press.

1991   The Museum in the Disciplinary Society. In *Museum Studies in Material Culture,* ed. S. M. Pearce, 61–72. London: Leicester University Press.

1992   *Museums and the Shaping of Knowledge.* London: Routledge.

HOOVER, ALAN, AND RICHARD INGLIS

1990   Acquiring and Exhibiting a Nuu-Chah-Nulth Ceremonial Curtain. *Curator* 4:272–88.

HORSE CAPTURE, GEORGE P.

1981   Some Observations on Establishing Tribal Museums. *History News* 36(1). Technical Leaflet 134.

1994   From the Reservation to the Smithsonian via Alcatraz. *American Indian Culture and Research Journal* 18(4):135–49.

1995   Field notes from an interview by Patricia P. Erikson, New York City. Erikson personal files.

HOTTOWE, EDIE MARKISHTUM

1995   Field notes from an interview by Patricia P. Erikson, Neah Bay, Washington. Erikson personal files.

HOWARD, KATHLEEN, AND DIANA PARDUE, EDS.

1996   *Inventing the Southwest: The Fred Harvey Company and Native American Art.* Flagstaff AZ: Northland.

HUELSBECK, DAVID R.

1988   Whaling in the Precontact Economy of the Central Northwest Coast. *Arctic Anthropology* 25(1):1–15.

HUNTER, MARY

1995   Field notes from an interview by Patricia P. Erikson, Neah Bay,
        Washington. Erikson personal files.

HYMES, DELL, ED.

1969   *Reinventing Anthropology.* New York: Random House.

IDES, ISABELLE ALLABUSH

1995   Field notes from an interview by Patricia P. Erikson, Neah Bay,
        Washington, MCRC Archives.

IRVING, MARGARET ALLABUSH

1995   Field notes from an interview by Patricia P. Erikson, Neah Bay,
        Washington. Erikson personal files.

JACKNIS, IRA

1985   Franz Boas and Exhibits: On the Limitations of the Museum
        Method of Anthropology. In *Objects and Others: Essays on Museums and
        Material Culture,* ed. G. W. Stocking Jr., 75–111. Madison: University
        of Wisconsin Press.

1991   Heafitz Hall of the North American Indian: Change and Continuity,
        Peabody Museum, Harvard. *Museum Anthropology* 15(2):29–34.

JACOBSEN, WILLIAM

1979   *First Lessons in Makah.* Forks WA: Olympic Graphic Arts.

JEWITT, JOHN R.

1824   The Adventures and Sufferings of John R. Jewitt, only survivor of
        the ship Boston during a captivity of nearly three years among the
        Savages of Nootka Sound. Edinburgh: Constable and Co.

JOCKS, CHRISTOPHER

1996   Spirituality for Sale: Sacred Knowledge in the Consumer Age. *American Indian Quarterly* 20:415–31.

JOHNSON, KEITH

1998   The Makah manifesto. *Seattle Times,* August 23, B9.

JOHNSON, SADIE

1995   Field notes from an interview by Patricia P. Erikson, Neah Bay,
        Washington. Erikson personal files.

JOHNSON, SHIRLEY WARD

1995   Field notes from an interview by Patricia P. Erikson, Neah Bay,
        Washington. Erikson personal files.

JONAITIS, ALDONA

1993   Pathways of Tradition: Indian Insights into Indian Worlds. Exhibit
        review. *Museum Anthropology* 17(1):76–82.

JONAITIS, ALDONA, ED.

1991 *Chiefly Feasts: The Enduring Kwakiutl Potlatch.* Seattle: University of Washington Press.

JONAITIS, ALDONA, AND RICHARD INGLIS

1992 Power, History, and Authenticity: The Mowachaht Whalers' Washing Shrine. *South Atlantic Quarterly* 91(1):193–213.

JONES, ANNA LAURA

1993 Exploding Canons: The Anthropology of Museums. *Annual Review of Anthropology* 22:201–20.

KAPLAN, FLORA EDOUWAYE

1996 Museum Anthropology. In *Encyclopedia of Cultural Anthropology*, ed. David Levinson and Melvin Ember, 813–16. New York: Henry Holt.

KARP, IVAN

1992 On Civil Society and Social Identity. In *Museums and Communities: The Politics of Public Culture*, ed. I. Karp, C. M. Kreamer, and S. D. Lavine, 19–33. Washington DC: Smithsonian Institution Press.

KARP, IVAN, CHRISTINE M. KREAMER, ET AL., EDS.

1992 *Museums and Communities: The Politics of Public Culture.* Washington. DC: Smithsonian Institution Press.

KARP, IVAN, AND STEVEN D. LAVINE, ED.

1992 *Exhibiting Cultures: The Poetics and Politics of Museum Display.* Washington DC: Smithsonian Institution Press.

KAVANAGH, THOMAS W.

1990 "A Brief Illustrated History of the Manikins, Statues, Lay-figures, and Life-Groups Illustrating American Ethnology in the National Museum of Natural History," Smithsonian Institution, June 16, 1990. Erikson personal files.

KELLER, ROBERT H., AND MICHAEL F. TUREK

1998 *American Indians and National Parks.* Tucson: University of Arizona Press.

KIDWELL, CLARA SUE

1999 Every Last Dishcloth: The Prodigious Collecting of George Gustav Heye. In *Collecting Native American, 1870–1960*, ed. Shepard Krech III and Barbara A. Hail, 232–58. Washington DC: Smithsonian Institution Press.

KING, DUANE

1976 History of the Museum of the Cherokee Indian. *Journal of Cherokee Studies* 1(1):60–64.

KIRK, RUTH

1973   Cape Alava — A Window to the Past for the Makahs. *Seattle Times*, November 4, 30–35.

1974   *Hunters of the Whale*. New York: William Morrow and Company.

1975   Ozette: The Search Goes On. *Pacific Search* (Mar.).

1980   The Pompeii of the Northwest. *Historic Preservation* 32(2):2–9.

KOPYTOFF, IAN

1986   The Cultural Biography of Things: Commoditization as Process. In *The Social Life of Things: Commodities in Cultural Perspective*, ed. A. Appadurai, 64–91. Cambridge: Cambridge University Press.

KUCHLER, SUSANNE, AND WALTER MELION

1991   *Images of Memory: On Remembering and Representation*. Washington DC: Smithsonian Institution Press.

LACHESTER, BATCH

1995   Field notes from an interview by Patricia P. Erikson, Neah Bay, Washington. MCRC Archives.

LANE, BARBARA

1972a   Makah Fishing and the Promises of the U.S.: A Brief Report. MCRC Archives, July 24.

1972b   Makah Fishing and the Promises of the U.S.: A Supplementary Report. MCRC Archives, December 13.

1974   Makah Fishing and the Promises of the U.S.: A Third Report. MCRC Archives, September 13.

LAWRENCE, JOSEPH

1995   Field notes from an interview by Patricia P. Erikson, Neah Bay, Washington. Erikson personal files.

LESTER, JOAN

1972   The American Indian: A Museum's Eye View. *Indian History* 5(2): 25–31.

LOHSE, E. S., AND FRANCES SUNDT

1994   History of Research: Museum Collections. In *Native America in the Twentieth Century: An Encyclopedia*, ed. M. B. Davis, 88–97. New York: Garland.

LOMAWAIMA, K. TSAININA

1994   *They Called It Prairie Light: A Story of Chilocco Indian School*. Lincoln: University of Nebraska Press.

LOMNITZ-ADLER, CLAUDIO

1992   *Exits from the Labyrinth: Culture and Ideology in the Mexican National Space.* Berkeley: University of California Press.

LOOMIS, ORMOND H.

1983   Cultural Conservation: The Protection of Cultural Heritage in the United States. A Study by the American Folklife Center, Library of Congress, carried out in cooperation with the National Park Service, Department of the Interior. Washington DC: Library of Congress.

LURIE, NANCY OESTREICH

1981   Museumland Revisited. *Human Organization* 40(2):180–87.

1988   Relations between Indians and Anthropologists. In *Indian-White Relations*, ed. W. E. Washburn, 548–56. Vol. 4 of *Handbook of North American Indians*, ed. William C. Sturtevant. Washington DC: Smithsonian Institution.

LYMAN, CHRISTOPHER

1982   *The Vanishing Race and Other Illusions: Photographs of Indians by Edward Curtis.* New York: Pantheon.

MACDONALD, SHARON, AND GORDON FYFE, EDS.

1996   *Theorizing Museums.* Oxford: Blackwell.

MCRC

n.d.   Reasons Why the MTC Should Forgive the Debt *AND* Make a Cash Contribution. MCRC Archives.

1979   [1995] Museum Exhibit Leaflet. Neah Bay, Washington: Makah Tribal Council.

1989   Riding in His Canoe: The Continuing Legacy of Young Doctor. An Exhibit in Celebration of our Tenth Year, 1979–1989. Neah Bay, Washington: Makah Tribal Council.

1991   Makah Dictionary Project Proposal. Application to the National Park Service Historic Preservation Fund Grant. MCRC Archives.

MAKAH TRIBAL COUNCIL

1979   MCRC Museum Exhibit Leaflet. Tacoma: Western Media.

1984   The Makah Claims Settlement Bill: An Honorable and Practical Resolution of Thirty-Four Years of Litigation. MCRC Archives.

1995a   MCRC Museum Exhibit Leaflet, second edition.

1995b   Rebounding Gray Whales Prompt Makah Tribe's Resumption of Treaty Harvest. Press Release. Neah Bay WA: Makah Tribal Council.

1999   Makah Whaling: Questions and Answers. Electronic document. Available from *http://www.makah.com/whales.htm*.

MAPES, LYNDA V.

1998a   Some Makahs Oppose Hunt. *Seattle Times*, October 30, A1, A18.

1998b   The Whale-Waiting Game. *Seattle Times*, October 8, A1, A20.

MARCUS, GEORGE E.

1986   Contemporary Problems of Ethnography in the Modern World System. In *Writing Culture: The Poetics and Politics of Ethnography*, ed. J. Clifford and G. Marcus, 165–93. Berkeley: University of California Press.

1995   Ethnography in/of the World System: The Emergence of Multi-Sited Ethnography. *Annual Review of Anthropology* 24:95–117.

MARCUS, GEORGE, AND DICK CUSHMAN

1982   Ethnographies as Texts. *Annual Review of Anthropology* 11:25–69.

MARCUS, GEORGE E., AND MICHAEL M. J. FISCHER

1986   *Anthropology as Cultural Critique: An Experimental Moment in the Human Sciences*. Chicago: University of Chicago Press.

MARR, CAROLYN, LLOYD COLFAX, ET AL.

1987   *Portrait in Time: Photographs of the Makah by Samuel G. Morse, 1896–1903*. Seattle: MCRC.

MARTINDALE, ROB

1994   Osage Tribal Museum Reopened. *Tulsa World*, March 26.

MAUGER, JEFFREY E.

1978   Shed Roof Houses at the Ozette Archaeological Site: A Protohistoric Architectural System. Washington Archaeological Research Center Project Report No. 73. Pullman: Washington State University.

1982   Ozette Kerfed-Corner Boxes. *American Indian Art Magazine* 8(1): 72–79.

1991   Part II: Shed-Roof Houses at Ozette and in a Regional Perspective. In *House Structure and Floor Midden*, ed. Stephan R. Samuels, 29–173. Vol. 1 of *Ozette Archaeological Project Research Reports*. Pullman: Washington State University Department of Anthropology.

1994   Oral history transcription from interview by Patricia P. Erikson, Neah Bay, Washington. Erikson personal files.

MAUGER, JEFFREY E., AND JANINE BOWECHOP

1995   Tribal Collections Management at the MCRC. *A Resource for Tribal Museums* 2.

MCBETH, SALLY

1983   Indian Boarding Schools and Ethnic Identity: An Example from the Southern Plains Tribes of Oklahoma. *Plains Anthropologist* 28: 119–28.

MCCURDY, JAMES G.

1981   *Indian Days at Neah Bay*. Seattle: Historical Society of Seattle and King County.

MCDONALD, LUCILE

1965   A Cultural Pillar of the Makahs. *Seattle Times*, December 26, 7.

1972   *Swan among the Indians, Life of James G. Swan, 1818–1900*. Portland OR: Binfords and Morts.

MCEVILLEY, THOMAS

1984   Docotor, Lawyer, Indian Chief: "Primitivism in Twentieth Century Art at the Museum of Modern Art in 1984." *Art Forum* 23(3):54–61.

MCGREEVY, SUSAN BROWN

1986   Daughters of Affluence: Wealth, Collecting, and Southwestern Institutions. In *Hidden Scholars: Women Anthropologists and the Native American Southwest*, ed. N. J. Parezo, 76–106. Albuquerque: University of New Mexico Press.

MCKENZIE, KATHLEEN H.

1974   Ozette Prehistory—Prelude. Master's thesis, University of Calgary.

MEDICINE, BEATRICE

1971   The Anthropologist and American Indian Studies Programs. *Indian Historian* 4(1):15–18, 63.

MERRILL, WILLIAM

1995   Field notes from an interview by Patricia P. Erikson, Washington DC. Erikson personal files.

MERRILL, WILLIAM L., EDMUND J. LADD, ET AL.

1993   The Return of the *Ahayu:da*: Lessons for Repatriation from Zuni Pueblo and the Smithsonian Institution. *Current Anthropology* 34(5): 523–67.

MEYER, EUGENE L., AND JACQUELINE TRESCOTT

1995   "Smithsonian Scuttles Exhibit: Enola Gay Plan Had 'Fundamental Flaw.'" *Washington Post*, Jan. 31, A1, A12.

MILLER, BEATRICE D.

1952   Neah Bay: The Makah in Transition. *Pacific Northwest Quarterly* 43(4): 262–72.

MINER, H. CRAIG

1972   The United States Government Building at the Centennial Exhibi-
        tion, 1874–77. *Prologue: The Journal of the National Archives* 4 (winter):
        211.

MINTZ, SIDNEY

1996   The Anthropological Interview and the Life History. In *Oral History:
        An Interdisciplinary Anthology*, ed. David K. Dunaway and Willa K.
        Baum, 298–305. Walnut Creek CA: Altamira.

MOHANTY, CHANDRA TALPADE

1984   Under Western Eyes: Feminist Scholarship and Colonial Discourses.
        Boundary 2(12):333–58.

MOORE, S.

1987   Federal Indian Burial Policy—Historical Anachronism or Contem-
        porary Reality? *Native American Rights Fund Legal Review* 12:1–7.

MORALES LERSCH, TERESA, AND CUAUHTÉMOC CAMARENA OCAMPO

1991   La participacion social en los museos. In *Etnia y Sociedad en Oaxaca*,
        ed. Alicia Castellanos Guerrero and Gilberto Lopez y Rivas, 181–90.
        Mexico DF: INAH.

1993   The Community Museums of Oaxaca: A Case of Cultural Appropri-
        ation through the Cargo System. Paper presented at the American
        Anthropological Association Meeting, Washington DC.

MORALES LERSCH, TERESA, CUAUHTÉMOC CAMARENA OCAMPO,
AND MANUEL CAMARENA OCAMPO

1987   La experiencia de constitutución del Museo "Shan-Dany," de Santa
        Ana del Valle, Tlacolula, Oaxaca. *Antropología, Boletín Oficial del Insti-
        tuto Nacional de Antropología e Historia* 14 (May–June): 9–11.

MOZINO, JOSE MARIANO, ED.

1970   *Noticias de Nutka: An Account of Nootka Sound in 1792.* American Eth-
        nological Society Monograph 50. Seattle: University of Washington
        Press.

NASON, JAMES

1995   Field notes from an interview by Patricia P. Erikson, Seattle. Erik-
        son personal files.

NICHOLSON, LINDA, ED.

1997   *The Second Wave: A Reader in Feminist Theory.* New York: Routledge.

NICKS, TRUDY

1996   Dr. Oronhyatekha's History Lessons: Reading Museums Collections
        as Texts. In *Reading beyond Words: Contexts for Native History*, ed.

Jennifer S. H. Brown and Elizabeth Vibert, 483–508. Orchard Park, N.Y.: Broadview.

NICKS, T., AND T. HILL

1991   Turning the Page: Forging New Partnerships between Museums and First Peoples. Ottawa: Canadian Museum Association.

NMAI REPORT

1996   Latin America Vital to NMAI Mission. Native Peoples 9(2):66–67.

N. N.

1993   Indianism in Hungary. European Review of Native American Studies 7(1):37–42.

NOEL, TED

1995   Field notes from an interview by Patricia P. Erikson, Neah Bay, Washington. Erikson personal files.

NORA, PIERRE

1989   Between Memory and History: Les Lieux de Memoire. Representations 26:7–25.

NORKUNAS, MARTHA K.

1993   The Politics of Public Memory: Tourism, History, and Ethnicity in Monterey, California. Albany: State University of New York Press.

ONG, AIHWA

1988   Colonialism and Modernity: Feminist Re-Presentations of Women in Non-Western Societies. Inscriptions 3(4):79–93.

OROSZ, JOEL J.

1990   Curators and Culture: The Museum Movement in America 1740–1870. Tuscaloosa: University of Alabama Press.

ORTIZ, ALFONSO

1971   An American Anthropologist's Perspective on Anthropology. Indian Historian 4(1):11–14.

OWSLEY, DOUGLAS W.

1984   Human Bones from Archaeological Context: An Important Source of Information. Council for Museum Anthropology Newsletter 8 (April): 2–8.

OXENDINE, LINDA ELLEN

1992   Tribally Operated Museums: A Reinterpretation of Indigenous Collections. Ph.D. diss., University of Minnesota.

PASCUA, MARIA PARKER

1991   A Makah Village in 1491: Ozette. National Geographic 184(10):38–53.

PERROT, PAUL

1995   Field notes from an interview by Patricia P. Erikson, Washington DC, Erikson personal files.

PETERSON, BRENDA

1996   Makah Have Another Way to Hunt and Honor whales. *Seattle Times*, October 2.

1998   Elders Call for a Spiritual Dialogue on Makah Tribe's Whaling Proposal. *Seattle Times*. December 22, B8.

PETHICK, DEREK

1980   *The Nootka Connection: Europe and the Northwest Coast, 1790–1795*. Vancouver BC: Douglas and McIntyre.

PHILLIPS, RUTH B.

1998   *Trading Identities: The Souvenir in Native North American Art from the Northeast, 1700–1900*. Seattle: University of Washington Press.

PRATT, MARY LOUISE

1985   Scratches on the Face of the Country; Or, What Mr. Barrow Saw in the Land of the Bushmen. *Critical Inquiry* 12 (Autumn): 119–43.

1992   *Imperial Eyes: Travel Writing and Transculturation*. New York: Routledge.

PRICE, RICHARD

1983   *First Time: The Historical Vision of an Afro-American People*. Baltimore: Johns Hopkins University Press.

PROSLER, MARTIN

1996   Museums and Globalization. In *Theorizing Museums*, ed. Sharon Macdonald and Gordon Fyfe, 21–44. Oxford: Blackwell.

QUIMBY, ED

1977   Cedar Canoe Live Again. *Pacific Search* (September): 18–19.

QUIMBY, GEORGE I., AND JAMES D. NASON

1977   Two Specialized Training Programs: New Staff for a New Museum. *Museum News* (May–June): 50–52.

1995   Field notes from an interview by Patricia P. Erikson, Seattle. Erikson personal files.

RAPPAPORT, JOANNE

1988   History and Everyday Life in the Colombian Andes. *Man* 23: 718–39.

REINGOLD, NATHAN, AND MARC ROTHENBERG

1985   The Exploring Expedition and the Smithsonian Institution. In

Magnificent Voyagers: The U.S. Exploring Expedition, 1838–1842, ed.
H. J. Viola and C. Margolis, 243–53. Washington DC: Smithsonian
Institution Press.

RENKER, ANN

1994   Makah. In *Native America in the Twentieth Century: An Encyclopedia,*
ed. M. B. Davis, 326–27. New York: Garland.

RENKER, ANN M., AND GREIG W. ARNOLD

1988   Exploring the Role of Education in Cultural Resource Management: The MCRC Example. *Human Organization* 47(4):302–7.

RENKER, ANN, AND ERNA GUNTHER

1990   The Makah. In *Northwest Coast,* ed. Wayne Suttles, 422–30. Vol. 7
of *The Handbook of North American Indians,* ed. William C. Sturtevant.
Washington DC: Smithsonian Institution.

RHEES, WILLIAM J., ED.

1901   *The Smithsonian Institution: Documents Relative to Its Origin and History,
1835–1899.* Washington DC.

RICE, DAVID G.

1997   The Seeds of Common Ground: Experimentations in Indian Consultation. In *Native Americans and Archaeologists: Stepping Stones to
Common Ground,* ed. Nina Swidler, Kurt E. Dongoske, Roger Anyon,
and Alan S. Downer, 217–26. Walnut Creek CA: Altamira.

RICHARDS, KENT D.

1990   The Young Napoleons: Isaac Stevens, George McClellan, and the
Northern Railroad Survey. *Columbia: The Magazine of Northwest History* 3(4):21–23.

RICHARDSON, DAVID

1996   Coming Together in Brazil. *Native Peoples* 9(2):42–46.

RIEGEL, HENRIETTA

1996   Into the Heart of Irony: Ethnographic Exhibitions and the Politics
of Difference. In *Theorizing Museums,* ed. Sharon Macdonald and
Gordon Fyfe, 83–104. Oxford: Blackwell.

RILEY, CARROLL L.

1968   The Makah Indians: A Study of Political and Social Organization.
Ethnohistory (15)1: 57–95.

ROBINSON, JOHN A.

1981   Personal Narratives Reconsidered. *Journal of American Folklore*
94(371):58–85.

ROSALDO, RENATO

1989   Culture and Truth: The Remaking of Social Analysis. Boston: Beacon Press.

RUBY, ROBERT H., AND JOHN A. BROWN

1992   Guide to the Indian Tribes of the Pacific Northwest.

SACCO, ELLEN

1996   Racial Theory, Museum Practice: The Colored World of Charles Willson Peale. Museum Anthropology (20)2:25–32.

SADONGEI, ALYCE

1995   Field notes from an interview by Patricia P. Erikson, Washington DC, Erikson personal files.

SAID, EDWARD

1978a   Orientalism. New York: Pantheon.

1978b   The Problem of Textuality: Two Exemplary Positions. Critical Inquiry 4(4):673–714.

1989   Representing the Colonized: Anthropology's Interlocutors. Critical Inquiry 15:205–25.

SAMUELS, STEPHAN R., AND RICHARD D. DAUGHERTY

1991   Part 1: Introduction to the Ozette Archaeological Project. In House Structure and Floor Midden, ed. Stephan R. Samuels, 2–27. Vol. 1 of Ozette Archaeological Project Research Reports. Pullman: Washington State University Department of Anthropology.

SHARPE, JIM

1991   History from Below. In New Perspectives on Historical Writing, ed. P. Burke, 24–41. Cambridge: Polity.

SIDER, GERALD M.

1993   Lumbee Indian Histories: Race, Ethnicity, and Indian Identity in the Southern United States. New York: Cambridge University Press.

SILVA, WENONA

1975   A Wampanoag at the Smithsonian. CENA News 2(3).

SIMPSON, MOIRA G.

1996   Making Representations: Museums in the Post-Colonial Era. London: Routledge.

SINGH, AMRITJIT, JR., JOSEPH T. SKERRETT, ET AL., EDS.

1994   Memory, Narrative, and Identity: New Essays in Ethnic American Literatures. Boston: Northeastern University Press.

SMALL, CATHY A.

1997   *Voyages: From Tongan Villages to American Suburbs.* Ithaca: Cornell University Press.

SMITH, FRANK

1995   Field notes from an interview by Patricia P. Erikson, Neah Bay, Washington. Erikson personal files.

SPECTOR, JANET

1993   *What This Awl Means: Feminist Archaeology at a Wahpeton Dakota Village.* St. Paul: Minnesota Historical Society.

SPIVAK, GAYATRI CHAKROVORTY

1987   *In Other Worlds.* New York: Methuen.

STEWART, SUSAN

1984   *On Longing: Narratives of the Miniature, the Gigantic, the Souvenir, the Collection.* Baltimore: Johns Hopkins University Press.

STOCKING, GEORGE W., JR.

1976   Ideas and institutions in American Anthropology: Thoughts toward a History of the Interwar Years. In *Selected Papers from the American Anthropologist, 1921–1945,* 1–53. Washington DC: American Anthropological Association.

1983   The Ethnographer's Magic: Fieldwork in British Anthropology from Tylor to Malinowski. In *Observers Observed: Essays on Ethnographic Fieldwork,* ed. G. Stocking, 70–119. Madison: University of Wisconsin Press.

1985   Philanthropoids and Vanishing Cultures: Rockefeller Funding and the End of the Museum Era in Anglo-American Anthropology. In *Objects and Others: Essays on Museums and Material Culture,* ed. G. W. Stocking Jr., 112–45. Madison: University of Wisconsin Press.

STOCKING, GEORGE W., JR., ED.

1985   *Objects and Others: Essays on Museums and Material Culture.* Madison: University of Wisconsin Press.

STURTEVANT, WILLIAM C.

1969   Does Anthropology Need Museums? *Proceedings of the Biological Society of Washington* 182:619–50.

1995   Field notes from an interview by Patricia P. Erikson, Washington DC, Erikson personal files.

SUTTLES, WAYNE

1991   The Shed-Roof House. In *A Time of Gathering: Native Heritage in Wash-*

ington State, ed. Robin K. Wright, 212–22. Seattle: University of Washington Press.

SWAN, JAMES G.

1870   The Indians of Cape Flattery. *Smithsonian Contributions to Knowledge* 16:1–105.

1971   *Almost Out of the World: Scenes in Washington Territory.* Tacoma: Washington State Historical Society.

SWINDLER, NINA, ET AL., EDS.

1997   *Native Americans and Archaeologists: Stepping Stones to Common Ground.* Walnut Creek CA: Altamira.

TAYLOR, COLIN F.

1988   The Indian Hobbyist Movement in Europe. In *Indian-White Relations,* ed. W. E. Washburn, 562–69. Vol. 4 of *Handbook of North American Indians,* ed. William C. Sturtevant. Washington DC: Smithsonian Institution.

TAYLOR, HERBERT C.

1969   Anthropological Investigation of the Makah Indians Relative to Tribal Identity and Aboriginal Possession of Lands. Unpublished report. Department of Anthropology. Western Washington University, Bellingham.

1974   [1975] Anthropological Investigation of the Makah Indians Relative to Tribal Identity and Aboriginal Possession of Lands. In *American Indian Ethnohistory: Indians of the Northwest—Coast Salish and Western Washington Indians,* vol. 3:27–115. New York: Garland.

TEDLOCK, DENNIS

1987   Questions Concerning Dialogical Anthropology. *Journal of Anthropological Research* 43:325–37.

THOMAS, NICHOLAS

1989   Material Culture and Colonial Power: Ethnological Collecting and the Establishment of Colonial Rule in Fiji. *Man* 24(1):41–56.

1991   *Entangled Objects: Exchange, Material Culture, and Colonialism in the Pacific.* Cambridge: Harvard University Press.

THORNTON, RUSSELL

1994   Repatriation of Human Remains and Artifacts. In *Native American in the Twentieth Century: An Encyclopedia,* ed. M. B. Davis, 542–44. New York: Garland.

TIZON, ALEX

1998   The Whale Hunt. *Seattle Times.* September 20, A1.

1999   E-mails, Phone Calls Full of Threats, Invective. *Seattle Times,* May 23, A1, A16.

TOLLEFSON, KENNETH

1994   The Snoqualmie Indians as Hop Pickers. *Columbia: The Magazine of Northwest History* 8(4):39–44.

TRENNERT, ROBERT A., JR.

1974   A Grand Failure: The Centennial Indian Exhibition of 1876. *Prologue: The Journal of the National Archives* 6(2):118–29.

TWEEDIE, ANN

1999   "Drawing Back Culture": The Makah Tribe's Struggle to Implement the Native American Graves Protection and Repatriation Act. Ph.D. diss., Harvard University.

U.S. OFFICE OF INDIAN AFFAIRS

1863–71 *Report of the Commissioner of Indian Affairs.* Washington DC: Government Printing Office.

1872–88 *Annual Report of the Commissioner of Indian Affairs to the Secretary of the Interior.* Washington DC: Government Printing Office.

1889   *Fifty-Eighth Annual Report of the Commissioner of Indian Affairs to the Secretary of the Interior.* Washington DC: Government Printing Office.

1890   *Fifty-Ninth Annual Report of the Commissioner of Indian Affairs to the Secretary of the Interior.* Washington DC: Government Printing Office.

1891   *Sixtieth Annual Report of the Commissioner of Indian Affairs to the Secretary of the Interior.* Washington DC: Government Printing Office.

1892   *Sixty-First Annual Report of the Commissioner of Indian Affairs to the Secretary of the Interior.* Washington DC: Government Printing Office.

1893   *Sixty-Second Annual Report of the Commissioner of Indian Affairs to the Secretary of the Interior.* Washington DC: Government Printing Office.

1894–97 *Annual Report of the Commissioner of Indian Affairs to the Secretary of the Interior.* Washington DC: Government Printing Office.

VERHOVEK, SAM HOWE

1998   Protesters Shadow a Tribe's Pursuit of Whales and Past. *New York Times,* October 2, A1, A13.

1999   Reviving Tradition, Tribe Kills a Whale. *New York Times*, May 18, A1, A14.

VIOLA, HERMAN J.

1978   American Indian Cultural Resources Training Program at the Smithsonian Institution. *American Archivist* 41(2):143–46.

1985   The Story of the U.S. Exploring Expedition. In *Magnificent Voyagers: The U.S. Exploring Expedition, 1838–1842*, ed. H. J. Viola and C. Margolis, 9–22. Washington DC: Smithsonian Institution Press.

1990   *After Columbus: The Smithsonian Chronicle of the North American Indians.* Washington DC: Smithsonian Books.

1995   Field notes from an interview by Patricia P. Erikson, Washington DC. Erikson personal files.

VIOLA, HERMAN J., AND CAROLYN MARGOLIS, EDS.

1985   *Magnificent Voyagers: The U.S. Exploring Expedition, 1838–1842.* Washington DC: Smithsonian Institution Press.

WACHENDORF, KIRK

1995   Field notes from an interview by Patricia P. Erikson, Neah Bay, Washington. Erikson personal files.

WALLERSTEIN, IMMANUEL

1966   *Social Change: The Colonial Situation.* New York: John Wiley.

1974   *Capitalist Agriculture and the Origins of the European World-Economy in the Sixteenth Century.* New York: Academic Press.

WARD, HELMA SWAN

1995   Field notes from an interview by Patricia P. Erikson, Neah Bay, Washington. Erikson personal files.

WARD, IRENE

1995   Field notes from an interview by Patricia P. Erikson, Neah Bay, Washington. MCRC Archives.

WARREN, DAVID

1974   Cultural Studies in Indian Education. BIA Education Research Bulletin 2(1):2–18.

1995   Field notes from an interview by Patricia P. Erikson, Washington DC. Erikson personal files.

WASHBURN, WILCOMB E.

1967   Joseph Henry's Conception of the Purpose of the Smithsonian Institution. In *A Cabinet of Curiosities*, 106–66. Charlottesville: University Press of Virginia.

WATANABE, JOHN M.

1995   Unimagining the Maya: Anthropologists, Others, and the Inescapable Hubris of Authorship. *Bulletin of Latin American Research* 14: 25–45.

WATERMAN, T. T.

1920   The Whaling Equipment of the Makah Indians. *University of Washington Publications in Anthropology* 1(1):1–67.

WATSON, PAUL

1999a   Sea Shepherd Returning to Makah Whale Hunt: Patrol Vessel Will Rally Anti-Whaling forces in Neah Bay, Washington, May 4 (on-line). *Http://www2.seashepherd.org/orgs/sscs/wh/us/mkssret.html.*

1999b   *Today Show.* National Broadcasting Corporation, May 18.

WEIL, STEPHEN

1990   Rethinking the Museum. *Museum News* (Mar.–Apr.): 56–61.

WEI TCHEN, JOHN KUO

1992   Creating a Dialogic Museum. In *Museums and Communities: The Politics of Public Culture,* 285–326. Washington DC: Smithsonian Institution Press.

WENZEL, GEORGE

1991   *Animal Rights, Human Rights: Ecology, Economy and Ideology in the Canadian Arctic.* Toronto: University of Toronto Press.

WESSEN, GARY

1988   The Use of Shellfish Resources on the Northwest Coast: The View from Ozette. *Research in Economic Anthropology* (Supplement 3): 179–207.

1995   Oral history transcription from interview by Patricia P. Erikson, Neah Bay, Washington. MCRC Archives.

WEST, RICHARD

1995   Field notes from an interview by Patricia P. Erikson, Washington DC, Erikson personal files.

WESTERMAN, WILLIAM

1994   Central American Refugee Testimonies and Performed Life Histories in the Sanctuary Movement. In *Migration and Identity,* ed. R. Benmayor and A. Skotnes, 167–81. Vol. 3 of the International Yearbook of Oral History and Life Stories. Oxford: Oxford University Press.

WILKIE, DONNA

1995   Field notes from an interview by Patricia P. Erikson, Neah Bay, Washington. Erikson personal files.

WOLF, ERIC

1982   *Europe and the People without History*. Berkeley: University of California Press.

WRIGHT, R. K., ED.

1991   *A Time of Gathering: Native Heritage in Washington State*. Seattle: University of Washington Press.

YENGOYAN, ARAM

1994   Culture, Ideology, and World's Fairs: Colonizer and Colonized in Comparative Perspectives. In *Fair Representations: World's Fairs and the Modern World*, ed. Robert W. Rydell and Nancy Gwinn, 62–83. Amsterdam: VU University Press.

ZEGAS, JUDY BRAUN

1976   North American Indian Exhibit at the Centennial Exposition. *Curator* 19(2):162–73.

ZIMMERMAN, LARRY J.

1996   Epilogue: A New and Different Archaeology? *American Indian Quarterly* (20)2:297–307.

THE ZUNI PEOPLE [QUAM, ALVINA, TRANS.]

1972   *The Zunis: Self-Portrayals*. Albuquerque: University of New Mexico Press.

Index

colonial expeditions, 43
colonial experience: of Makahs, 70–95
Colson, Elizabeth, 52
Community Action Program (CAP), 110, 111, 114
contact zone: museum as, 6
Cook, James, 9
cultural center: definition of, 174, 198

dance: wand, 102; elk, 102
Daugherty, Richard, 22, 121, 123–24, 127, 140–41, 169
Denney, Mary Lou, 60–61, 64, 78, 121–23, 125–26, 128–29
Densmore, Frances, 186, 207

education: Ba'adah boarding school, 71, 73–75, 139; Cushman boarding school, 77–78; day school, 71, 135; public school, 79, 99, 109–19; resistance to, 72, 75
epidemics, 45
Evans, Clifford, 149

Fidalgo, Salvador, 24
fisheries, 80, 82
fishing rights, 133–34

gender restrictions, 184
Greene, Frances, 114
Greene, Hamilton, 176
Greene, Mary, 106–7, 115
Greene, Norman, 105
Greene, Walter, 114
Gunther, Erna, xi, 52, 139

Hamatsa Club, 105
Heilman, Meredith (Flinn), 156–58
Henry, Joseph, 44
Heye, George Gustav, 153

Hill, Rick, 162
Holden, Virginia, 111
hop picking, 83–85, 90
Horse Capture, George, 152–56
houses, 94
human remains: collecting of, 45, 148
Hunter, James, 102
Hunter, Mary, 99
Hunter's Hall, 102, 105

Ides, Harold, 129, 169
Ides, Hildred, 62–64
indigenization, 37
intellectual property, 58–67, 124, 185–89, 197
Irving, Hillary, 122
Irving, Margaret, 1–4, 102

Johnson, Sadie, 113
Johnson, Shirley, 112, 176

Kachook, 73
Kallappa, Alice Anderson, 109
Kloopoose, 73
knowledge-making, 15, 55–67

LaChester, Batch, 102
LaChester, Sebastian, 102, 114
LaChester, Ralph, 102
LaChester, Jack, 111
language, Makah, 9, 10; repression of, 76–80, 114, 115; revitalization of, 117–18, 171, 182–85, 193–94
Lawrence, Joseph, 122, 171
longhouse, 18, 94, 103–4, 143; reproduction of, 180–81, 195–96
Luna, James, 68–69

Makah Arts and Crafts Club, 103–5
Makah Club, 105–6
Makah Cultural and Research Center: collections management of,